The
MYSTERY
—◦ *of* ◦—
IRMA VEP

AND OTHER PLAYS

Charles Ludlam

The
MYSTERY
of
IRMA VEP

AND OTHER PLAYS

Charles Ludlam

THEATRE COMMUNICATIONS GROUP
NEW YORK

This publication is made possible in part with public funds from
the New York State Council on the Arts, a State Agency.

TCG books are exclusively distributed to the book trade by
Consortium Book Sales and Distribution, 1045 Westgate Dr., St. Paul, MN 55114.

LIBRARY OF CONGRESS CATALOGING-IN-PUBLICATION DATA
Ludlam, Charles
The Mystery of Irma Vep and other plays / by Charles Ludlam. —1st ed.
p. cm.
ISBN 1-55936-173-5 (pb : alk. paper)
1. American farces. I. Title.
PS3562.U258 A6   1999
812'.54—dc21   99-044196

Book design and typography by Lisa Govan
Frontis photo copyright © Henry Groskinsky
Cartouche illustration by Rochelle Krause based on a drawing by Everett Quinton
Cover design by Mark Melnick

First edition, June 2001

Contents

~ *A Fan's Foreword* ~

BY TONY KUSHNER

I HAD A MAD CRUSH on Charles Ludlam. I never met him. I saw him onstage. You always fall in love with really funny people—nothing's sexier than genuine laughter—and a comic genius like Ludlam was world-class crush material, in spite of the fact that, or more likely because of the fact that he always seemed so dangerous. All great comic actors do. Ralph Richardson was scary in a similar way. Ludlam had these eyes, you see, no one had ever had eyes like Ludlam's, so piercing, so smart, so beautiful, so alarming. One little look, one sideways glance from Ludlam onstage and an audience would scream—in terror? Certainly in joy! Those eyes were forever warning us: He sees how ridiculous the world is, he can make us see how ridiculous the world is, and look out! he sees through you, he's learned your secret, he knows what you hope no one has noticed, that you too are ridiculous; and though now, at this instant, we are sharing a laugh at some other idiot and his absurdities, at any instant, the idiot we are watching and laughing at could easily be you!

You feared his judgment and longed for it in equal measure. Since nothing was safe from his gaze, everything was included. A lot of what he did on stage was appalling, very wicked, but never mean. Mean-spirited comedy, the comedy of the right, makes some bully feel better. Ludlam's was a comedy that reassured nobody. The theater of Ludlam was a delirous, glorious, ransacking of the contents of the entire world, all of history, everything written, every story ever told; nothing human was spared, but no oppressive Norm was secretly being fortified at the expense of that which provided the occasion for laughter. It was wonderfully sharp and bloody comedy, but the blood was stage blood. Everything seemed ridiculous, but nothing, no one was mocked. Mocking is impossible when no position of superiority can be assumed.

I replay Ludlam moments in my head, all the time. I try to make my eyes do the things his did—a luxurious rolling, the merest hint of a squint, a goosepimple-producing narrowing of the lids—when circumstance calls for it. (It almost always does.) The AIDS epidemic has robbed us of so much it would be impossible to countenance the loss and still feel life is worth living, so we don't count or countenance, not all of it all at once, but oh oh oh do I miss Charles Ludlam. Those evenings at One Sheridan Square fed my soul, and since 1987 my soul has not stopped asking for more of that particular food.

If you never saw him, you might think this excessive. If you saw him you probably know exactly what I mean. We, his audience, adored him. No one will ever do what he did.

The Complete Plays of Charles Ludlam was published by Harper & Row in 1989. It's now out of print, one further bit of proof, if you needed any, that we're slipping into barbarism. The book was over nine hundred pages long and it contained twenty-nine plays. Ludlam's is a dazzling and significant body of work, and it should be accorded a place of greatest regard and honor in the American dramatic literary canon. The plays are funny, erudite, poetic, transgressive, erotic, anarchic, moving, and so theatrical they seem the Platonic ideal of everything we mean when we use that word. His vocabulary! What other American playwright has ever used so many different words? The endless references, the quotes, the great arias of perversion, the Great Silliness—they defy easy categorization, these plays, but among other traditions they belong to that of Lewis Carroll and Edward Lear, and no finer tradition exists.

TCG is doing us the good service of bringing back the most famous Ludlam titles in this volume, along with the invaluable Steven Samuels biography, originally published in *The Complete Plays*. The selection should whet the appetite of any serious lover of the theater to read everything Ludlam wrote, his essays (many of which are available from TCG in *Ridiculous Theatre: Scourge of*

Human Folly), and most importantly, all twenty-nine plays, the well-known and instantly stageworthy like *Irma Vep*, and the darker, stranger wilder texts like *Turds in Hell*, *Caprice*, *Der Ring Gott Farblonjet*. Like Shakespeare, like most great playwrights, everything Ludlam wrote is, in varying degrees, stageworthy. The plays await serious study, exploration, reinterpretation, rediscovery. They are the sublime expressions of what Ludlam insisted was not an aesthetic, but a moral vision: anti-Puritan, unsentimentally utopian, sexually destabilizing—a transporting, a transcendence by means of deflation, a joyous and a subversive, even dangerous revelry leading to revelation, a wise and ecstatic celebration of the world.

New York
April 2001

TONY KUSHNER is the author of *Angels in America* (Parts One and Two), *A Bright Room Called Day* and *Slavs!* His current projects include *Homebody/Kabul*, *Henry Box Brown or The Mirror of Slavery*, *St. Cecilia or The Power of Music* and *Caroline or Change*. He is the recipient of numerous awards, including the Pulitzer Prize and two Tony Awards for *Angels in America*. He grew up in Lake Charles, Louisiana, and lives in New York.

∽ Charles Ludlam: A Brief Life ∽

BY STEVEN SAMUELS

*I*N 1984, when he was forty-one years old, *The Mystery of Irma Vep* brought Charles Ludlam surprisingly close to his long-term goal of conquering the universe. Possessor of a personal yet influential vision of modern American stage comedy as a synthesis of "wit, parody, vaudeville farce, melodrama and satire," he had, since 1967, pursued this vision as a superb actor, inventive director, delightful designer, and—most significantly—prodigious playwright, with a year-round company dedicated exclusively to producing his works. New York's Ridiculous Theatrical Company had had major successes before (*Bluebeard, Camille, The Ventriloquist's Wife* and *Reverse Psychology* among them), but even the back-to-back hits *Le Bourgeois Avant-Garde* (a tribute to and transfiguration of Ludlam's revered French comedic master, Molière, and a declaration of independence from aesthetic labels he had found confining since the sixties) and *Galas* (the life of opera singer Maria Callas conceived as a "modern tragedy," with Ludlam himself as the diva), could not prepare the press or the public for *The Mystery of Irma Vep.*

An astonishing tour-de-force in which two performers—Ludlam and his longtime lover, Everett Quinton—portrayed men, women and an assortment of monsters in a full-length quick-change act, *The Mystery of Irma Vep* was inspired by the "penny dreadful," that quintessentially Victorian melange of sensationalism and sublime poetry. Ludlam had always ransacked the history of art for the form and content of his crafty comic engines; this time he introduced a vampire, a werewolf and an Egyptian mummy into his usual assortment of jokes and puns, trademark stage business such as cross-dressing and billowing fog, and literary references ranging from *Jerusalem Delivered* to *Little Eyolf*. An uproarious, thought-provoking paean to love everlasting, *The Mystery of Irma Vep* garnered praise, awards, adoring audiences and an embarrassment of offers for Ludlam from the worlds of film, television, opera and the legitimate stage.

Armed with strong opinions and big plans, Ludlam set out to remake all the theatrical arts. Tempted as he was by wider arenas, and fully intending to invade them, he never forgot that the conquest of the universe could best be conducted from his 145-seat theater in the heart of Greenwich Village, where the unusually creative conditions he had developed for himself let him concentrate on his most important work: the writing and staging of plays.

⌒ *Early Years* ⌒

One is tempted to say Charles Ludlam's father was Aristophanes, the ancient Greek satirist, but he was born, in fact, in Floral Park, New York, April 12, 1943, the middle son of Joseph William Ludlam, a witty, eccentric, ambitious master plasterer, an independent man who built the family home in New Hyde Park himself (as the witty, eccentric, ambitious Charles Ludlam would later establish his own theater). His mother, the former Marjorie Braun, may have started her six-year-old son's career by losing him at the Mineola Fair, where he wandered into a Punch and Judy show, which enthralled him, and then a freak show, where he saw armless black dwarves painting pictures with their toes.

Soon he was watching puppet shows on TV (*Foodini and Pinhead* was his favorite), then performing his own in the basement. By the age of seven he was out in the backyard, stringing up sheets to serve as curtains, making up lines for the little girls next door to say. He was also appearing in productions at school (beginning in second grade with *Santa in Blunderland*), the once-a-year chance for an otherwise withdrawn child to shine.

Other children played games, but Ludlam lived in the intense world of his imagination. The Catholic church, with its drama, mystery, role-playing, rhetoric, philosophy and spirituality, would prove an enduring influence. Of equal importance was the movie theater conveniently located directly across the street. Until he was ten years old and the family moved to Greenlawn, his mother took him to the movies whenever the marquee changed.

Always somewhat "different," Ludlam was a rebel and an outcast by his high school years, wearing long hair a decade before it became fashionable. A voracious reader of the classics, he was obsessed with theater. In 1958, an apprenticeship at the Red Barn Theater, a local summer stock company, gave him his first true glimpse of actors' lives and—since the performers lived together in an adjoining barn—bohemian life as well.

He went to New York to attend Living Theatre performances of *Tonight We Improvise* and *The Connection*. Inspired by this first glimpse of an expressive, noncommercial company, Ludlam founded his own avant-garde troupe, the Students Repertory Theatre, above a Northport liquor store, in an abandoned Odd Fellows' meeting hall, at the age of seventeen, directing and acting in such dramatic obscurities as *Madman on the Roof*, a modern Nōh play by Kikuchi Kahn, and Nikolai Yevreinov's *Theatre of the Soul*, a Russian late-romantic work set inside the human body, as well as Eugene O'Neill's *The Great God Brown* and August Strindberg's *Dream Play*.

In 1961, he matriculated at Hofstra University on Long Island with an acting scholarship and clashed with his professors immediately. His behavior was outrageous and his acting excessive; so excessive that the staff insisted he concentrate on writing and directing. One result was his first full-length play, *Edna Brown*—expressionistic, semiautobiographical, and never performed. (Ludlam later destroyed it, although he did work fragments of it into subsequent efforts.)

Ludlam would always refer to his Hofstra experience as crucial, since it provided him the opportunity to master the techniques of classical stagecraft. But his college sojourn also had significant personal ramifications. In long conversations with his old friend Christopher Scott, Ludlam finally discovered the source of his outrageous, excessive "difference": he was queer. Graduated from Hofstra with a degree in dramatic literature, he headed straight for

New York City, immersing himself completely in the almost indistinguishable artistic and homosexual undergrounds.

On the Lower East Side (where Ludlam lived for many years before settling in the West Village), 1965 was characterized by great aesthetic exuberance and cross-fertilization, rock and roll, happenings, experimental filmmaking and the flowering of Off-Off-Broadway. Among the many on the cutting edge were playwright Ronald Tavel and director John Vaccaro, who formalized their nascent collaboration in 1966 with the founding of the Play-House of the Ridiculous in a loft on 17th Street. Ludlam made his first New York stage appearance as Peeping Tom in the Ridiculous's premiere production, *The Life of Lady Godiva*.

"We have passed beyond the absurd; our situation is absolutely preposterous," Tavel declared in a program note, and his play gave ample evidence. Like most subsequent efforts in the divergent strains of the Ridiculous, *The Life of Lady Godiva* was a self-conscious mix of high and low culture, an anarchic, psychosexual phantasmagoria filled with camp, drag, pageantry, grotesquerie and literary pretension. Its impact on Ludlam cannot be overestimated.

A subsequent Play-House production proved equally telling. In *Screen Test*, intended as a half-hour curtain-raiser, a director (Vaccaro himself) was to interview and humiliate an actress and a transvestite (an important early member of Ludlam's Ridiculous, Mario Montez). The introduction of another female character provided Ludlam with his first drag performance opportunity: wearing a wig that had passed through Salvador Dali's hands, he found himself transformed instantly and almost magically into Norma Desmond, the fading star played by Gloria Swanson in the movie *Sunset Boulevard*. Improvising both character and lines, Ludlam turned *Screen Test* into a two-hour star turn before he was finished with it.

Despite subsequent difficulties, Ludlam was always grateful to Vaccaro for freeing him as an actor. Before Vaccaro, he had been accused of being "too pasty, corny, mannered, campy." After Vaccaro, he knew these weren't deficiencies but assets.

Epic Theater

Soon after *Screen Test*, Tavel and Vaccaro quarreled and parted. In search of new material, Vaccaro turned to Ludlam, whom he had heard was writing a Ridiculous play.

Big Hotel was originally intended as an exercise, fun for Ludlam to have with a notebook. With a very loose plot and a bizarre assortment of characters having little in common but occupancy at a metropolitan hotel, *Big Hotel* drew on dozens of movies, songs, comic books, television ads and great works of literature for its material.

Its staging encouraged Ludlam's next play, *Conquest of the Universe*, a collage epic partially patterned on Christopher Marlowe's *Tamburlaine the Great*. Whereas *Big Hotel* had been modeled on movies, *Conquest of the Universe* demonstrated Ludlam's flair for Elizabethan dramaturgy. Because of Ludlam's talent for exaggeration, his Tamberlaine could never be satisfied with conquering mere continents; Ludlam's Tamberlaine's hubris demanded the subjugation of planets and allowed him to reenact passages from *Hamlet* and to imitate the Last Supper.

Ludlam himself was slated to star as Tamberlaine's twin opponents, Cosroe and Zabina, but in the middle of rehearsals the famously temperamental Vaccaro fired him. Half of the company walked out with Ludlam and, at a subsequent meeting, encouraged him to stage the play himself. Then they elected him to lead their new troupe, The Ridiculous Theatrical Company.

Its first shoestring performances—weekends after midnight at Tambellini's Gate, on Second Avenue and 10th Street, after the company had taken down Tambellini's movie screen—were *When Queens Collide* (otherwise *Conquest of the Universe*, the same play presented simultaneously by Vaccaro's newly christened Theater of the Ridiculous, which owned the rights to the play), and *Big Hotel*, revived in repertory. Over the next several years—despite limited attendance and continual moves from venue to venue—the company continued to perform and to add new plays to its repertoire: Bill Vehr's *Whores of Babylon* (a verse play by the actor/filmmaker who was, at the time, Ludlam's closest associate; a play so intriguing that Ludlam staged it on three separate occasions, once as a shadow puppet play); *Turds in Hell* (a collaboration with Vehr which recapitulated the mythic search for a lost parent, with the hero in this case being a hunchback, pinhead, sex maniac with goat's hooves and gigantic cock and balls), and *The Grand Tarot* (an aleatoric experiment inspired by Commedia dell'Arte methods, with stock characters created from cards in the Tarot deck, and the order of the scenes at each performance determined by the luck of the draw).

These were chaotic, nonconformist, often all-night affairs. Even in an era of experimental theater, Ludlam's must have seemed *supremely* experimental. He was simultaneously devoted to the virtuosic use of language and the sheer physicality of stage presentation, energized by the clash of opposing philosophies and by divergent acting styles. Tawdry, flamboyant sets and costumes, nudity and simulated sex were juxtaposed with the words of Wilde, Joyce, Shakespeare and Baudelaire. Ludlam stood in awe before the world's art and literature, viewing himself as a recycler not only of cultural detritus, but also of neglected and abused masterworks. He collaged his plays because he didn't feel worthy of adding one word to the canon, anxious instead to use his gifts to reanimate tradition-bound classics and to revive outmoded theatrical techniques.

Ludlam wasn't only making theater, he was remaking himself. Theater had replaced Catholicism as his religion. Whatever was rejected anywhere else was welcome on his stage. East and West could meet there, dramatically, spiritually, philosophically.

Formerly confused about his sexuality, Ludlam was now a man without a closet, intent on setting his actors and audiences free of culturally enforced conformity and prejudice. Polemical, furrowed-brow theater was not for him. Ludlam knew life was "a comedy to those who think / a tragedy to those who feel," and he was an irrepressible thinker. Laughter was the great liberator, and the great equalizer. Anything carried to an extreme was, willy-nilly, ridiculous.

Ridiculous, too, was critical neglect by mainstream publications. Ludlam and the Ridiculous had their champions, but their champions' influence, unlike that of the mainstream's, did not extend to the box office. Glorious as these adventurous productions may have been, they didn't bring in any money.

Ludlam survived by working in a health-food store, packaging rare books, doing stunts on *Candid Camera*, occasionally receiving help from Christopher Scott. Few of the ever-changing caravan of gypsies which made up his troupe seemed as serious or disciplined as he was. As the sixties came to a close, Ludlam knew it was time for a change.

⌐ *Classic Repertory* ⌐

In 1970, Ludlam dreamed of a stage career that would pay his way and of installing a classic repertory company in a permanent home. He gathered his most dedicated players (including Vehr, Black-Eyed Susan, John Brockmeyer and Lola Pashalinski, who were to remain with him for many years) and set about creating a much more focussed and carefully worked-out play than those which had preceded, writing his own dialogue as well as quoting favorite sources. In *Bluebeard*, based on H. G. Wells's *Island of Dr. Moreau*, Ludlam played Khanazar von Bluebeard, a mad vivisectionist in search of a third sex, obsessed with the creation of "some new and gentle genital." Despite opening on a plank of wood on top of the bar at Christopher's End, *Bluebeard* was the first Ridiculous production to win major critical plaudits and was the company's first financial success, leading to an acclaimed European tour, modest funding from the New York State Council on the Arts and the National Endowment for the Arts (which increased substantially with the passing years) and a Guggenheim playwrighting fellowship.

A natural satirist whose tendency was to take any idea and stand it on its head, Ludlam found himself freed of the limitations of autobiography, able to enter into any time or place and, chameleon-like, make it his own. New and diverse plays appeared at the rate of one a year: in 1971, the prerevolutionary China of *Eunuchs of the Forbidden City* provided an exotic terrain in which Ludlam could explore the perversions of power; in 1972, *Corn*, a country-western musical, produced long before most city slickers took country-western music to heart, retold the hoary story of the Hatfield-McCoy feud with enormous inventiveness and charm, and hinted at Ludlam's burgeoning interest in macrobiotics; and, in 1973, *Camille* gave full reign to Ludlam's unsentimental romanticism.

The triumph of *Camille*, when Ludlam was thirty, overshadowed the brilliance of Ludlam's other work for the next ten years. Based on Dumas fils' *La Dame aux Camélias*, which had served as a theatrical warhorse on stage, at the opera and in the movies for 120 years, Ludlam's *Camille* was a *Camille* with a difference: the tubercular courtesan, Marguerite Gautier, was impersonated by Charles Ludlam in drag. Ludlam's was a comic creation, but he subtitled *Camille* a "tearjerker" with good reason: at every one of the more than 500 performances he gave over seven years, he brought his audiences directly from laughter to tears. A bald man of modest height and build, with large hands, a big nose and startling blue eyes, Ludlam mocked his assumed femininity with decolletage that revealed his hairy chest; yet, his convincing characterization so completely imprinted on theatergoers' minds Ludlam's identity as a drag artist, they seemed not to notice that he did not write another woman's role for himself until 1983.

In the meantime, 1974's *Hot Ice* pitted the forces of cryogenics against the Euthanasia Police in a parody of the James Cagney gangster movie, *White Heat*, simultaneously providing a de-illusionistic view of theater, with actors-as-audience interrupting the show, company members addressing each other onstage by their real names, a narrator proffering a critical history of the play in progress, and multiple endings. 1975's *Stage Blood* offered even more dramatic commentary, as the Caucasian Theatrical Company performed *Hamlet* in Mudville, U.S.A.; freely mixing his own dialogue with occasionally doctored Shakespeare, Ludlam held the mirror up to the Bard, adding infinite complexity to the familiar narrative by recapitulating the Danes' intrafamilial battle royal in the Caucasian actors' backstage life, and then inventing a happy ending. (*Stage Blood* premiered at the Evergreen, a theater which might have remained The Ridiculous Theatrical Company's home had Grove Press not sold the building to the Baha'i Foundation.)

Staging annual New York seasons, touring nationally and internationally, the company won applause, awards and a growing following, but money was scarce and life difficult. There were times Ludlam starved, and he would starve again, but several grants in the mid-seventies helped him tremendously. A commission from the New York State Council on the Arts allowed him to write a proletarian and vegetarian *Jack and the Beanstalk*. An award from the Rockefeller Brothers Fund enabled the creation, in 1976, of *Caprice*, a gloss on the fashion industry and a uniquely unapologetic representation of homosexual characters. (*Caprice* also marked the first stage appearance of Everett Quinton, the man with whom Ludlam was to live for the rest of his life.) A most unusual offer to write the book for a Broadway musical about Catherine de' Medici added *Isle of the Hermaphrodites or The Murdered Minion* to the growing corpus, although it was never produced.

As if this weren't enough activity, Ludlam served three years on the New York State Council's theater panel, taught Commedia dell'Arte at several colleges, including New York University, received a CBS fellowship to coach graduate playwrighting students at Yale and created "Aphrodisiamania," a scenario for Paul Taylor's dance company. (He also performed periodically *Professor Bedlam's Educational Punch and Judy Show*, an ever-changing one-man multicharacter puppet play for children, originally presented in 1974.) Nothing, it seemed, could diminish his productivity.

In 1977, the Ford Foundation's New American Plays Program provided the means for the writing of *Der Ring Gott Farblonjet*, a Wagnerian send-up for which Ludlam invented his own language. Of all contemporary American dramatists, only Ludlam had consistently concerned himself with the creation of a stage language which went beyond the diction of everyday speech. In *Der Ring Gott Farblonjet*—inspired by the Joyce of *Finnegans Wake*—Ludlam sought a comic, theatrical esperanto, hoping to make his work accessible to as broad an audience as Wagner's operas.

The largest Ridiculous production since *Eunuchs of the Forbidden City*—and the first in which Ludlam did not perform—*Der Ring Gott Farblonjet* attracted almost no paying customers.

Exhausted by the responsibilities of his expanded company, Ludlam decided to work alone—or rather, in tandem with a ventriloquial figure he had acquired, Walter Ego. After hiring Black-Eyed Susan for secretarial assistance, he ended up building her into the fabric of 1978's comic thriller, *The Ventriloquist's Wife*, which rang new changes on the notion of a piece of wood acquiring a life of its own. Successful in nightclubs and on tour across the United States (even in the lounge of a Las Vegas casino), *The Ventriloquist's Wife* earned the down payment for a ten-year lease on the theater at One Sheridan Square which became the company's long-sought permanent home.

Ludlam had been scouring old joke books for years in pursuit of the notion of a play constructed entirely out of jokes. The result, *Utopia, Incorporated*—about the shipwreck of two marijuana-smoking sailors on an idyllic, ecologically-sound island entered through the Bermuda Triangle—was the first new play in the new space, and a fiasco which catapulted the company into hyperactive repertory. Sometimes as many as six different shows were performed in one week, including *Anti-Galaxie Nebulae*, a sci-fi puppet serial improvised with Vehr and Quinton.

The suggestion that appearing in his own plays prevented the directorial polish that might lead to greater success kept Ludlam off the stage for an entire year. *The Enchanted Pig* (a charming fairy tale with echoes of *King Lear* as well as popular children's stories), the 1979 revival of *Conquest of the Universe* (which proved the play was more stringently constructed than viewers of its earlier incarnations could have guessed) and *The Elephant Woman* (a "midnight frolic" consisting of a frame tale and specialty acts having nothing whatever to do with *The Elephant Man*, the popularity of which it wished to capitalize on), were all presented without Ludlam's special onstage presence. Since this left him with a great deal of time on his hands, he taught a course in eccentric comedy at New York University, took a major role in Mark Rappaport's film, *Impostors*, and began to make a movie of his own, *The Sorrows of Dolores*, a silent, black and white, comedy-adventure starring Quinton in the title role. (Filmed over many years, *The Sorrows of Dolores* contains a rogues' gallery of actors who appeared in Ludlam's plays.)

By the end of the year, Ludlam returned to the stage triumphantly as Scrooge in Charles Dickens' *A Christmas Carol*. His adaptation was so scrupulously faithful to the source that even most of the stage directions were crafted from Dickens' prose.

A relatively straightforward presentation of *A Christmas Carol* may seem a strange programming choice for Ludlam to have made at this point in his career, but it helped to demonstrate how completely within the classic mold his theater was (an unmodified Dickens seeming so perfectly Ridiculous) and was very much in keeping with the two-track approach he had been taking toward audience development, alternating plays for adults with plays for children. He had often spoken of modeling The Ridiculous Theatrical Company after modern dance troupes such as those of Martha Graham and Merce Cunningham; now the plan was to emulate the New York City Ballet, with *A Christmas Carol* serving as the company's *Nutcracker*, providing an annual Christmas bonus at the box office. Unfortunately, the unavoidably large cast made a mockery of this scheme, monetarily, and the production was dropped after its second season.

Meanwhile, the company made its final tour in the first months of 1980. No matter what marvels Ludlam introduced, only three plays were wanted on the road: *Bluebeard*, *Stage Blood* and *Camille*. The stress of repetition had finally worn Ludlam and his cohorts down. The core of the acting ensemble, whose members had worked steadily together for thirteen years, finally broke up under personal and—not coincidentally—financial pressures.

Farce and Invented Genres

Ludlam articulated a new policy for the new decade: rather than tour and revive plays, he would stay home and establish a working repertoire of entirely new works, inspired by a restructured company of old friends and fresh faces. Turning to farce and a contemporary American setting, he scored a huge hit with *Reverse Psychology*, concerning a pair of married psychiatrists having affairs with each other's patients (another married couple) and an experimental drug which—in its *Midsummer Night's Dream* way—made them all fall in love with whomever they were least attracted to. (Ludlam performed the play weekends while commuting to Pittsburgh to direct William Wycherly's *The Country Wife* for the drama department at Carnegie-Mellon University.)

1981's *Love's Tangled Web*, with its mismatched lovers, psychic phenomena and escaped gorilla supported Ludlam's contention that farce, with plots of multiple complexity, was the most modern medium for the exploration of ideas. Its critical failure, caused primarily by a too-short development period, added one more rule to Ludlam's formula for success: since the plays were produced as he wrote them, and often performed before they were complete, only extensive previews could ensure that the works would be ready before bowing for the press.

A quick trip to Coney Island in late 1981 resulted in a second silent, black and white film, *Museum of Wax*, in which Ludlam starred as a homicidal maniac. A playwrighting fellowship from the National Endowment for the Arts helped him produce two new plays in 1982: *Secret Lives of the Sexists* (which Ludlam called "The Farce of Modern Life"), an exposé of modern mores indebted to Aristophanes' *Thesmophoriazusae*, and *Exquisite Torture*, a surrealistic comedy about the last of the Neros inspired by Salvador Dali's remarkable novel, *Hidden Faces*. *Exquisite Torture* ("A Romantic Ecstasy") was Ludlam's last box office flop, somewhat ameliorated by another stint as a playwrighting professor at Yale University.

Le Bourgeois Avant-Garde ("A Comedy Ballet"), presented early in 1983, with Ludlam as Rufus Foufas, a successful greengrocer who wanted to become "avant-garde," was Ludlam's knowing, loving attack on those theatrical brethren he believed had mistakenly thrown out character and plot in a misguided search for the new. This production—which Ludlam considered a public service—inaugurated an unprecedented string of hits including *Galas* (the first woman he had portrayed since Marguerite Gautier, and a secretly autobiographical vision of a demanding, original, overworked artist) and *The Mystery of Irma Vep* (for which Ludlam turned down Broadway and world tour invitations).

Contractual obligations led, in the space of two months, to the writing of *Medea* (which Ludlam chose not to play, so disturbing did he find the notion of killing his own children), and *How to Write a Play* ("An Absolute Farce" hilariously depicting the playwrighting process—with Ludlam and Quinton featured in mock renditions of themselves—which was, unfortunately, performed publicly only twice). Ludlam spent the summer of 1984 with the American Ibsen Theater, appearing in the title role of *Hedda Gabler*.

The success of *The Mystery of Irma Vep*, and one last National Endowment fellowship, provided Ludlam with financial security for the first time in his life and gave him the nerve to attempt another epic, an adaptation of Gustave Flaubert's historical novel of the siege of Carthage, *Salammbô*. (Ludlam's version was "An Erotic Tragedy.") Bodybuilders were hired to play the barbarian hordes; five-hundred-pound Katy Dierlam took on the cross-dressed role of the decadent, decaying suffete Hanno; and Ludlam himself portrayed the title character, the thirteen-year-old virgin priestess of the moon. The opening was delayed while Ludlam directed the Santa Fe Opera in Henze's *English Cat* and filmed a guest spot on "Miami Vice" (having made his network television debut the previous year as a guest star on Madeline Kahn's "Oh, Madeline"). When it opened in the fall of 1985, *Salammbô* was a *succès de scandale* and proved Ludlam could be popular without losing his bite.

More opportunities followed. *The Production of Mysteries*, a short opera he had written with the company's resident composer, Peter Golub, in 1980, was performed by Lukas Foss and the Brooklyn Philharmonic Orchestra. He directed his own libretto of *Die Fledermaus* for the Santa Fe Opera. He filmed an episode of *Tales from the Dark Side* for television and was featured in two movies, *Forever Lulu* and *The Big Easy*.

But Ludlam remained dedicated to The Ridiculous Theatrical Company and his life on the stage, and triumphed again, in the fall of 1986, with *The Artificial Jungle* ("A Suspense Thriller"). Indebted to the writings of James M. Cain, but more particularly to Emile Zola's *Thérèse Raquin*, *The Artificial Jungle* was set in a pet shop on the Lower East Side and showed Ludlam being murdered onstage six times a week. The audience could not have known that their beloved clown was actually dying then. Neither could he, at first.

⌒

Ludlam, who had often said "no one is promised tomorrow," had long feared AIDS, but he refused to be tested for the virus. His many plans and obligations distracted him: an adaptation of *Der Ring Gott Farblonjet* for Broadway; direction of *Titus Andronicus* for the Public Theater's Free Shakespeare in the Park; completion of *The Sorrows of Dolores* for a showing at the Collective for Living Cinema; and a new play, *Houdini, A Piece of Pure Escapism*—all these meant too much to him for him to consider that they would never happen. *Houdini*, particularly, was intended to be his noblest creation, a masterful blend of history, comedy and stage illusion, a philosophical disquisition on the tragedy of Harry Houdini's desperate attempts to escape the bonds of this life. Ludlam had received a generous grant to make a film of himself creating *Houdini*, a documentary which would have opened still more doors for him and the company.

When his illness was confirmed at Thanksgiving, 1986, he would not surrender to it. He convinced himself he would be the first man to beat this disease, through strict application of macrobiotic principles. He sought to lessen stress by devotion to his hobbies—his plants, his fish, his birds, watercolor and Sumi-e painting—but he relinquished none of his dreams, rehearsing Houdini's death scene when he was too weak to get out of his chair, negotiating a second ten-year lease on the theater at One Sheridan Square, finishing—with much assistance—*The Sorrows of Dolores* the very day of its premiere, April 30, 1987. That same evening, he was hospitalized with pneumocystis. Along with other complications, it ended his life on May 28th.

He was only forty-four. He had planned, but not accomplished, his greatest work.

⌒

We mourn the man, this priceless theatrical resource, determined to free us with laughter. We mourn the works that might have been: *Houdini, Twilight of the Surrealists, The Lonely Communist* . . . In the end, we must be grateful for the wisdom and grace with which he packed a lifetime's achievement into his brief span.

Using bawdy, shameless humor and a larger-than-life stage presence, Ludlam had spent twenty years leading The Ridiculous Theatrical Company's rise from a small, out-of-the-way, avant-garde theater to a major attraction and theatrical influence. Theater was his intellectual and sociological battleground. The intensely active life of the mind manifested so richly in his works was the greatest gift he gave his public.

We are lucky to have the plays collected here to continue Ludlam's conquest of the universe. Not since Molière have we been blessed with such a playwright, and it may be several centuries more before we see his like again.

New York City
1989

The
MYSTERY
of
IRMA VEP

A Penny Dreadful

1984

This version of *The Mystery of Irma Vep: A Penny Dreadful* was that used for the 1998 revival at the Westside Theatre in New York City, and reflects cuts to the original text made by Everett Quinton and Eureka. These cuts are retained here and appear in brackets.

The Mystery of Irma Vep: A Penny Dreadful was first presented by The Ridiculous Theatrical Company at the Sheridan Square Theatre in New York City on 1984. Scenic design was by Charles Ludlam, costume design was by Everett Quinton, lighting design was by Lawrence Eichler and original music was by Peter Golub. It was directed by Charles Ludlam. The cast was as follows:

LADY ENID HILLCREST	Charles Ludlam
LORD EDGAR HILLCREST	Everett Quinton
NICODEMUS UNDERWOOD	Charles Ludlam
JANE TWISDEN	Everett Quinton
AN INTRUDER	Everett Quinton
ALCAZAR	Charles Ludlam
PEV AMRI	Charles Ludlam
IRMA VEP	? ? ?

The Mystery of Irma Vep: A Penny Dreadful was remounted October 1, 1998 at the Westside Theatre in New York City. Scenic design was by John Lee Beatty, costume design was by William Ivey Long, lighting design was by Paul Gallo, sound design was by One Dream Sound and original music was by Peter Golub. It was directed by Everett Quinton and Eureka. The cast was as follows:

LADY ENID HILLCREST	Everett Quinton
LORD EDGAR HILLCREST	Stephen DeRosa
NICODEMUS UNDERWOOD	Everett Quinton
JANE TWISDEN	Stephen DeRosa
AN INTRUDER	Stephen DeRosa
ALCAZAR	Everett Quinton
PEV AMRI	Everett Quinton
IRMA VEP	? ? ?
VALIANT SWING UNDERSTUDY	Mike Finesilver

LADY ENID HILLCREST

LORD EDGAR HILLCREST

NICODEMUS UNDERWOOD

JANE TWISDEN

AN INTRUDER

ALCAZAR

PEV AMRI

IRMA VEP

~ *Author's Note* ~

The Mystery of Irma Vep is a full-length quick-change act.
All roles are portrayed by two performers.

⌒ Act One

The library drawing room of Mandacrest, the Hillcrest estate near Hampstead Heath, between the wars.

The study is a large room with French doors at the back that open out on a garden. There is a side table. A fireplace with a mantel over which is a portrait of Lady Irma in her bloom. Two deep armchairs flank the fireplace. There are signs that the Hillcrests have traveled: African masks, an Egyptian mummy case and a painted Japanese screen. There is a bookcase with morocco-bound volumes and a door stage right. At rise, a lit candle is seen moving across the stage carried by Jane. Nicodemus enters from the French doors with a crash of thunder. He has a deformed right leg and the sole of his shoe is built up with wood.

JANE: Watch what you're doing! You're soaking wet! Don't track mud in here!

NICODEMUS: It's God's good rain, my girl!

JANE: It's the devil's rain. That's what it is!

(Lightning flashes, then loud thunder is heard.)

NICODEMUS: Would you rather that the drought went on and on? It's thankful you should be. And that mightily. ,

JANE: And don't clump so with that wooden leg. You'll wake Lady Enid.

NICODEMUS: And wasn't it to save Lord Edgar from the wolf that me leg got mangled so? I should think she'd be glad to hear me clump after what I did for him.

7

JANE: That was a long time ago. Lady Enid doesn't know anything about it.

NICODEMUS: She'll find out soon enough.

JANE: Now, now Nicodemus, I won't have you frightening Lord Edgar's new bride with your wolf tales.

NICODEMUS: And the sooner she does find out the better, I say!

JANE: Hush. Your tongue will dig your grave, Nicodemus. There are some things better left unsaid.

NICODEMUS: Pah! It's a free country, ain't it?

JANE: Shhhh!

NICODEMUS: Well, ain't it?

JANE: If Lord Edgar hears you you'll see how free it is. You'll find yourself without a situation.

NICODEMUS: That's a little too free for me. I'll bite me tongue. *(He bites his tongue)*

JANE: We must stand by Lord Edgar. I'm afraid he'll be needing us now more than ever.

NICODEMUS: Why now more than ever? I'd say the worst was over. He's finally accepted the fact that Miss Irma's in her grave.

JANE: Don't talk like that. I can't bear the thought of her in a grave. She was always so afraid of the dark.

NICODEMUS: He's accepted it and you must, too. Life has begun again for him. He mourned a more than respectable length of time and now he's brought home a new Lady Hillcrest.

JANE: That's just it. That's just the very thing! I don't think Lady Enid will ever make a fit mistress for Mandacrest.

NICODEMUS: And why not?

JANE: She's so, so . . . common. She'll never live up to the high standard set by Lady Irma.

NICODEMUS: That, my girl, is not for you or me to decide.

JANE: I can't stand taking orders from that vulgarian.

NICODEMUS: Come, come, I won't have you talking that way about Lady Enid.

JANE: Lady Irma had a commanding presence and her manners were impeccable.

NICODEMUS: It takes more to please a man than fancy manners.

JANE: I would think a man—a real man—would find nothing more pleasing than fine breeding and savoir faire.

NICODEMUS: If that French means what I think it does you'd better wash your mouth out with soap. Here's eggs and milk. *(Hands her a basket)* The turtle was laying rather well today.

JANE: And where's the cream?

NICODEMUS: I skimmed it.

JANE: Again? Ah, you're incorrigible.

NICODEMUS: In what?

JANE: Now what will I tell Lord Edgar when he wants cream for his tea, huh?

NICODEMUS: Tell him what you like.

(Lightning and a loud clap of thunder.)

JANE *(Shrieks)*: Ahhh! *(The basket goes flying)*

NICODEMUS *(Catches the basket)*: There there. Don't be skeered. Nicodemus is here to protect you. *(Tries to put his arm around her)*

JANE *(Eluding his embrace)*: Keep your hands to yourself. You smell like a stable.

NICODEMUS: If you slept in a stable you'd smell like one, too.

JANE: Keep your distance.

NICODEMUS: Someday, Janey my girl, you're going to smile on me.

JANE: Yeah, when hell freezes over and little devils go ice-skating.

NICODEMUS: If I was cleaned up and had a new white collar and smelled of bay rum and Florida water, you'd think different.

JANE: Don't get any ideas about me. You are beneath me and beneath me you are going to stay.

NICODEMUS: Someday you might want to get beneath me.

JANE: UGH! How dare you speak to me in such a manner. I've had education.

NICODEMUS: What education have you ever had?

JANE: I've read Bunyan's *Pilgrim's Progress* from cover to cover, the Holy Bible, the almanac and several back issues of *Godey's Lady's Book*.

NICODEMUS: Well, I've read the *Swineherd's Manual* from kiver to kiver.

JANE *(Contemptuously)*: Hurmph!

NICODEMUS: You got no reason to look down your nose at me, Miss. We're cut from the same bolt of goods.

JANE: Don't go giving yourself airs. Go on back to your pigsty
before I say something I'll be sorry for.

NICODEMUS: I'm not leaving until you give me a kiss.

JANE: I'll see you hanged first.

NICODEMUS *(Chasing her around the room)*: Give me a little kiss
and I'll show you how I'm hung.

JANE: Get away from me you beast with your double entendres.

NICODEMUS: Double what?

(Thunder, footsteps above.)

JANE: Now you've done it. You've waked Lady Enid. Go quick
before she sees you in the house.

NICODEMUS: What she getting up now for? It's just about
evening.

JANE: That's her way. She sleeps all day and she's up all night.

NICODEMUS: It's them city ways of hers. Lord Edgar told me
she'd been on the stage.

JANE *(Shocked)*: The stage! Ugh! How disgusting!

NICODEMUS: To think, a real live actress here at Mandacrest!

JANE: Yes, it's utterly degrading. But she is the mistress of the
house now and we must adjust to her ways.

NICODEMUS: That's not what I meant. I think Lord Edgar has
done really well for himself.

JANE: You men are all alike. You're so easily taken in.

(Footsteps.)

I hear footsteps. Go!

NICODEMUS: But I want to get a look at her.

JANE: She's an ordinary woman and she doesn't need you gawking at her. Go on back to your pigsty.

NICODEMUS: I found better company there than ever I found at
Mandacrest. *(Exits)*

LADY ENID *(From offstage)*: Jane.

JANE: Yes, Lady Enid.

LADY ENID *(Off)*: Were you talking to someone?

JANE: Just Nicodemus. He came to bring the eggs.

LADY ENID *(Off)*: Is he gone?

JANE: Yes, Lady Enid.

LADY ENID *(Off)*: Has the sun set?

JANE: It's pouring down rain, your Ladyship. There's very little out there that could be called sun.

LADY ENID *(Off)*: Draw the draperies and light a fire. I'm coming down.

JANE: Ah, Lord, my work is never done. *(Draws the draperies across the French doors, cutting off the view of the garden. She takes a quick look at herself in the mirror, straightens her hair, then takes a bellows to the fire)*

LADY ENID *(Entering)*: Ah, you've made the room warm and cheery. Thank you, Jane.

JANE: Can I fix you a nice cup of tea?

LADY ENID: If it's no trouble.

JANE *(Sternly)*: That's what I'm here for.

LADY ENID: Is Lord Edgar about?

JANE: He was up and out at the crack of dawn.

LADY ENID: Out? Out where?

JANE: He goes riding in the morning. It's a custom with him.

(Teakettle whistles off.)

Ah, there's the kettle calling. *(Exits)*

(Lady Enid begins to look around the room. Rearranges figurines on the table near the door. Walks up to the French doors and opens the drapes and the doors slightly, looking out on the garden. The portrait over the mantel catches her attention; she crosses to the mantel and stares at the portrait.

Jane enters with tea things. She sees the figurines moved and puts them back to their former locations.)

How do you take it?

LADY ENID: I beg your pardon?

JANE: Your tea, Miss.

LADY ENID: Plain.

JANE *(Incredulous)*: No cream or sugar?

LADY ENID: No, quite plain.

JANE: That's queer.

LADY ENID: Queer?

JANE: Tea ain't much without cream and sugar.

LADY ENID: I'm on an eternal diet. The stage you know.

JANE: But that's all behind you now.

LADY ENID: Yes, I suppose it is. But the habit's ingrained. I shall probably refuse bread and potatoes 'til I die. *(Indicating the portrait)* Who is that woman?

JANE: Why, that's Lady Hillcrest . . . I mean, that's the last Lady Hillcrest.

LADY ENID: She was very beautiful, wasn't she?

JANE: There will never be another woman who's her equal—oh, I beg your pardon, Miss.

LADY ENID: That's all right, Jane. You were very fond of her, weren't you?

JANE *(Bringing her a cup of tea)*: She was like a part of meself, Miss.

LADY ENID: I see. *(Sips tea. Sharp reaction to the tea)* You do make strong tea, don't you?

JANE *(Indignant)*: When I makes tea, I makes tea. And when I makes water, I makes water.

LADY ENID: God send you don't make them in one pot.

(Beat.)

JANE *(Realizing that a joke was made at her expense)*: Hurmph!

LADY ENID: You don't like me, do you, Jane?

JANE: I don't hate you.

LADY ENID: I should hope not! That would be a terrible thing, wouldn't it? If you hated me and we had to live here together.

JANE: Yes, I suppose it would. I said I don't hate you.

LADY ENID: You don't hate me. But you don't like me.

JANE: I'm not used to you. You'll take getting used to.

LADY ENID *(Shivers)*: I felt a chill. A cat walked over my grave.

JANE: Isn't there a draft there, where you're sitting, Lady Enid?

LADY ENID: Yes, there is a little. Perhaps you'd better close the French doors.

JANE: Did Nicodemus leave them open again? If I've told him once I've told him a thousand times . . . Why, isn't that the master coming over there?

LADY ENID *(Quickly)*: Where? *(Gets up. Hands Jane the teacup)* Yes, it's he. *(Hiding behind curtain)* Stand back! Don't let him see us.

JANE: What's that he's carrying? Armsful of heather and he's dragging something behind.

LADY ENID: Dragging something?

JANE: It looks like a big animal. Why, I believe he's killed the wolf.

LADY ENID *(Nervously)*: Wolf?

JANE: The wolf that's been killing our lambs. Well, we'll all sleep better too, without that devil howling all night.

LADY ENID: He killed a wolf?

JANE: Yes, and he's brought the carcass back with him.

LADY ENID: Is it dead? Is it really dead?

JANE: It's dead and it won't get any deader.

LADY ENID: Which way is he coming?

JANE: He's taking the path by the pyracanthas.

LADY ENID: He's done that before. But will he take the foot-bridge?

JANE: That's just what I was asking meself. He's getting closer— no he's turned off—he's going the long way 'round and through the ivy arches.

LADY ENID: Then he's still not over it.

JANE: Ah, you can't blame him for not taking the footbridge after what happened there.

LADY ENID: They cling to their dead a long time at Mandacrest.

JANE: Nay, I think it's the dead that cling to us. It's as if they just don't want to let go. Like they can't bear to leave us behind. *(Comes back to herself abruptly)* The master will be wanting his dinner. *(Turning at the door)* How do you like your meat, Miss?

LADY ENID: Well done.

JANE: No red meat?

LADY ENID: Not for me.

JANE: See, there's another difference. Miss Irma liked it bloody. *(Exits)*

(The lights change and music plays. Lady Enid turns sharply and looks at the portrait.)

LADY ENID: Don't look at me like that. I didn't take him away from you, you know. Someone was apt to take your place sooner or later. It happened to be me. I know how you must feel seeing us so happy under your very nose. But there's nothing to be done about it, old girl. Life must go on.

(Lord Edgar enters through the French doors and throws the wolf carcass on the floor.)

LORD EDGAR *(With armsful of heather)*: Rough weather.

LADY ENID *(Rushing to Lord Edgar and planting a kiss on his lips)*: Edgar, darling, you're back.

LORD EDGAR: Please, Enid, not in front of . . .

LADY ENID: In front of who? *(She closes doors)* There's no one looking. *(Pauses)* Unless you mean her. *(Points to the painting)*

LORD EDGAR: It does seem a bit odd. I mean kissing right in front of her.

LADY ENID: She looks vaguely sinister.

LORD EDGAR: Please, Enid. She's dead.

LADY ENID: Perhaps that's the reason.

LORD EDGAR: Let's don't talk about her.

LADY ENID: Yes, let's don't.

LORD EDGAR: Are you quite comfortable?

LADY ENID: Yes, quite. Jane doesn't like me, but I think I'll win her over.

LORD EDGAR: I hope you'll like it here.

LADY ENID: I'm sure I will. Oh, Edgar, Edgar.

LORD EDGAR: Oh, Enid, Enid.

LADY ENID: Oh Wedgar, Wedgar, Wedgar.

LORD EDGAR: Oh Wenid, Wenid, Wenid.

LADY ENID *(With a qualm)*: Edgar.

LORD EDGAR *(Slightly reprimanding)*: Enid.

LADY ENID *(Reassured)*: Edgar.

LORD EDGAR *(Condescendingly)*: Enid.

LADY ENID *(Snuggling his chest, with a sigh)*: Edgar Edgar Edgar.

LORD EDGAR *(Comforting and comfortable)*: Enid Enid Enid.

LADY ENID *(Passionately)*: Edgar!

LORD EDGAR *(Aroused)*: Enid!

LADY ENID *(More passionately)*: Edgar!

LORD EDGAR *(More passionately)*: Enid!

LADY ENID *(Rapturously)*: Edgar!

LORD EDGAR *(Likewise)*: Enid!

LADY ENID *(Climactically)*: Edgar!!
LORD EDGAR *(Orgasmically)*: Enid!!
LADY ENID *(Cooling)*: Edgar.
LORD EDGAR: Enid.

(Lord Edgar and Lady Enid snore.)

LADY ENID *(Waking Edgar)*: Edgar.
LORD EDGAR *(Drowsily)*: Enid.
LADY ENID: Take the painting down.
LORD EDGAR: I couldn't do that.
LADY ENID: Why not?
LORD EDGAR: I just couldn't.
LADY ENID: She's been dead three years.
LORD EDGAR: Yes, I know, but . . .
LADY ENID: Let's make a fresh start. Forget about the past.
LORD EDGAR: I want to, Enid, believe me, I do.
LADY ENID: We'll never feel comfortable with her watching
   every move we make.
LORD EDGAR: No, I suppose not.
LADY ENID: Then, why not put her things away in a chest some-
   where or make a little shrine where you can visit her once in
   a while? But not our home.
LORD EDGAR: You're right, of course. I know you are. It's just
   that . . .
LADY ENID: What?
LORD EDGAR: She made me promise that I would always keep a
   flame burning before her picture.
LADY ENID: What nonsense.
LORD EDGAR: I tell you she made me promise.
LADY ENID: Blow it out.
LORD EDGAR: I couldn't break my word.
LADY ENID: I thought you belonged to me now. That we
   belonged to each other.
LORD EDGAR: We do, but that was before we met.
LADY ENID: Which means more to you? Your love for me or your
   promise to her?
LORD EDGAR: Enid, please. Don't put it that way.
LADY ENID: Which is it, Edgar? Which will it be?

LORD EDGAR: Please don't make me choose.
LADY ENID: Do you love me?
LORD EDGAR: How can you doubt it?
LADY ENID: Then the choice is already made. Blow it out!
LORD EDGAR: Dare I? *(Blows out candle)*
LADY ENID: You see, nothing happened.
LORD EDGAR: Weird that we thought it would.

(They laugh.)

LADY ENID: And now, darling, as to this matter of dragging dead animals into the drawing room—it's really got to stop.
LORD EDGAR: I say, you're really out to reform me, aren't you?
LADY ENID: Just a little.
LORD EDGAR: I'll have Nicodemus tend to it. Why don't you change for dinner?
LADY ENID: Good. I'm famished.
LORD EDGAR: Don't be long.
LADY ENID: I won't, I promise. *(Exits)*
LORD EDGAR *(Goes for painting)*: Forgive me, Irma, please. Please forgive me!

(Nicodemus enters.)

NICODEMUS: Where's the new lady?
LORD EDGAR: Changing. You know how slow women are.
NICODEMUS: So you've finally killed the beast, eh, Lord Edgar?
LORD EDGAR: Yes, I've killed it. It will rage no more.
NICODEMUS: But what about the beast within? Is that through with raging?
LORD EDGAR: It's resting peacefully at the moment. That's about the most we can expect, don't you think?
NICODEMUS: You're a man of will, you are, Edgar Hillcrest.
LORD EDGAR: Nicodemus, take the guts out and burn it.
NICODEMUS: Don't you want me to save the skin?
LORD EDGAR: No, burn every hide and hair of it.
NICODEMUS: And the ashes? What should I do with them?
LORD EDGAR: Scatter them on the heath.
NICODEMUS: And let the wind take up its howling?
LORD EDGAR: Then throw them in the mill run.

NICODEMUS: After her?

LORD EDGAR: Yes, after her. And Nicodemus . . .

NICODEMUS: Yes, Lord Edgar?

LORD EDGAR: Take down the painting.

NICODEMUS: And what do you want me to do with it?

LORD EDGAR: Burn it with the wolf. *(Exits)*

> *(Nicodemus goes toward the mantel and tries to take down the painting. Jane enters.)*

JANE: And what do you think you're doing?

NICODEMUS: The master wants the painting down.

JANE: You can't do that. You can't take Lady Irma!

NICODEMUS: I can and I will. It's the master's orders.

> *(Jane runs to pull him away from the painting.)*

JANE: Stop it! Stop it! Don't touch that picture. Ahgh! The sanctuary light's gone out. Oh God, this will never do.

NICODEMUS: Don't blame me. It was out when I came in. Lord Edgar must have extinguished it.

JANE *(Indicating the carcass)*: And what's this here?

NICODEMUS: You've got eyes in your head to see with. It's the wolf. He's killed the wolf.

JANE: Glory be! Is it possible?

NICODEMUS: It's a cause for rejoicing.

JANE *(Approaching the carcass warily, holding a poker)*: It's no rejoicing there'll be this night, Nicodemus Underwood. He's killed the wrong wolf.

> *(Blackout.)*

SCENE 2

The scene is as before. It is late evening. The household is asleep. Jane is stoking the last embers of the fire. Lady Enid enters silently in her dressing gown. She stands over Jane, whose back is to her, and watches. Jane suddenly becomes aware of her presence and, frightened, gasps. This in turn frightens Lady Enid, who gasps also.

LADY ENID: I didn't mean to frighten you.

JANE: I didn't mean to frighten you either. You shouldn't creep up on a person like that.

LADY ENID: I'm sorry, Jane. You have lived here a considerable time. Did you not say sixteen years?

JANE: Eighteen, Miss. I came when the mistress was married, to wait on her; after she died, the master retained me as his housekeeper. Though I knew him from childhood. I was raised at the Frambly Parsonage.

LADY ENID: Indeed.

(Long silence between them.)

JANE: Ah, times have greatly changed since then!

LADY ENID: Yes, you've seen a good many alterations, I suppose?

JANE: I have. And troubles, too.

LADY ENID: The Hillcrests are a very old family, aren't they?

JANE: Oh, Lord yes. Why the Hillcrests go back to . . . back to . . . well, I don't know exactly who. But they've been descending for centuries.

LADY ENID: Lord Edgar told me he was an only child.

JANE: Yes, a strange flower upon the old solid wood of the family tree.

LADY ENID: Was he always so fond of hunting, even as a child?

JANE: Nay, he only took that up after the mistress passed away. Oh, but that's a long story. I won't be after boring you with it.

LADY ENID: Oh, do go on, Jane. Everything about Lord Edgar fascinates me.

JANE: Where is himself?

LADY ENID: Sleeping soundly. Jane, it will be an act of charity to tell me something of the family history. I know I shall not be able to rest if I go to bed, so be good enough to sit and chat for an hour.

JANE: Oh, certainly, Miss! I'll just fetch a little sewing and then I'll sit as long as you please. *(Gets her sewing basket)* Listen to that wind! It's an ungodly night. Can I get you a hot toddy to drive out the cold?

LADY ENID: If you're having one.

JANE *(Pulls a bottle from the basket)*: Sure, I loves me toddy and me toddy loves me.

(Jane pours out two toddies from a pan she has nestled among the embers. She gives one drink to Lady Enid and settles into the chair opposite her before the fire. Howling sound.)

LADY ENID: That wind!

JANE: That's not the wind. That's a wolf howling.

LADY ENID: It seems you've been troubled by wolves of late.

JANE: Not wolves. It's one wolf in particular. Victor!

LADY ENID: Victor?

JANE: He was captured as a pup and tamed. But his heart was savage. Miss Irma kept him as a pet.

LADY ENID: Like a dog.

JANE: He was bigger than a dog, so big the boy used to ride about on his back. Though Victor didn't like that much, I can tell you. Though he bore it for the mistress's sake, for it was to her he belonged. His happiest hours were spent stretched out at Miss Irma's feet, his huge purple tongue lolling out of his mouth. He never left her side the whole time she was carrying. Lord Edgar locked him out when it came time for her to deliver. And when he heard her labor pains, he howled.

LADY ENID: Lord Edgar told me that he'd had a son but that he died when he was still a child.

JANE: Ah, there's a tragic story, Miss. But your toddy's getting cold. Finish that and I'll fix you another.

LADY ENID *(Drains her cup and passes it to Jane)*: He was taken off with chicken pox, wasn't he?

JANE: Chicken pox? Now who told you that?

LADY ENID: No one told me. I was just supposing.

JANE: If Lord Edgar told you it was chicken pox, then chicken pox it was. We'd better leave it at chicken pox.

LADY ENID: No, really, he didn't tell me anything. The chicken pox was pure conjecture.

JANE: It's understandable that he didn't go into it. It's not an easy subject to talk about. Here's your toddy.

LADY ENID: Thanks.

JANE: And here's one for me.

LADY ENID: I'd like to know the true history, if you don't mind relating it.

JANE *(The toddy loosening her tongue)*: One clear winter day Victor and the boy went out to the heath to play in the new fallen snow. The wolf came back without the boy. We waited. We watched. We called ourselves hoarse. And at dusk we found him in the mill run, dead. His throat had been torn apart.

LADY ENID: Horrible.

JANE: Lord Edgar wanted Victor destroyed. But Lady Irma fought against it. She said it wasn't Vic had done it.

LADY ENID: Perhaps it wasn't.

JANE: His throat was torn. What else could it have been? They fought bitterly over it. He said she loved the wolf more than her own child. But I think it was the double loss she dreaded, for when Victor was gone she'd have nothing, you see. When the master came to shoot Victor, Lady Irma turned him loose upon the heath and drove him away with stones, crying, "Run, Vic, run and never come back!" I don't think the poor beast understood what happened because he still comes back to this day, looking for Lady Irma.

LADY ENID: Poor Victor. Poor boy. Poor Irma.

JANE *(Reprimanding her)*: Poor Lord Edgar.

LADY ENID: Yes, poor poor Lord Edgar!

JANE: But here's the strangest part of all.

LADY ENID: Yes?

JANE: The fresh snow is like a map. I traced their tracks meself. Victor's trail turned off. The boy was killed by a wolf that left human tracks in the snow.

LADY ENID: Human? You mean the boy was murdered?

JANE: But that takes us to the subject of werewolves.

LADY ENID: Werewolves?

JANE: Humans who take the form of a wolf at night.

LADY ENID: But that's just superstition.

JANE: Yes, superstition, the realm beyond the explainable where science is powerless. Of course everything pointed to Victor. The boy fell down and skinned his knee. He let the loving beast lick his wound. He tasted blood. The killer was aroused. He turned on the child and sank his fangs into his tender neck. A perfectly logical explanation. But then there were those tracks in the snow. Wouldn't it be convenient for a werewolf to have a real wolf to blame it on?

LADY ENID: Didn't you show them to anyone? The tracks, I mean.

JANE: Ah, they wouldn't listen. They said they were my tracks. That I'd made them meself. I didn't push it, Miss, or they'd have packed me off to Dottyville. It's hard to convince people of the supernatural. Most people have enough trouble believing in the natural.

LADY ENID: Of course you're right. But those footprints.

JANE: I wish I had 'em here as evidence. But where are the snows of yesteryear? And that's the werewolf's greatest alibi— people don't believe in him. Well Miss, I must be gettin' meself to bed. My rheumatism is starting to act up again.

LADY ENID: Leave the light, Jane. I think I'll stay up and read for a while.

JANE: Here's a good book for you. It's the master's treatise on ancient Egyptian mythology.

LADY ENID: Thanks!

JANE *(Heading toward the door)*: Don't stay up too late now. We're having kippers and kidneys for breakfast and I know you wouldn't want to miss that.

LADY ENID: Jane, what was the boy's name?

JANE: Didn't you know? That was Victor, too. Goodnight, Lady Enid. *(Exits)*

(Lady Enid sits in a chair with her back to the glass doors and reads. The shadow of the stranger can be seen through the sheer curtains, illuminated intermittently by flashes of lightning. A bony, almost skeletal, hand feels for the latch. It drums its fingernails against the window pane.)

LADY ENID *(Seeing something)*: What—what was it? Real or a delusion? Oh God, what was it?

(Suddenly a single pane of the French door shatters. The bony hand reaches through the curtains and opens the latch. A gaunt figure enters the room slowly. A ray of light strikes the pallid face. He fixes her with a stare.)

Who are you? What do you want?

(The clock chimes one. The intruder emits a hissing sound.)

What do you want? Oh God, what do you want of me?

(She tries to run to the door but the intruder catches her by her long hair and, winding it around his bony fingers, drags her back toward the mantel. She grabs a burning log from the fireplace and thrusts it into the intruder's eye. The intruder lets out a cry and releases her. She runs across the room, trips and falls to the ground. He follows her. She stabs him with scissors from Jane's sewing basket. Intruder staggers back and falls through open door down right. Lady Enid crosses to the mantel and tries to get control of herself. She sighs with relief. Intruder reenters and, clapping his hand over her mouth, drags her to the door, locks it, then crosses up center to the double doors where shriek follows strangled shriek as he seizes her neck in his fanglike teeth and a hideous sucking noise follows. Lady Enid emits a high-pitched scream made at the back of the throat by drawing a breath in. Running footsteps are heard off.)

LORD EDGAR *(From offstage right)*: Did you hear a scream, Jane?

JANE: *(From offstage right)*: I did. Where was it?

LORD EDGAR *(Off)*: God knows. It sounded so near, yet far away. I got up and dressed as soon as I heard it.

JANE *(Off. No pause)*: All is still now.

LORD EDGAR *(Off)*: Yes, but unless I was dreaming there was a scream.

JANE *(Off)*: We couldn't both have dreamed it?

LORD EDGAR *(Off)*: Where is Lady Enid?

JANE *(Off)*: Isn't she with you?

(Lady Enid emits another high-pitched scream.)

LORD EDGAR *(Off)*: There it is again. Search the house! Search the house. Where did it come from? Can you tell?

(Lady Enid screams again as before.)

Good God! There it is again! *(He tries the door from offstage right. But it will not open)* Enid! Enid! Are you in there? Speak for heaven's sake! Speak! Good God, we must force the door.

(They beat on the door.)

Get the crowbar.

JANE *(Off)*: Where is it?

LORD EDGAR *(Off)*: In the cellar. Hurry! Hurry! Run! Run! Enid!
Oh Enid!

JANE *(Off)*: Here it is.

(They force the door open and Lord Edgar bursts into the room.)

NICODEMUS *(From offstage up center)*: Lady Enid! Lady Enid! Oh
God no! Lady Enid!

*(Nicodemus enters carrying the limp body of Lady Enid. Her
long hair hangs on her nightgown.)*

Help oh help oh heaven oh help! *(He carries her body out the
door stage right)* Now where the blue hell am I bringing her,
beyond the veil?

LORD EDGAR *(Following them)*: What is it? What's happened?
Who's done this thing to you?

NICODEMUS *(Reentering)*: Who or what? I saw something moving on the heath.

LORD EDGAR: Something? What kind of something?

NICODEMUS: Dog's skull. Dog's body. Its glazing eyes staring out
of death's candle to shake and bend my soul.

*(Suddenly something with a horrible face appears at the window.
It lets out a frightening, earsplitting sound and then, laughing,
bangs against the windowpanes.)*

(Growling in a hoarsened, raspy voice) There! There it is.

*(The thing emits a shrill laugh like the sound of electronic feed-
back.)*

LORD EDGAR: Lord help us!

NICODEMUS: Be it whatever thing it may—I'll follow it!

LORD EDGAR: No! No! Do not!

NICODEMUS: I must! I will!

LORD EDGAR: Not without a gun! Don't be a fool!

NICODEMUS: Let whoever will come with me—I'll follow this dread form! *(Exits)*

LORD EDGAR: Wait for me you fool! *(Takes a gun from the mantel)*

NICODEMUS *(From offstage)*: I see it! I see it! It goes down the wall and through the wisterias.

LORD EDGAR: It's dark down there. There isn't any moon.

(There are animal sounds, the sounds of a struggle and then a few agonized cries. The doors fly open and a wooden leg, one that had formerly belonged to Nicodemus, is thrown in.)

Great Scott! *(He rushes out. And is heard calling from off)* Which way? Which way?

NICODEMUS *(Off)*: This way. Over here. Help! Oh help me! *(Exits)*

(There is the sound of shots off.)

JANE *(Entering from stage right)*: Was them shots I heard?

LADY ENID *(Sticking her head in through the door stage right)*: Jane. Jane.

JANE: Yes, Lady Enid.

LADY ENID: Come. I need you. I'm afraid to be alone. *(She withdraws)*

JANE: I'll come and I'll bring the ghost candle to light your agony. It's the curse of the Druids that's what it is. The Druidy Druids. *(She withdraws)*

(Animal sounds.)

NICODEMUS *(Entering up center)*: I saw it. I touched it. I struggled with it. It was cold and clammy like a corpse. It can't be human.

LORD EDGAR *(Entering)*: Not human? No, of course not human. You said it was a dog.

NICODEMUS: Then it looked like a wolf, then it looked like a woman! It tore off me leg and started chewing on it.

LORD EDGAR: Great Scott! It can't be.

NICODEMUS: If it hadn't been wood I swear it would have eaten it.

LORD EDGAR: No!

NICODEMUS: Yes! Yes! Ghoul! Chewer of corpses! And all the while it made this disgusting sucking sound. It sucked the very marrow from me bones. I can feel it now. It's very near. Bride bed. Child bed. Bed of death! She comes, pale vampire, through storm her eyes, her bat sails bloodying the seas! Mouth to her mouth's kiss! Her eyes on me to strike me down. I felt the green fairy's fang.

(Howling off.)

LORD EDGAR: What was that?

NICODEMUS: Just a wolf.

LORD EDGAR: No! It's Victor! Victor come back to haunt me! *(Starts out)* Give me that pistol there. This time I'll get him! *(Fur at the door)* Look! There it is now! It won't escape me this time.

NICODEMUS *(Clinging to his leg)*: No! Master, do not go! There is no help for it!

(Keening lament is heard on the wind.)

LORD EDGAR: Let go of my leg. Goblin damned, I'll send your soul to hell! *(Exits)*

NICODEMUS: No! Master! Master! It's Irma, Irma Vep! A ghost woman with ashes on her breath, alone, crying in the rain.

(Shots, running footsteps and howling heard off.)

JANE *(Rushing in)*: What's all this yelling? You'll wake the dead.

NICODEMUS: The master's at it again—hunting.

JANE: Is it wolves again?

NICODEMUS: This time he's sure it's Victor.

JANE: Victor?

NICODEMUS: That's what he says!

JANE: Well, don't just stand there gawking! Go after him! Be some help!

NICODEMUS: Oh no. Not me! There's something on that heath that would make your blood run cold.

JANE: Ah, you big sissy. If you don't go to his aid I'll go meself.

NICODEMUS: Oh, very well, woman. Wait until I screw in me leg. *(He goes off, screws it in noisily, returns)*

JANE: It seems that more than your leg got bitten off. There's also been a loss of virility.

(She takes a gun down off the wall.)

NICODEMUS: Where are you going with that gun?

JANE: Let go! Let go! Get out of my way. Lord Edgar needs me.

(The gun goes off and the bullet hits the painting. The painting bleeds.)

NICODEMUS: Now see what you've done. You've shot Lady Irma. The painting is bleeding! *(Wrests the gun from her grasp and exits in the same direction as Lord Edgar)* Lord Edgar!

JANE *(Calling after him)*: Down past the mill run and out onto the moors. The other way, Nicodemus! The other way! Take the shortcut through the cedar grove. Faster. Faster, Nicodemus! Faster!

LADY ENID *(Enters)*: Where is Lord Edgar?

JANE: He's searching the moors. He thinks he's seen Victor.

LADY ENID: The wolf or the boy?

JANE: Both.

(Blackout.)

SCENE 3

It is nearly dawn of the same night. Lady Enid sits in a chair by the fire; Lord Edgar hovers near her.

LORD EDGAR: Can you tell me how it happened, Enid dearest?

LADY ENID: Jane and I sat up late, she regaling me with tales of Mandacrest, its history, legends and such. As the hour grew late I prepared myself for bed as is my wont. When I had completed my beauty ritual I went straight to our bed chamber and discovered that you had fallen asleep over one of your books. I crawled in beside you. But unable to sleep myself got up again and came downstairs. As there were some embers of the fire still aglow, I instructed Jane to leave the light when she went to bed, which she did. Then I sat in that chair and began reading your treatise on lycanthropy and the dynasties of Egypt. There was a light rain as you will recall. Then it turned to hail. And as I read, I listened to the patter of the hailstones on the windowpanes. It was during that chapter on how the priests of Egypt perfected the art of mummification to the point that the Princess Pev Amri was preserved in a state of suspended animation and was known as She Who Sleeps . . .

LORD EDGAR: . . . but Will One Day Wake.

LADY ENID: Yes, that's it! She Who Sleeps but Will One Day Wake. And how her tomb was guarded by Anubis the Jackal-headed god. But that her tomb had never been found.

LORD EDGAR: That is what is generally believed.

LADY ENID: Then suddenly the pattering at the window caught my attention, for the hail had stopped but the pattering went on. The glass shattered. I turned. It was in the room. I think I screamed. But I couldn't run away! I couldn't run away! It caught me by the hair and then . . . I can tell no more! I can tell no more!

LORD EDGAR: You seem to have hurt your neck. There is a wound there.

LADY ENID: Wound?!! I feel so weak. I feel so faint. As though I had almost bled to death.

LORD EDGAR: But you couldn't have bled very much. There were no more than five little drops of blood on your dressing gown. Now you'd better get some sleep.

LADY ENID: No sleep! No sleep for me! I shall never sleep again! Sleep is dead. Sleep is dead. She hath murthered sleep. I dare not be alone to sleep. Don't leave me alone. Don't ever leave me alone again. For sleep is dead. Sleep is dead. *(She moves offstage)* Who murthered sleep?

LORD EDGAR: Jane will sit with you. *(Stands with door open talking to Jane)* Take care of her, Jane.

JANE: I will Lord Edgar.

LORD EDGAR: Good girl, Jane.

(Nicodemus enters from French doors.)

NICODEMUS: Is Lady Enid alive?

LORD EDGAR: She is weak and will sleep long. *(Sighs)*

NICODEMUS: You sigh . . . some fearful thoughts, I fear, oppress your heart.

LORD EDGAR: Hush. Hush. She may overhear.

NICODEMUS: Lord Edgar, look at that portrait.

LORD EDGAR: Why, that's blood isn't it?

NICODEMUS: You must muse upon it.

LORD EDGAR: No, no. I do wish, and yet I dread . . .

NICODEMUS: What?

LORD EDGAR: To say something to you all. But not here—not now—tomorrow.

NICODEMUS: The daylight is coming quickly on.

LORD EDGAR: I will sit up until sunrise. You can fetch my powder flask and bullets. And if you please, reload the pistols.

NICODEMUS: Lady Enid is all right, I presume?

LORD EDGAR: Yes, but her mind appears to be much disturbed.

NICODEMUS: From bodily weakness, I daresay.

LORD EDGAR: But why should she be bodily weak? She was strong and well but a few hours ago. The glow of youth and health was on her cheeks. Is it possible that she should become bodily weak in a single night? Nicodemus, sit down. You know that I am not a superstitious man.

NICODEMUS: You certainly are not.

LORD EDGAR: And yet I have never been so absolutely staggered as I am by the occurrences of this night.

NICODEMUS: Say on.

LORD EDGAR: I have a frightful, hideous suspicion which I fear to mention to anyone lest I be laughed to scorn.

NICODEMUS: I am lost in wonder.

LORD EDGAR: Nicodemus, swear to me that you will never repeat to anyone the dreadful suggestion I am about to make.

NICODEMUS: I swear.

LORD EDGAR: Nicodemus, you have heard of the dreadful superstition which, in some countries, is extremely rife, wherein it is believed that there are beings who never die.

NICODEMUS: Never die?

LORD EDGAR: In a word you have heard of a—heard of a—oh God in heaven! I dread to pronounce the word, though I heard you speak it not three hours past. Dare I say? . . . Dare I say? . . .

NICODEMUS: Vampire?

LORD EDGAR *(Excitedly)*: You have said it. You have said it. Nosferatu. But swear to me once more that you will not repeat it to anyone.

NICODEMUS: Be assured I shall not. I am far from wishing to keep up in anyone's mind suspicions which I would fain, very fain refute.

LORD EDGAR: Then let me confide the worst of my fears, Nicodemus.

NICODEMUS: Speak it. Let me hear.

LORD EDGAR: I believe the vampire . . . is one of us.

NICODEMUS *(Uttering a groan of almost exquisite anguish)*: One of us? Oh God! Oh God! Do not readily yield belief to so dreadful a supposition, I pray you.

LORD EDGAR: Nicodemus, within a fortnight I shall embark for Cairo, there I will organize an expedition to Giza, and certain obscure Numidian ruins in the south.

NICODEMUS: Are you taking Lady Enid?

LORD EDGAR: No, I fear that in her delicate mental state the trip might be too much for her. I will arrange for her to rest in a private sanitarium. Look after Mandacrest until I return. I believe the desert holds some secrets out there among its pyramids and sacred mummies. At least I know I shall be far away from her.

NICODEMUS: From Lady Enid?

LORD EDGAR: No, from Lady Irma. For Nicodemus, it is she I believe has extended her life by feasting on human gore.

NICODEMUS: Say not so!

LORD EDGAR: Irma could never accept the idea of death and decay. She was always seeking consolation in the study of spiritualism and reincarnation. After a while it became an obsession with her. Even on her deathbed she swore she would come back.

NICODEMUS: Do you think she will come again?

LORD EDGAR: I know not. But I almost hope she may. For I would fain speak to her.

NICODEMUS: It is said that if one burns a love letter from a lover who has died at the third crowing of the cock on Saint Swithin's Day, you will see the lover ever so briefly.

LORD EDGAR: More superstition.

NICODEMUS: Very like. Yet after the occurrences of this night I can scarcely distinguish truth from fancy.

(Cock crows off.)

There's the cock. 'Twill soon be dawn. Damned spirits all, that in crossways and floods have burial, already to their wormy beds have gone, for fear lest day should look their shames upon.

LORD EDGAR *(Amazed)*: Nicodemus, you know your Shakespeare!

NICODEMUS: I paraphrase. *(Exits)*

(The cock crows again.)

LORD EDGAR: The second crowing of the cock. *(Takes out letters bound with a ribbon)* Irma's letters. Of course it's ridiculous . . . but what harm can it do? I'd best part with them anyway. *(Quotes)* "In all the world. In all the world. One thing I know to be true. You'd best be off with the old love before you're on with the new."

(Burns letter in front of the painting using a piece of flash paper. Cock crows. Painting flies out. A woman's face appears in the painting. She screams.)

Irma!

(Curtain.)

⟶ Act Two

SCENE I

Various places in Egypt.

LORD EDGAR: Ah Egypt! It looks exactly as I pictured it!

ALCAZAR: Osiris hear you!

LORD EDGAR: This invocation is certainly permissible opposite the ancient Diospolis Magna. But we have failed so often. The treasure seekers have always been ahead of us.

ALCAZAR: In recent years our work has been made doubly difficult by the activities of certain political groups seeking to halt the flow of antiquities from out of the country. These armed bandits use this high moral purpose to seize any and all treasures. And this, after the excavators have spent a great deal of time and money to unearth these precious objects, the existence and whereabouts of which these scum were totally unaware.

LORD EDGAR: If we can but find an untouched tomb that can yield up to us its treasures inviolate!

ALCAZAR: I can spare you the disappointments of places I know to be quite empty because the contents have been removed and sold for a good price long ago. [I believe I can take you to a syrinx that has never been discovered by the miserable little jackals who take it into their heads to scratch among the tombs.

LORD EDGAR: The idea fascinates me. But to excavate an unopened tomb—not to mention the difficulties of locating

31

one—would require manpower and organizational abilities almost equal to those the pharaohs employed to seal it.

ALCAZAR: I can place at your disposal a hundred intrepid fellahs, who, incited by baksheesh and a whip of hippopotamus hide would dig down into the bowels of the earth with their fingernails. We might tempt them to bring to light some buried sphinx, to clear away the obstructions before a temple, to open a tomb.

LORD EDGAR *(Smiles dubiously)*: Hmmm.

ALCAZAR: I perceive that you are not a mere tourist and that commonplace curiosities would have no charm for you. So] I shall show you a tomb that has escaped the treasure seekers. Long it has lain unknown to any but myself. It is a prize I have guarded for one who should prove worthy of it.

[LORD EDGAR: And for which you will make me pay a round sum.

ALCAZAR: I will not deny that I hope to make money. I unearth pharaohs and sell them to people. Pharaohs are getting scarce these days. The article is in demand and it is no longer manufactured.]

LORD EDGAR: Let's not beat about the bush. How much do you want?

ALCAZAR: [For a tomb that no human hand has disturbed since the priests rolled the rocks before the entrance three thousand years ago,] Would it be too much to ask a thousand guineas?

LORD EDGAR: A thousand guineas!

ALCAZAR: A mere nothing. After all, the tomb may contain gold in the lump, necklaces of pearls and diamonds, earrings of carbuncle formed from the urine of lynxes, sapphire seals, ancient idols of precious metals; why, the currency of the time, that by itself would bring a good price.

LORD EDGAR *(Aside)*: Artful scoundrel! He knows perfectly well that such things are not to be found in Egyptian sepulchres.

ALCAZAR: Well, my lord, does the bargain suit you?

LORD EDGAR: Yes, we will call it a thousand guineas. If the tomb has never been touched and nothing—not even a stone—has been disturbed by the levers of the excavators, and on condition that we can carry everything away.

ALCAZAR: I accept. You can risk the bank notes and gold without fear. It seems your prayer has been answered.

LORD EDGAR: Perhaps we are rejoicing too soon and are about to experience the same disappointments encountered by Belzoni when he believed he was the first to enter the tomb of Menepha Seti. [He, after having passed through a maze of corridors, pits and chambers, found only an empty sarcophagus with a broken lid, for the treasure seekers had attained the royal tomb by mining through the rocks from the other direction.]

ALCAZAR: Oh no! [This tomb is too far removed for those accursed moles to have found their way there.] I have lived many years in the Valley of the Kings and my eyes have become as piercing as those of the sacred hawks perched on the entablatures of the temples. For years I have not so much as dared to cast a glance in that direction, fearing to arouse the suspicions of the violators of the tombs. This way, my lord.

(They exit.
The lights fade and come up somewhere in the tomb. It is very dark. From time to time some detail emerges from the darkness in the light of their lanterns.)

LORD EDGAR: The deuce! Are we going down to the center of the earth? The heat increases to such a degree that we cannot be far from the infernal regions.

ALCAZAR: It is a pit, *(With an echo)* pit, pit. Milord, lord, lord. What's to be done, done, done?

LORD EDGAR: We must lower ourselves on ropes, *(Echo)* ropes, ropes. *(Ropes drop out of the ceiling. They climb in place)* These cursed Egyptians were so cunning about hiding the entrances of their burial burrows. [They could not think of enough ways to puzzle poor people.] One can imagine them laughing beforehand at the downcast faces of the excavators.

ALCAZAR: Another dead end.

LORD EDGAR: It looks like they've beaten us this round. It's a bit low, we'll have to crawl on our faces.

ALCAZAR: Oy!

LORD EDGAR: Rap on the floor and listen for a hollow sound.

(They do so. After much rapping, the wall gives back a hollow sound.)

Help me to remove this block.

ALCAZAR: Oy!

(They remove an imaginary block, which puts the set change into action, revealing the tomb.)

[Look there,] Milord.

[LORD EDGAR: The familiar personages of the psychostasia Osiris as judge. *(Stands)* Well well, my dear Alcazar. So far you have kept your part of the bargain. We are indeed the first human beings who have entered here since the dead, whoever he may be, was abandoned to eternity and oblivion in the tomb.

ALCAZAR: Oh, he must have been a very powerful personage— prince of the royal household at least.

LORD EDGAR: I will tell you after I decipher his cartouche.]

ALCAZAR: [But first let us enter the] We have entered the most beautiful room of all, the room the ancient Egyptians called The Golden Room.

[LORD EDGAR: Really, I have some compunction of conscience about disturbing the last rest of this poor unknown mortal who felt so sure that he would rest in peace until the end of the world. Our visit will be a most unwelcome one to the host of this mansion.

ALCAZAR: You'll be wanting a proper introduction and I have lived long enough among the pharaohs to make you one. I know how to present you to the illustrious inhabitant of this subterranean palace.

LORD EDGAR: Look, a five-toed footprint in the dust.

ALCAZAR: Footprint?

LORD EDGAR: It looks as though it were made yesterday.

ALCAZAR: How can that be?

LORD EDGAR: It must have been the last footprint made by the last slave leaving the burial chamber thirty-five hundred years ago. There has not been a breath of air in here to disturb it.

Why, mighty civilizations have risen and fallen since this footprint was made. Their pomp, their power, their monuments of stone have not lasted as long as this insignificant footprint in the dust.]

(Sarcophagus revealed.)

ALCAZAR: [My lord! My lord!] The sarcophagus *(Pronounced "sarcoFAGus")* is intact!

LORD EDGAR: Is it possible, my dear Alcazar—is it intact? *(Examines the sarcophagus then exclaims rapturously)* Incredible good fortune! Marvelous chance! Priceless treasure!

ALCAZAR *(Aside)*: I asked too little. This my lord has robbed me.

LORD EDGAR: There there, Alcazar. A bargain is a bargain. Here are the vases that held the viscera of the mummy contained in the sarcophagus. [Nothing has been touched in this palace of death since the day when the mummy, in its coffins and cerements, had been laid upon its couch of basalt.]

ALCAZAR: Observe that these are not the usual funerary offerings.

LORD EDGAR: Don't touch it! [Touch nothing!] It might crumble. First I must decipher this cartouche. "She Who Sleeps but Will One Day Wake." A lotus sarcophagus. Hmmmm. Notice that the lotus motif recurs as well as the ankh, emblem of eternal life. Must you smoke those nasty musk-scented cigarettes? [There's little enough air in here as it is.]

ALCAZAR: Shall we open the sarcoFAGus?

LORD EDGAR: Certainly. [But take care not to injure the lid when opening it, for I want to remove this monument and make a present of it to the British Museum.]

(They remove the cover.)

ALCAZAR: A woman! A woman!

LORD EDGAR: Astonishing novelty! But [the necropolis of the queens is situated farther off, in a gorge of the mountains.] the tombs of the queens are very simple. Let me decipher the cartouche. "She Who Sleeps but Will One Day Wake."

ALCAZAR *(Pointing to the "but")*: This is a very primitive hieroglyph.

LORD EDGAR: It's a little behind.

SHE

WHO SLEEPS

BUT WILL

ONE DAY

WAKE

*Deciphered hieroglyphic
cartouche: "She Who
Sleeps but Will One
Day Wake."*

[ALCAZAR: It's almost more than I can believe.

LORD EDGAR: It's *altogether* more than *I* can believe.

ALCAZAR: What? You see these things before your very eyes and
still you do not believe.

LORD EDGAR: The women of the East have always been considered inferior to the men, even after death. The greater part
of these tombs, violated at very remote epochs, have served
as receptacles for deformed mummies, rudely embalmed,
that still exhibit traces of leprosy and elephantiasis. By what
means, by what miracle of substitution, had this woman's
coffin found its way into this royal sarcophagus, in the midst
of this palatial crypt, worthy of the most illustrious and
powerful of the pharaohs? This unsettles all of my opinions
and theories and contradicts the most reliable authorities on
the subject of the Egyptian funeral rites so uniform in every
respect for thousands of years.

ALCAZAR: We have no doubt alighted on some mystery, some obscure point lost to history. Had some ambitious woman usurped the tomb as she had the throne?

LORD EDGAR: What a charming custom. To bury a young woman with all the coquettish arsenal of her toilette about her. For there can be no doubt that it is a young woman enveloped in these bands of linen stained yellow with age and essences.

ALCAZAR: Compared with the ancient Egyptians we are veritable barbarians: dragging out a mere animal existence. We no longer have any delicacy of sentiment connected with death. What tenderness, what regret, what love are revealed in this devoted attention, this unlimited precaution, this vain solicitude that no one would ever witness, the affection lavished upon an insensible corpse, these efforts to snatch from destruction an adored form, and to present it to the soul intact upon the great day of the resurrection.

LORD EDGAR: Someday we may attain to such heights of civilization and refinement of feeling. In the meantime let us disrobe this young beauty, more than three thousand years old, with all the delicacy possible.

ALCAZAR: Poor lady, profane eyes are about to rest upon charms unknown to love itself, perhaps.

LORD EDGAR: Strange, I feel embarrassed at not having the proper costume in which to present myself before a royal mummy.

ALCAZAR: There is no time here. In this tomb, far away from the banal stupidities of the modern world, we might just as well be in ancient Egypt on the day this cherished being was entrusted to eternity.

LORD EDGAR: Extraordinary! In most cases the mummification is accomplished through the use of bitumen and natron. Here, the body, prepared by a longer, safer and more costly process has preserved the elasticity of the flesh, the grain of the epidermis, and a color that is almost natural. The skin has the fine hue of a new Florentine bronze and the warm amber tint of a Titian.

ALCAZAR: By the knees of Amon Ra] —Behold—there is a scroll clasped in her hand!

37

(They unwrap the mummy's hand, which holds a scroll.)

LORD EDGAR: [Bring that electric torch here.] "She Who Sleeps but Will One Day Wake." It is the same cartouche unmistakably. *(Reads on silently, then mutters)* Good God! It can't be! It can't be!

ALCAZAR: What does it say?

LORD EDGAR *(Awed)*: It is the formula to revive the princess. To return her to life once more.

ALCAZAR: But surely you don't . . .

LORD EDGAR: It's more than I can believe at the moment, Alcazar. But something inside me wants to believe. *(He reads more)* Well! This is simple enough. These caskets and bottles and bowls contain the ingredients in the formula. *(Reads)* The priest must wear certain vestments and douse the lid with wine. The wine in these bottles has dried up over the centuries. Oh drat! I have no wine. I am an abstainer.

ALCAZAR *(Produces a bottle of wine from his pocket)*: I have wine. Very good wine. And although it is a Madeira, of somewhat more recent vintage, I believe it may suffice. The wine may very well be the least important element in the formula.

LORD EDGAR *(Reads)*: It says here that the priest must be alone with the mummy when the soul is called back from the underworld.

ALCAZAR: Permit me to withdraw and leave you alone with your newfound lady friend. [But before I go, may I make one request?

LORD EDGAR: Certainly, Alcazar, what is it?

ALCAZAR: Leave some wine for the return trip.

LORD EDGAR: I'll use only what is absolutely necessary to complete the ritual.

ALCAZAR: Thank you.]

(Alcazar exits backward making a salaam as he goes out. Lord Edgar closes the door to the sarcophagus. He dresses himself in the costume of the Egyptian priest. Lights the charcoal braziers in the perfuming pans on either side of the sarcophagus. And intones the following invocation:)

LORD EDGAR: Katara katara katara rana! Ecbatana ecbatana soumouft! Soumouft! Fahata fahata Habebe! Oh Habebe! Oh Habebe! Habebe tay! *(He opens the sarcophagus, revealing the living Pev Amri)*

PEV AMRI *(Flutters her eyelashes and opens her eyes)*: Habebe? Habebe tay? *(Unfolds her arms revealing her naked breasts)*

LORD EDGAR *(Cries out)*: Oh God!

PEV AMRI *(Dances, then)*: Fahouta bala bala mem fou ha ram saha-di Karnak!

LORD EDGAR: Oh exquisite! Exquisite beauty!

PEV AMRI: Han fu bazaar danbazaar.

LORD EDGAR: Forgive me divine one, but your spoken language is lost on me.

PEV AMRI: Mabouka. Giza. *(Laughs, then looking into sarcophagus and touching herself)* Ankh! Ankh!

LORD EDGAR *(Exclaims)*: Ankh! Life! Ankh! Life! Life!

PEV AMRI: Ankh . . . life?

LORD EDGAR: Ankh . . . life.

PEV AMRI: Life. Life!

LORD EDGAR: Life!

PEV AMRI *(Writhing indicates stiffness of spine)*: Cairo! Cairo! Practor! [*(If audience hisses:)* Asp!] *(Gestures, pointing to mouth)*

LORD EDGAR: Those lips. Silent for three thousand years now beg to be kissed. But do I dare? *(Kisses her)*

PEV AMRI *(She slaps him)*: Puna kha fo ha na ba bhouna. *(Makes gesture that she is hungry)* Bhouna! Bhouna!

LORD EDGAR: Hungry? Of course you must be hungry after not having eaten in three millennia. I'll get you food. A loaf of bread, a jug of wine, a book of verse and thou beside me in the wilderness and wilderness is paradise enow! *(Kisses her hand)*

PEV AMRI: Amon! Amon Ra! Ahmin-hotep. Memphis. Giza. Aswan. Hatshepsut. Toot 'n' come in!

(Edgar runs off.)

(Scurries back into the mummy case, sniffs) Sphinx! *(Closes the door after her)*

LORD EDGAR *(From offstage)*: Alcazar! Alcazar! She's hungry! She wants food!

ALCAZAR *(From offstage)*: She wants? Surely you don't mean . . .

LORD EDGAR: Yes it's true! It's true! She's alive! She's alive. In flesh and blood.

ALCAZAR: My boy you have stayed too long in the tomb. Your mind is playing tricks on you.

LORD EDGAR: Come if you don't believe me. See for yourself.

(Lord Edgar rushes onto the stage. Alcazar follows behind somewhat slowly and dubiously. He is obviously totally unconvinced.)

Where is she? She's gone . . . She was here a minute ago.

ALCAZAR: Akh—naten!

[LORD EDGAR: I tell you she spoke! I kissed those divine lips. Look! She gave me this ring!

ALCAZAR: We must leave before dawn. If they find us looting the tomb they will report us to the authorities.]

LORD EDGAR: But she's alive, I tell you, alive! *(Calling)* Princess! Princess, where are you? Where are you, Pev Amri? Pev!

ALCAZAR: Is this what you are looking for? *(Opens the lid)*

(Inside the sarcophagus stands a mummy as before, only this time the wrappings have been partially removed, revealing a hideously decomposed face through the dried flesh of which the skull protrudes.)

LORD EDGAR *(Screams)*: No! It can't be! It can't be! Pev. Pev. I should never have summoned you, Alcazar. It broke the spell and sent her back to the underworld.

ALCAZAR: The hour grows late. We must leave before dawn. Pack up whatever you want to take along.

LORD EDGAR: I must take her with me. I must find a way to bring her back again. If it's the last thing I do, I'll bring her back again!

ALCAZAR: Let us remove the sarcoFAGgus. The most dangerous part is over. Rain is what we have to fear now.

(They carry out the mummy case. Lights fade.)

~ Act Three

The scene is Mandacrest. The time is autumn. Jane is dusting the mummy case. Nicodemus looks on. The portrait over the mantel is now of Lady Enid.

NICODEMUS: It was a devil of a time we had getting it in here. The thing must weigh a ton.

JANE: Did you bring Lady Enid's trunk upstairs?

NICODEMUS: Yes.

JANE: Where is she?

NICODEMUS: Alone with her secrets: [old feather fans, tasseled dance cards, powdered with musk, a gaud of amber beads locked away in her drawer. A program from Antoine's when she appeared with Bonita Bainbridge in *The Farfelu of Seville*.]

JANE: It's the paralysis of the insane. She sleeps all day and she's up all night.

NICODEMUS: That was always her way.

JANE: She's got terrible insomnia.

NICODEMUS: Can't remember a thing, eh?

JANE: And when she's up—she walks.

NICODEMUS: And why shouldn't she walk? It's daft she is, not crippled.

JANE: I haven't slept a wink since they brought her home a week ago.

NICODEMUS: You're doing the work of three people.

JANE: I asked Lord Edgar if I could get a slight raise in pay and he said he'd consider it.

NICODEMUS: And to think of you having to beg from these swine. I'm the only one who knows what you are. Why don't you trust me more? What have you got up your nose against me?

JANE *(Crosses to the mirror)*: Come to the glass, Nicodemus, and I'll show you what you should wish. Do you mark those [two lines between your eyes? And those thick brows that instead of rising, arched, sink in the middle? And that] couple of black fiends, so deeply buried, [who never open their windows boldly, but lurk glinting under them,] like devil's spies? Wish and learn to smooth away the surly wrinkles, [to raise your lids frankly] and change the fiends to confident, innocent angels, [suspecting and doubting nothing and always seeing friends where they are not sure of foes.] Don't get the expression of a vicious cur that appears to know the kicks it gets are its dessert, and yet hates all the world, as well as the kicker, for what it suffers.

NICODEMUS: In other words, I must wish for Edgar Hillcrest's great blue eyes and even forehead. I do, but that won't help me to them. I was abandoned. Found on the doorstep of a London doss house. My own mother didn't want me.

JANE: Who knows but your father was emperor of China and your mother was an Indian queen, each of them able to buy up Mandacrest with one week's income. And you were kidnapped by wicked sailors and brought to England. Were I in your place, I would frame high notions of my birth, and the thoughts of what I was should give me courage and dignity.

NICODEMUS: Thank you Janey. In the future while I'm shoveling shit I'll try to think of myself as a prince in disguise.

JANE *(Looking out of the door windows)*: Why don't you do some washin' and combin' and go to the village and visit that dairy maid you've taken a fancy to.

NICODEMUS: She's a cute little baggage but she smells of cheese.

JANE: It's a good night for wooing for the moon is full. *(Bell off)* There's the bell. The mistress wants me. *(Exits)*

NICODEMUS: The moon is full? *(Goes upstage and looks out through the doors)* A full moon. *(He begins to make jerky movements)* A full moooooon! *(Howls as Nicodemus, with his back to the audience, raises one arm, which has become a wolf's paw)* No! No! No! Oh God! God help me! Don't let it happen! It's the moooooon! Moooooooooon! *(He turns to the audience. His face has become that of a wolf. He runs about the stage on his tiptoes with his knees bent. He sniffs, scratches, lifts his leg against a piece of furniture, howls and runs out)*

JANE *(Enters)*: Nicodemus, Lady Enid wants to have a word with you. *(Sees the door left open)* He's gone and he's left the door wide open again. God, he'll never change.

(There is the sound of a wolf howling in the distance.)

LADY ENID *(Enters)*: Do you hear that? First you think it's a wolf. Then you tell yourself it's the wind. But you know that it's a soul in pain. *(Crosses to the fireplace)* Get that flower out of here!

JANE: I thought it looked so lovely.

LADY ENID: I can stand neither its color nor its scent. Take it away.

JANE: It's the last rose of summer. *(Exits with vase)*

(Lady Enid takes down a dulcimer, lays it across her lap and begins to play "The Last Rose of Summer." Jane returns with another dulcimer. She sits on the other side of the fireplace and joins Lady Enid in a duet.)

LADY ENID *(Staring at the portrait over the mantel)*: Who is that woman?

JANE: Why that's yourself, Lady Enid.

LADY ENID: No, no, that's not me. She's a virgin.

JANE: It was painted a long time ago.

LADY ENID: She still has her illusions. She still has her faith. No, that isn't me.

JANE: Virginity is the balloon in the carnival of life. It vanishes with the first prick.

[LADY ENID *(Stops playing abruptly)*: In all of England I don't believe I could have married into a situation so completely removed from the stir of society. A perfect misanthropist's heaven—and Lord Edgar and I are such a perfect pair to divide the desolation between us.

JANE: It's a refuge, it is, from the chatter of tongues.]

LADY ENID: Mine eyes itch. Doth that bode weeping?

JANE: Maybe you've got something in your eye, Lady Enid.

LADY ENID: Where is Nicodemus? I want to have a word with him.

JANE: I'm afraid that's not possible, [Lady Enid.]

LADY ENID: And why not? Send for Nicodemus. I demand to see him at once.

JANE: Nicodemus can't come, Lady Enid. For obvious reasons.

LADY ENID: Obvious reasons? *(The light dawns)* Oh! Oh! For obvious reasons. Oh, I see. In that case, I'll go to him.

JANE: Are you fond of Nicodemus?

LADY ENID: Fond of Nicodemus? Sometimes I feel that I am Nicodemus. That Nicodemus and I are one and the same person.

JANE: Now now, Lady Enid, what have you got up your sleeve?

LADY ENID: Up my sleeve? Up my sleeve? *(She looks up her sleeve. Her own hand comes out in a clawlike gesture. She screams)*

JANE: Don't be frightened, Lady Enid. That's your own hand.

LADY ENID: I frighten myself sometimes. Jane, I fear that Lord Edgar and I are drifting apart. It's a terrible thing to marry an Egyptologist and find out he's hung up on his mummy. [*(If audience hisses:)* That wind!]

JANE: He's an incurable romantic. If you really want to please him, you should try to appeal to that side of his nature. I have a lovely old dress you could wear. It's a family heirloom. It's full of nostalgia.

LADY ENID: We could have it cleaned.

JANE: I'll lay it out in your room. Wear it tonight. It's sure to get a strong reaction.

[LADY ENID: Thank you, Jane.]

(Jane exits. Lady Enid picks up dulcimer, plays "Skip to My Lou." Lord Edgar enters.)

LADY ENID: Edgar, darling, where have you been?

LORD EDGAR: I've been to the jewelers.

LADY ENID: To buy jewelry?

LORD EDGAR: No, bullets. Silver bullets. The young dairymaid in the village was found badly mauled. It seems the werewolf has struck again. I must go to the morgue.

LADY ENID: Oh Edgar. Why don't you just go and live at the morgue instead of making a morgue of our home. *(She flings out)*

LORD EDGAR *(Calling after her)*: Enid. Enid, darling. Please be reasonable.

(Nicodemus appears in the French doors up. He has blood on his hand.)

NICODEMUS: Lord Edgar.

LORD EDGAR: Nicodemus. I'll be needing your help tonight. The werewolf has struck again. This time, the cur must die.

NICODEMUS: Must he die? Is there no other help for him? Can't he be put away somewhere where he could receive therapy? Perhaps someday, science will discover a cure for what he has.

LORD EDGAR: There is only one cure for what he has. The barrel of a gun and a silver bullet. *(Exits)*

NICODEMUS: Oh miserable me. Must I, like Tancred in *Jerusalem Delivered*, ever injure what I love beyond all else? Unloved I lived. Unloved I die. My only crime was having been born.

(Jane enters.)

JANE: And who are you talking to, Nicodemus Underwood?

NICODEMUS: Myself. The only one who'll listen.

JANE: Did you see the milkmaid tonight, Nicodemus?

NICODEMUS: The milkmaid, oh, the milkmaid. Would that I had never seen the milkmaid.

JANE: There's blood on your hand. Did you hurt yourself?

NICODEMUS: No. It's her blood. The blood of the tender maid you spoke of. The werewolf got her.

JANE: Werewolf?

NICODEMUS: Yes, you know, a person who dons the skin of a wolf in the full of the moon and turns into a wolf to prowl at night. A woman is usually the victim. It makes a horrible story.

JANE: And where is it now, this hound of hell?

NICODEMUS: Wipe the blood from my palm with your dainty little hankie, and see the mark of Cain.

(Jane spits on her hankie and wipes some of the blood from Nicodemus's palm. She gasps and jumps back.)

JANE: The pentagram! When did this happen to you?

NICODEMUS: Tonight, in the full of the moon! I turned into a wolf! And took the life of the only fair creature who'd ever shown me any love.

JANE: But the moon is still full. How come you're not a wolf now?

NICODEMUS: I'm in remission since a cloud passed over the moon.

JANE: Unspeakable horror!

NICODEMUS: Unspeakable shame! For I fear what I may do next. For it is the thing I love I kill. And I love you Janey, with all my heart.

JANE: No you don't. It's just infatuation tinged with lust.

NICODEMUS: And I love Lady Enid.

JANE: Lady Enid?

NICODEMUS: Yes. I'd have never dared confess it until this moment. But now I fear I may be some danger to her person. All must out!

JANE: Run away, Nicodemus. Run away and never come back!

NICODEMUS: Where shall I go? I've never known any life but Mandacrest! I have no money, no luggage!

JANE: Go upstairs to my room. On the table by my bed you will find a copy of Lord Lytton's *Zanoni*. In it I have saved a few pounds. Take them. You may need them.

NICODEMUS: Thank you, Janey. *(Exits)*

JANE: Sufficient unto the night are the horrors thereof. *(Falls on knees and prays)* Please God, don't let anything happen to Lord Edgar, don't let anything happen to Lady Enid, and please God, don't let anything happen to me!

LADY ENID *(Enters in a different frock)*: How do I look?

JANE: Lovely, Lady Enid. It's sure to put Lord Edgar into a romantic mood. This dress was always his favorite.

LADY ENID: Are you sure he really likes it?

JANE: Positive. He's even worn it himself when in an antic mood, in younger, happier days. *(Exits)*

LADY ENID *(Goes over to the mantel and looks up at the portrait)*: Well, any man who dresses up as a woman can't be all bad!

(To herself in the portrait) If you continue at this rate you'll
be an even greater actress than Bonita Bainbridge!

VOICE *(From offstage left, moans twice, then)*: Help me. Help me!
Turn the figurine. Turn the figurine!

*(Lady Enid moves an ornament on the fireplace, triggering a
sliding panel. The bookcase slides back, revealing a cage. She
jumps back, startled. A shrouded figure appears within the cage.)*

LADY ENID: Who are you? What are you doing in there?

VOICE: They keep me here! I'm their prisoner! They torture me!
[Please help me! Help me!]

LADY ENID: Who? Who tortures you?

VOICE: Edgar! Edgar tortures me!

LADY ENID: You poor thing. Who are you?

VOICE: Why, I'm his wife, Irma.

LADY ENID: Irma!

VOICE: Irma Vep! The first Lady Hillcrest.

LADY ENID: But I thought you were dead!

IRMA: That's what they want you to think! That's what they want
everyone to think!

LADY ENID: Why have they put you here?

IRMA: There are jewels hidden in the house. I alone know where
they are. But I'll never tell! For if I tell, they'll kill me! If you
help me, I'll tell you where the jewels are, and I'll share them
with you.

LADY ENID: Poor woman! Of course I'll help you. But this cage
is locked!

IRMA: Jane has the key! Steal it from her! But don't tell her you've
seen me! Don't tell anyone! Not Jane. Not Nicodemus! Not
Lord Edgar! *(Footsteps are heard)* I hear someone coming.
Turn the figurine! And please, please remember me!
Remember me!

LADY ENID: Remember you? Of course I'll remember you! How
could I forget you. You poor darling. Poor, poor darling!

*(She turns the figurine. The bookcase starts to close but sticks.
Enid struggles with the figurine. The bookcase closes finally as
Lord Edgar enters.)*

47

LORD EDGAR: Enid!

LADY ENID *(Turning)*: Edgar.

LORD EDGAR: Where did you get that dress?

LADY ENID: Do you like it?

LORD EDGAR: Like it? I hate it! I despise it! I loathe it! Take it off! Take it off!

[LADY ENID: But Edgar! I only wanted to please you!

LORD EDGAR: Please me? You wanted to torture me! You wanted to make me suffer! I'll never forgive you for this Enid! Never!]

LADY ENID: But Edgar! I only wanted to be nearer to you!

LORD EDGAR: You've only driven me further away. I'd rather see you locked away in rags in the deepest, darkest dungeon I could find than see you in that dress!

LADY ENID: No!

LORD EDGAR: Take it off, I said! You're making me hate you!

LADY ENID: What are you saying?

LORD EDGAR: It was her dress.

LADY ENID: *Her* dress?

LORD EDGAR: Irma's!

LADY ENID: Jane didn't tell me that!

LORD EDGAR: Jane told you to wear that? She should have known better. She knows how it upsets me to see the dress Irma wore the night she died!

LADY ENID: Died? But she . . . she didn't . . .

LORD EDGAR: Didn't what?

LADY ENID *(Catching herself)*: . . . die in this dress, did she?

LORD EDGAR: Oh don't talk about it anymore! You'll only make me hate you more. *(He tears her dress. Lady Enid bursts into tears and runs to the door)* Stop, Enid! I'm sorry. I didn't mean it.

LADY ENID: You don't love me and you never have.

LORD EDGAR: You're wrong! I love no one else but you.

LADY ENID: Then why, why, why must we go on living here as brother and sister? Why can't you live with me as a wife?

LORD EDGAR: Because of the terror I feel of *her* . . .

LADY ENID: Terror?

LORD EDGAR: Yes, terror! Terror! A terror so great that I've never been able to communicate it to anyone.

LADY ENID: Even your wife?

LORD EDGAR: Very well, then, I'll tell you. Sometimes I see her standing before me as big as life.

LADY ENID: How does she look?

LORD EDGAR: Oh, very well. Exactly as she did when I saw her last, three years ago.

LADY ENID: Three years ago?

LORD EDGAR: She won't let me go. I'm her prisoner.

LADY ENID: *She* won't let *you* go?

LORD EDGAR: Yes, yes, she's horrible. I'll never get rid of her.

LADY ENID: But you have gotten rid of her. On your trip to Egypt. You said you'd found something in the tomb that had made you forget all about her.

LORD EDGAR: Don't talk about it. Or think of it, even. There was no help for me there. I can feel it in my bones. I didn't get rid of it out there either.

LADY ENID: Of what? What do you mean?

LORD EDGAR: I mean the horror. The fantastic hold on my mind, on my soul.

LADY ENID: But you said it was over.

LORD EDGAR: No, no, that's just the thing. It isn't.

LADY ENID: Not over?

LORD EDGAR: No Enid, it's not over, and I'm afraid it never will be.

LADY ENID *(In a strangled voice)*: Are you saying then that in your heart of hearts you'll never be able to forget this woman?

LORD EDGAR: She comes toward me and puts her arms around me. Then she presses her lips to mine.

LADY ENID: To kiss you?

LORD EDGAR: As if to kiss me—but she doesn't kiss. She sucks.

LADY ENID: Sucks?

LORD EDGAR: She sucks my breath until I feel I'm suffocating. *(Turns blue)*

LADY ENID: Good God! Edgar! You're sick! You're much sicker than you thought. Than either of us thought.

LORD EDGAR *(Clutching at his throat)*: Yes! Yes! I can't breathe! I'm suffocating, and her fingers are tightening! Tightening around my throat. Help me. Help me.

LADY ENID: Oh, my dear Lord Edgar! Then you've been suffering in silence all this time and you've never told me anything about it?

LORD EDGAR: I couldn't tell you. I couldn't speak the unspeakable, name the unnameable. *(Gasps for breath)* And her fingers are tightening. Tightening more and more. Help me! Help me!

LADY ENID: Nicodemus! *(Runs off calling)* Nicodemus.

NICODEMUS *(From offstage)*: You called, Lady Enid?

LADY ENID *(From offstage)*: Yes please, please help me. Lord Edgar is having an attack. *(She weeps)*

NICODEMUS *(Off)*: There, there, Lady Enid. Calm yourself.

LADY ENID *(Off)*: Oh please, hurry, hurry!

NICODEMUS *(Off)*: Stay here. I'll go to him. *(Enters)* There, there, Lord Edgar. Doing poorly? Have you got the horrors again?

LORD EDGAR *(Rolling about on the floor, clutching his throat)*: Yes, yes, the horrors. It's her. I'll never be free of her.

NICODEMUS *(Offering his flask)*: [Here you go.] You must fight fire with fire and spirits with spirits!

LORD EDGAR: No, I won't break my rule. You know I am an abstainer.

NICODEMUS Oh well then, in that case . . . *(Drinks himself)*

LORD EDGAR *(Seeing this)*: On second thought, maybe just a drop.

NICODEMUS *(Passing him the flask)*: For medicinal purposes only.

(Lord Edgar drains the flask.)

(Turning over the empty flask) Feeling better?

LORD EDGAR: Yes, much. Thanks. Nicodemus, stay with Lady Enid tonight.

NICODEMUS: With Lady Enid?

LORD EDGAR: Yes, there's a wolf about, and I don't want her left alone. *(Exits up center)*

NICODEMUS: No, no, Lord Edgar. Not that! Don't ask me that! Anything but that! Horror. Horror. Horror. For I fear the gibbous moon. Oh horror! Oh horror!

JANE *(Enters with wolfsbane)*: Did you find the money?

NICODEMUS: Yes, thank you Janey.

JANE: Now go, Nicodemus. I've never liked you, but I've never wished you any harm. May God help you!

NICODEMUS: Thank you, Janey. This is the only kindness anyone has ever shown me.

JANE: Ah, be off with you. I have to put up wolfsbane against you.

NICODEMUS: I understand. *(Exits)*

(Jane hangs up wolfsbane around the room. Lady Enid enters.)

LADY ENID: Where's Lord Edgar?

JANE: He's gone out, after the wolf.

LADY ENID: Is he hunting wolves again, with one of his villainous old guns?

JANE: I think he took a horse pistol.

LADY ENID: The blackguard.

JANE: Now Lady Enid, I won't have you talking this way about Lord Edgar.

LADY ENID *(Seizing her by the wrist)*: When a woman loves a man she should be willing to do anything for him. Cut off her little finger at the middle joint there. *(Twisting Jane's finger)*

JANE *(Loudly)*: Ow!

LADY ENID: Or cut off her dainty hand at the wrist.

JANE: Please, let go. You're hurting me!

LADY ENID: Or lop off her pretty little ear. *(Twists her ear and takes the keys from Jane's apron pocket)*

JANE: Ow! Ow! Ow! Please stop!

LADY ENID: When you're willing to do those things for Lord Edgar then entertain thoughts of loving him. Otherwise back off. *(Releases her)*

JANE *(Rubbing her wrist)*: Now look. You've left red marks on my wrist. You've got a devil in you. That's what it is. You know I'm nothing to Lord Edgar. I have no more hold over his heart than you have. It's Irma he loves! Irma Vep. It's no use our fighting over the same man—when he's in love with a dead woman.

LADY ENID: You scandalous little hypocrite! Are you not afraid of being carried away bodily whenever you mention the devil's name? I warn you to refrain from provoking me or I will ask your abduction as a special favor.

(Jane goes to leave.)

Stop Jane! Look here. I'll show you how far I've progressed in the Black Art. *(Taking down a book from the shelf)* I shall soon be competent to make a clear house of it. [The red cow didn't die by chance, and your rheumatism can hardly be reckoned among providential visitations!]

JANE: Oh wicked! Wicked! May the Lord deliver us from evil!

LADY ENID: No, reprobate! You are a castaway. Be off, or I'll hurt you seriously. I'll have you all modeled in wax and clay, and the first who passes the limits I fix, shall . . . I'll not say what he shall be done to . . . but you'll see! Go—I'm looking at you. *(Runs toward Jane)*

JANE *(Trembling with sincere horror, hurries out praying and ejaculating)*: Wicked! Wicked!

LADY ENID *(Laughing)*: Wicked, perhaps. But I have the keys! *(She approaches the bookcase. She turns the figurine. The bookcase slides back)* Psst! Psst! Irma! Irma, darling. Are you there?

IRMA: Where else would I be? Did you get the key?

LADY ENID: Yes, I have it.

IRMA: Open the door. Quickly. Quickly!

LADY ENID: But I don't know which one it is.

IRMA: Quickly! Quickly! Before someone comes.

LADY ENID *(Trying one key after another)*: Well, there are so many of them.

IRMA: Quickly! Save me! Save me!

LADY ENID *(Opening the door)*: Ah, there, Irma, dearest. You're free.

(Irma flies out of the door shrieking like a madwoman. She seizes Lady Enid by the throat, turns her back to the audience and leans over her. Lady Enid sinks to her knees.)

IRMA *(Calmly)*: Oh triple fool! Did you not know that Irma Vep is "vampire" anagrammatized!

(Lady Enid reaches up and rips off Irma's face, which is a rubber mask, revealing the other player.)

LADY ENID: Edgar?

JANE: No, Jane!

LADY ENID: Jane! You?

JANE: Yes, I did it! I killed the child, and Irma, too! I was the vampire, feeding on the lifeblood of my own jealousy! No more will I eat the bitter crust of charity, nor serve a vain mistress!

LADY ENID: You? You killed her?

JANE: Yes I killed her, and I'll kill again. I'd kill any woman who stood in my way.

LADY ENID: You're mad.

JANE: Mad? Mad? *(She laughs maniacally)* Perhaps I am. Love is a kind of madness. And hatred is a bottomless cup, and I will drink the dregs.

(Jane pulls out a meat cleaver and attacks Lady Enid. Lady Enid, who has backed over to the mummy case, deftly opens the door as Jane runs at her. Jane goes into the mummy case. Lady Enid slams the door and holds it shut. We hear Jane pounding within the mummy case.)

LADY ENID *(Crying out)*: Help me! Nicodemus! Edgar! Someone! Anyone! Help me!

LORD EDGAR *(Rushes in)*: Enid, what is it?

LADY ENID *(Hysterically)*: She's in the mummy case. She's in the mummy case. You can hear her rapping.

(The rapping stops.)

LORD EDGAR: I don't hear anything.

LADY ENID: I found it all out. Jane killed Irma, and the child! Irma Vep is "vampire" anagrammatized.

LORD EDGAR: Enid, I think your mind is affected.

LADY ENID: No, it's Jane. Jane is mad. Mad, I tell you. She attacked me with a meat ax. She's in the mummy case. Call Scotland Yard.

LORD EDGAR: Nonsense, Enid. *(Goes to open the mummy case)*

LADY ENID: What are you going to do?

LORD EDGAR: I'm going to open the mummy case.

LADY ENID: No, don't open the mummy case.

LORD EDGAR: I'm going to open the mummy case. Stand back.

LADY ENID: Don't open the mummy case.

LORD EDGAR: I'm going to open the mummy case.

LADY ENID: Don't open the mummy case. Don't open it. Don't open it. Don't . . .

LORD EDGAR *(Opens the mummy case)*: See Enid? The mummy case is perfectly empty.

LADY ENID *(Somewhat mollified)*: Well, she was in there a moment ago.

(The lights begin to dim.)

The lights. The lights are dimming. The lights. The lights are dimming.

(The lights come back up.)

LORD EDGAR: Nonsense, Enid. The lights are not dimming. Come and sit by the fire.

(Lights dim again.)

LADY ENID: The lights are dimming.

LORD EDGAR *(Escorts her to chair)*: If you don't stop, Enid, they'll put you back in the sanitarium and they'll never let you out again.

LADY ENID *(In a tiny voice)*: The lights are dimming.

LORD EDGAR *(Infuriated)*: Stop it, Enid! Stop it stop it stop it stop it! I don't want to hear you say that again!

(Lady Enid turns to the audience and silently mouths the words, "The lights are dimming.")

There's the good girl. There's the good girl. Go on, play your dulcimer like the good girl. Play with your dulcimer, Enid. *(Crosses to the door to exit)* And I'll have Jane fix you a nice hot cup of tea.

(Lady Enid winces.)

Tch tch tch! *(Exits)*

(Lady Enid begins to play "The Last Rose of Summer" on her dulcimer as ominous music swells.)

LADY ENID: Is it possible my mind is affected? And yet I saw it with my very eyes. *(There is a tapping at the window, as in Act One)* There it is again! Oh God. Oh God in heaven. There it is again. The rapping! The rapping! As if someone gently tapping. *(She takes the poker from the fireside and approaches the French doors stealthily and flies through them, brandishing the poker)* Tapping at my chamber door!

NICODEMUS *(From offstage)*: Hey, Lady Enid! What's going on? *(Poking his head through the door)* What's going on here? *(Ducks out)*

LADY ENID *(Appearing at the door)*: Oh Nicodemus. I heard a rapping, a rapping, as if someone gently tapping, tapping at my chamber door! *(She ducks out)*

NICODEMUS *(Popping in)*: There, there, Lady Enid. 'Tis the wind and nothing more. *(Ducks out)*

LADY ENID *(Popping in)*: Oh Nicodemus, I was so frightened, so terribly, terribly frightened!

NICODEMUS *(His arm comes through the door, pats her shoulder)*: There, there, Lady Enid. I'll never let any harm come to you.

LADY ENID *(Kissing his hand)*: Thank you, Nicodemus. Thank you.

NICODEMUS: There, there. *(His hand is withdrawn and reappears as a wolf's hand. Pats her cheek and squeezes her breast)* There, there.

LADY ENID *(Fully reenters the room, closing the French doors behind her)*: It's so good to know he's there! Is it possible my mind is affected? Or can I trust my senses five? I saw it with my very eyes. And yet, the mummy case is perfectly empty! *(Opens the mummy case)*

(Jane, in her maid's uniform once again, comes running out of the mummy case shrieking and wielding a meat ax. Lady Enid screams and runs out the door down right, slamming it behind her. The corner of her robe sticks out through the closed door.)

JANE *(Flies to the door, finds it locked and rants)*: Open the door. Open the door, Lady Enid. It's just a matter of time before I get in, you know. It was the same way when I killed Lady Irma. She was all alone in the house the night I strangled her.

LADY ENID *(From offstage)*: No, no! You're horrible!

JANE: And Victor, the little bastard. I drowned him in the mill run.

LADY ENID *(Off)*: No!
JANE: You should have seen the bubbles coming out of his ugly little nose.
LADY ENID *(Off)*: How could you? How could you?
JANE: Ah, glorious death. Glorious, glorious death!

(Nicodemus, as werewolf, bursts through French doors.)

Victor!

(Nicodemus grabs Jane by the throat and drags her out the way he came in, howling.)

LADY ENID *(Off)*: Edgar, is that you?

(Lord Edgar rushes in and fires shots. The werewolf falls and turns into Nicodemus.)

NICODEMUS: Each man kills the thing he loves. The coward does it with a kiss, the brave man with a sword. Yet, Nicodemus did love.
LORD EDGAR: Nicodemus, Nicodemus, I've killed you. In earnest.
NICODEMUS: Thank you. *(Dies)*
LORD EDGAR: The poor man is dead. From his fair and unpolluted flesh may violets spring! Bury him on the moors he loved so well, and may his soul ascend to heaven, for he lived in hell!

(Blackout.)

SCENE 2

Lights up on Lady Enid and Lord Edgar. Lord Edgar is sitting in his chair. Lady Enid is standing beside him.

LADY ENID: Poor Nicodemus. Poor Victor. Poor Irma. Poor Jane! Somehow it just doesn't make sense.
LORD EDGAR: Enid, there are more things on heaven and earth than are dreamed of in our philosophies! Enid, I had an uncanny experience in Egypt. And I've written it all up in a treatise, which I expect will cause some stir. [My very reputation as an Egyptologist would hang in the balance.] I've been warned by

all my colleagues not to publish it, but I must. [They say that it couldn't have happened. That an ancient mummy, a hideously shriveled, decaying object, could not have survived the ages and been brought to life by spells and incantations. And yet, I saw it with my very eyes! I must tell the world,] Even if it ruins my reputation! For I believe that we all lived before, in another time, in another age, and that you and I were lovers in ancient Egypt, thirty-five hundred years ago. She was so like you. You are so like her. Oh Enid, Enid!

LADY ENID: Stop! I can't bear it! I can't go on. Oh, you poor, poor man!

LORD EDGAR: What do you mean, Enid?

LADY ENID: Oh, stop. You're making me weep so terribly! I've done a terrible thing. I fear you'll never forgive me for it.

LORD EDGAR: What are you talking about?

LADY ENID: It was me in the tomb, Edgar.

LORD EDGAR: You? Impossible. But you were away in a sanitarium.

LADY ENID: No, I wasn't. I feigned madness. Alcazar is my father! He is actually Professor Lionel Cuncliff of Cambridge University.

LORD EDGAR: Not *the* Lionel Cuncliff! The leading Egyptologist and sarcophogologist.

LADY ENID: Yes, your old rival.

LORD EDGAR: Old Cuncliff your father? That's impossible! You couldn't have been in Egypt!

LADY ENID: If you could only believe that I did it for you, to win you away from . . . her. If I could make you believe that our love was destined, I thought I could bind you to me. But my father used it for his own purposes. To make a fool of you. To discredit you before the academic community and the world! He had never forgiven you for having won the Yolanda Sonabend fellowship he had so counted on. Can you ever forgive me?

LORD EDGAR: I can't believe that you pulled it off! How did you get in the tomb?

LADY ENID: The tomb was actually an Egyptian restaurant that had been closed quite a number of years. I simply came in through the kitchen.

LORD EDGAR: You little witch!

LADY ENID: We had only a few days to make it look like a tomb. We used a decorator from the theater. Oh, the hours he spent polishing that floor. [It gave us quite a turn when you discovered that footprint. But by then you wanted to believe so much, you convinced yourself.] Can you ever forgive me?

LORD EDGAR: Forgive you? I want to thank you. You've freed me at last. Somehow I've come to realize that we are all God's creatures every one of us. Big Victor and little Victor, too.

LADY ENID: You can say that.

LORD EDGAR: I mean it. Oh God I've been so selfish.

LADY ENID: Me, too. But we can make it all up somehow.

LORD EDGAR: There's a hard day's work ahead of us, Enid.

LADY ENID: But on the seventh day we'll rest.

LORD EDGAR *(Quietly, very moved)*: And in that stillness perhaps we'll hear the spirits visiting.

LADY ENID *(In a whisper)*: Spirits?

LORD EDGAR *(As before)*: Yes, perhaps they'll be all around us— those we've lost.

LADY ENID: Big Victor and little Victor, too?

LORD EDGAR: Yes, it may be that now and then throughout our lives we may still catch glimpses of them. *(Ardently)* If only I knew where to look. Where should I look, Enid?

LADY ENID *(Going to the doors and opening them)*: Out there through the fog—beyond the moors. *(Reaches out her hand to him and beckons him to come)*

LORD EDGAR *(His eyes fixed on her, he moves toward her slowly)*: Beyond the moors?

LADY ENID: And upward.

LORD EDGAR: Yes, yes, upward.

LADY ENID: Toward the stars and toward that great silence.

LORD EDGAR *(Taking her hand in his)*: Thank you.

(They stand in the doorway with their backs to us, looking up as the lights fade to darkness.)

THE END

GALAS

A Modern Tragedy

1983

Production History

Galas: A Modern Tragedy was first presented by the Ridiculous Theatrical Company at the Sheridan Square Theatre in New York City in 1983. Scenic design was by Jack Kelly, costume design was by Everett Quinton, lighting design was by Lawrence Eichler and original music was by Peter Golub. It was directed by Charles Ludlam. The cast was as follows:

MARIA MAGDALENA GALAS (LA GALAS)	Charles Ludlam
GIOVANNI BAPTISTA MERCANTEGGINI	Emilio Cubeiro
BRUNA LINA RASTA	Everett Quinton
ARISTOTLE PLATO SOCRATES ODYSSEUS/	
STATUESQUE BEAUTY	John Heys
ATHINA ODYSSEUS	Deborah Petti
HÜRE VON HOYDEN	Black-Eyed Susan
POPE SIXTUS VII/FRITALINI/	
ILKA WINTERHALTER	Julian Craggs
PRELATE/GHINGHERI	Bill Vehr
FRANCO COGLIONES/TICKET SELLER/	
WAITER IN TRAIN STATION	Edward McGowan
PEOPLE IN THE OPERA BOX	Fred Segilia
SAILORS ON ODYSSEUS'S YACHT	Edward McGowan
	Fred Segilia
	Bill Vehr

⎯⎯◠ *Characters* ◠⎯⎯

MARIA MAGDALENA GALAS, a famous diva

GIOVANNI BAPTISTA MERCANTEGGINI,
her aging husband, an industrialist

BRUNA LINA RASTA, a mad soprano, Galas's maid

ARISTOTLE PLATO SOCRATES ODYSSEUS,
a wealthy ship owner

ATHINA ODYSSEUS, his beautiful young wife

HÜRE VON HOYDEN, a courtesan, his ex-mistress

POPE SIXTUS VII

PRELATE

GHINGHERI, artistic director of La Scala

FRITALINI, his associate

FRANCO COGLIONES, a tenor

ILKA WINTERHALTER, a gossip columnist, confidante to Galas

TICKET SELLER

WAITER IN TRAIN STATION

STATUESQUE BEAUTY

PEOPLE IN THE TRAIN STATION

PEOPLE IN THE OPERA BOX

SAILORS ON ODYSSEUS'S YACHT

GUESTS ON ODYSSEUS'S YACHT

GALAS: Only my dogs
will not betray me.

⟶ *Act One*

THE VERONA TRAIN STATION

MERCANTEGGINI *(To Ticket Seller)*: Has the eleven-thirty train arrived from Naples?

TICKET SELLER: No, signore, I'm afraid it's late.

MERCANTEGGINI *(Laughs)*: Excellent!

TICKET SELLER: You aren't angry?

MERCANTEGGINI: No, I'm delighted. It's another delightful reminder that that bastard Mussolini has fallen. He made the trains run on time. I shall never complain about their being late again.

(Train is heard off.)

TICKET SELLER: Here it comes now. Do you want to buy a ticket?

MERCANTEGGINI: No, I'm meeting someone. The Verona Arena has appointed me the official escort for their prima donnas. I am here to welcome a new singer from America.

TICKET SELLER: Is she any good?

MERCANTEGGINI: She's supposed to be fabulous.

TICKET SELLER: Have you heard Baldini? Now, there is the voice of an angel.

MERCANTEGGINI: She has a nice middle and wonderful bottom. But I think she's a little short on top.

TICKET SELLER: Up your ass! What do you know? *(Exits)*

(The station fills with steam as the train arrives onstage. Assorted types get off. Mercanteggini watches them and looks eagerly for the prima donna he is expecting. A soldier greets a woman; they embrace, kiss and walk off. An old lady is greeted by a couple with a baby; he takes her bags, they exit. Suddenly a statuesque beauty wearing a fur stole, small hat with veil and tight skirt enters. Mercanteggini approaches her.)

MERCANTEGGINI: Signorina Galas?

STATUESQUE BEAUTY: I'm afraid you are mistaken. *(Seeing someone offstage)* Ciao, Guido! *(Runs off)*

(The train starts up again. Through the last cloud of steam enters a dowdy person with her cardboard suitcase tied with string. She wears sensible oxfords, a severe suit and a cloth coat. She carries a covered birdcage and (forgive me for saying so) she is fat. She looks about the train station wearily and sits down at a small table. Mercanteggini goes out on the platform.)

WAITER *(Entering)*: Yes, signora?

GALAS *(To the Waiter)*: I'd like the veal cutlet, please.

WAITER: I think there's just one.

GALAS: And a cup of coffee.

(Waiter exits.)

MERCANTEGGINI *(Reenters)*: No sign of her.

WAITER *(Reenters and serves Galas her veal cutlet and coffee)*: Here you are signora . . . the last one. *(Then to Mercanteggini)* Yes, signore?

MERCANTEGGINI *(Looking at the menu)*: I'll have the veal cutlet.

WAITER: The veal, she is finished.

MERCANTEGGINI: How's that?

WAITER: No more veal cutlet.

MERCANTEGGINI: Damn.

GALAS *(To Mercanteggini)*: I'm afraid I have the last one. Please take mine.

MERCANTEGGINI: Thank you, but I couldn't, signorina.

GALAS: No, please, don't be silly. Take it. I'm not hungry. *(Hands him the plate)*

MERCANTEGGINI: If you're sure you don't want it.

GALAS: Positive.

MERCANTEGGINI: You're very kind. *(Tears into the veal)*

GALAS: Not at all. I'm too exhausted to eat. I didn't get a seat on the train so I had to stand all the way from Naples. The train ride was more of an ordeal than crossing the Atlantic.

MERCANTEGGINI: Crossing the Atlantic?

GALAS: Yes. I couldn't afford to fly so I came by boat and train. And now it seems that no one has come to meet me. You see, I've been engaged to sing at the Verona Arena.

MERCANTEGGINI: Forgive me, signorina, I am Giovanni Baptista Mercanteggini, *(Kisses her hand)* your official escort.

GALAS: You work for the opera?

MERCANTEGGINI *(Moves his chair to join Galas at her table)*: Not exactly. I am what you call . . . how do you say . . . a fan.

GALAS: You are an opera lover?

MERCANTEGGINI: Yes, I'm a real aficionado. Now there's something we have in common, eh?

GALAS *(Smiles, a little embarrassed)*: What's that?

MERCANTEGGINI: We are both music lovers.

GALAS: I am not a music lover. I am a musician.

MERCANTEGGINI: But surely you love music.

GALAS: I am a musician. And because I am a singer I am a musical instrument. A music lover, no. I am music.

MERCANTEGGINI: But you don't love it? Not even a little bit?

GALAS: I wouldn't dare. Art is so great it frightens me sometimes.

MERCANTEGGINI: What do you like to do more than anything else?

GALAS To sing. What else is there?

MERCANTEGGINI: Do you have any other interests?

GALAS Whatever do you mean? Of course I have no other interests . . .

MERCANTEGGINI: What about as a little girl?

GALAS: I never had any childhood. *(Lashing out bitterly)* And forgive me for saying this, because it may sound cruel, but I really do think there must be a law against making children perform like dogs. It makes them old before their time. My mother robbed me of my childhood.

MERCANTEGGINI: Don't tell me you never went to parties or on outings.

GALAS *(Amused)*: No. No parties. No outings. Only music. In Greece, during the war, I sang to the soldiers for food. Some of the girls sold their bodies. But I could sing so I never had to do *that*. We knew hunger then. As you can see I've made up for it since. *(Laughs)* In fact I had a chance to sing at the Metropolitan but I turned it down because of it.

MERCANTEGGINI: Why? Because of your weight? But that's quite usual in singers.

GALAS: The role was Madame Butterfly. I couldn't see myself as the fragile little geisha. Opera is more than singing, you know.

MERCANTEGGINI: Personally, I've never cared for skinny women. I like them more Rubenesque

GALAS *(Laughing, embarrassed)*: Really?

MERCANTEGGINI: Yes! I like a woman with some flesh on her bones.

GALAS *(Slightly annoyed, but enjoying the attention)*: Oh really? Enough of talking about me now. You haven't told me a thing about yourself. What do you do?

MERCANTEGGINI: I make bricks.

GALAS: No! Really? Bricks of all things! You don't look it.

MERCANTEGGINI: I don't make them myself. I own a chain of factories that make them.

GALAS: Oh, I see! That's more like it.

MERCANTEGGINI: I'd like to help you.

GALAS: Help me? How?

MERCANTEGGINI: We could make a little arrangement. I will support you for a year.

GALAS: I'm afraid I couldn't . . .

MERCANTEGGINI: Please don't get the wrong idea. This would be purely a business arrangement. I have helped other singers before but none of them ever went on to make a successful career.

GALAS: I'm sorry. I didn't know that.

MERCANTEGGINI: I will, as I said, support you for one year and act as your manager. You will devote yourself entirely to your singing. You study and I will take care of the rest. If at the end of the year we are both satisfied with the arrangement then we will continue. If not, we can let it go at that.

GALAS: Could I have a day to think this over?

MERCANTEGGINI: Of course you should think it over. You must be tired now and you have your Gioconda at the Verona Arena to think about.

(Galas lifts birdcage and whistles to her bird.)

Is that your pet?

GALAS: Pet? No, this is my music teacher.

(Waiter brings the check.)

Ah, here's the check.

MERCANTEGGINI: Allow me. *(Gives money to Waiter)* Since I ate your veal cutlet, I'll pay for your coffee.

GALAS: I couldn't let you do that. *(Looks at check myopically, then counts change)* Sixteen, seventeen, eighteen—there.

MERCANTEGGINI: Have you ever seen Venice?

GALAS: No.

MERCANTEGGINI: Tomorrow if you're free we could drive there.

GALAS: Oh well, that would be nice, but I think I'd better not.

MERCANTEGGINI: Oh, but I insist. If you've never seen Venice it's an absolute must.

GALAS: I would really love to—but I only brought one change of clothes and I wouldn't have a clean blouse to wear.

MERCANTEGGINI: I see nothing wrong with the one you're wearing.

GALAS: I suppose if I washed it out tonight it could be dry by tomorrow.

MERCANTEGGINI: If not, I'll buy you a new one. You need a holiday before you start working. Have you ever sung in the open air before?

GALAS: Not since I sang for those soldiers during the war.

MERCANTEGGINI: It's tricky. Sometimes it's difficult to be heard over the orchestra.

GALAS: Oh don't worry about that. That's one thing I'm sure of. I will be heard.

(Lights fade.)

SCENE 2

VILLA MERCANTEGGINI

Mercanteggini is reading a newspaper. Bruna is sweeping.

MERCANTEGGINI: Was there any mail, Bruna?

BRUNA: There is a letter from la Signora Mercanteggini.

MERCANTEGGINI: From my mother?

BRUNA: From your wife.

MERCANTEGGINI: From Magdalena? At last. I thought she'd never answer my letters. *(Opens letter and reads; Bruna sits and listens)* "Caro, caro Giovanni. Forgive me for not writing sooner but I have been ill, terribly ill. The weather here is beastly. Their seasons are just the reverse of ours. So that while you are having spring, autumn has come here and I apparently got a chill. It's damp and gray, that kind of cold that pierces your bones. I never really feel warm. Anyway, the cold became a flu. And I had to sing with runny eyes and nose. Sometimes the voice obeys and sometimes it does not. We have received very good critics and they have asked me to stay longer and sing a Norma but I told them no. I am homesick, darling. I long only to be in the arms of my Giovanni. I cover you with a thousand kisses on your eyes on your lips and other naughty places. Hold me close and never let me go again. Leaving for Argentina on our wedding night I felt like one of my opera heroines. After not hearing from you for weeks one day a packet arrived with all your letters at once. Tomorrow I leave to return to you forever. The mails are so slow that by the time you get this I will probably be home. I long to see the villa. I want to see if it is exactly as I imagined it from your description. I love you so much that I would die happy if I could die in your arms. Magdalena." Bruna, what's today's date?

BRUNA: February thirtieth.

MERCANTEGGINI: March first? My God! She'll be home today! Bruna, prepare her room.

(A bell is heard off.)

See who it is.

(With a grand operatic gesture, Bruna exits. She reenters with Galas, in fur. She is blond and has undergone a dramatic weight loss.)

GALAS: Is this the Mercanteggini residence?

MERCANTEGGINI: Yes, signora, can I . . . Magdalena!

GALAS *(Flying into his arms)*: Giovanni, my darling Giovanni! It's so good to be home. *(Removes her coat)*

MERCANTEGGINI: What happened to you? You got so skinny. How did you lose so much weight?

GALAS: Misery. I've been pining away for you.

MERCANTEGGINI: And your hair. You're like a different person.

GALAS: Don't worry. It's still me. Don't you like me blond?

MERCANTEGGINI: It's just that it seems a little vulgar. It makes you look hard.

GALAS: Don't worry. If you don't like it I'll change it back.

MERCANTEGGINI: So tell me, how was your tour? The reviews I've read have all been glowing.

GALAS: Argentina is a miserable country. Every Fascist in the world must be there. And the climate is very bad for the voice.

MERCANTEGGINI: And you met the Peróns?

GALAS: Yes.

MERCANTEGGINI: What was that like?

GALAS: Well, Evita is a bit of a bitch. I couldn't stand her. You know they run that country almost entirely at their caprice. Although she did do one thing I am thankful of.

MERCANTEGGINI: What's that?

GALAS: She prevented Rigal from singing at the state gala and demanded me instead.

MERCANTEGGINI: Delia Rigal, the great Argentine soprano?

GALAS: Yes, poor Rigal. I really had to laugh. *(Sits)*

MERCANTEGGINI: Bruna?

BRUNA: Yes, Giovanni?

MERCANTEGGINI: This is your new mistress, Magdalena. Magdalena, this is Bruna, our housekeeper.

GALAS *(Rising to shake her hand)*: How do you do, Bruna?

BRUNA: Very well, thank you. I'm pleased to meet you, Magdalena.

GALAS: Really Giovanni, I think the servants should show more respect and not address us by our first names.

MERCANTEGGINI: What, Bruna?

GALAS: Yes. Bruna, in the future I would like you to cultivate a manner of excessive politeness. In the future you will please call the master of the house "Commendatore Mercanteggini" and you will refer to me as "madam."

BRUNA: Yes, madam.

GALAS: And I really do think you ought to wear a uniform.

MERCANTEGGINI: Yes, Bruna, we'll have to get you a uniform.

BRUNA: Yes, Commendatore Mercanteggini. *(Exits with grand operatic gesture)*

MERCANTEGGINI: You know Bruna was a singer herself once.

GALAS *(Skeptically)*: Really?

MERCANTEGGINI: Perhaps you've heard of her. Bruna Lina Rasta.

GALAS: Bruna Lina Rasta! Of course I've heard of her. She was one of the greatest. But how did she come to this . . . I mean being a servant?

MERCANTEGGINI: I don't really think of Bruna as a servant. She's more like a mother to me. She once had a great career but one night she went mad and started singing *Il Trovatore* during a performance of *Aïda* and threw herself into the orchestra pit.

GALAS: Her voice is preserved on only one seventy-eight R.P.M., very speeded up but you can tell she was incredible. I'll bet I could learn a lot from her if she were willing to teach me.

MERCANTEGGINI: And she is a great cook. I'm going to tell her to fatten you up again.

GALAS: Oh no you don't! Now that the weight is off it's going to stay off. I've had quite enough of the critics comparing me to the elephants when I sing Aïda.

MERCANTEGGINI: There's such a thing as being too thin too, you know. It's like you're not the same old Magdalena.

GALAS *(Embracing Mercanteggini)*: But you still love me, don't you?

MERCANTEGGINI: Sure I love you. It's just that there's not as much to hold onto. *(Feels her bottom)*

GALAS: I never want to be away from you again. I don't mind touring if you go with me. But going to Argentina all by myself was almost unbearable. I was so lonely without you.

MERCANTEGGINI: I missed you, too. But bookings are where you find them. You only got sixty lira at the Verona Arena. In Buenos Aires you made several thousand. That's some difference.

GALAS: Yes, but they wouldn't let me take the money out of the country. I didn't know what to do, so at the last minute I spent it all on fur coats.

MERCANTEGGINI: Every time you sing your fee goes up a little higher. That's good business.

GALAS *(Sits)*: But what about La Scala? Has there been any word?

MERCANTEGGINI: Your audition went so well, I was sure it was in the bag. But no matter how often I write or call, I get no response. Something is blocking your way. I don't know what it is. *(Sits)*

GALAS: To sing at La Scala. That's every singer's dream. It's the most one could hope for in a career.

MERCANTEGGINI: I hardly know how to break this news to you, cara. Look at this advertisement in today's paper. *(Hands her the paper)*

GALAS *(Puts on her glasses and reads)*: "Physiological Pizza—dietetic foods from the great Roman industries of nourishment—The Pastaciutta Mills and Pizza Factories." What of it?

MERCANTEGGINI: Read the paragraph underneath the caption, "Certificate."

GALAS: "Certificate: In my capacity as the doctor treating Maria Magdalena Galas, I certify that the marvelous results obtained in the diet undertaken by Signora Galas (she lost close to sixty kilos) was due in large part to her eating the miraculous dietetic spaghetti and no-cal pizza dough produced in Rome's Pastaciutta Mills and Pizza Factories. —Giuseppi Gazozza." That worm, Vermicelli! He followed me all over Buenos Aires trying to get that endorsement. I told him he was wasting his time to ask me of all people.

I never eat that sort of thing. *(Dials phone)* "Miraculous spaghetti" indeed!

MERCANTEGGINI: What are you doing?

GALAS: I'm calling my lawyer. I'll sue Pastaciutta Mills!

MERCANTEGGINI: But Magdalena, the firm's president is Prince Marcantonio Pucelli, a lawyer and nephew to Pope Sixtus VII.

GALAS: I don't care whose nephew he is! I want these frauds exposed. *(Into phone)* Ciao, Borsa, it's Magdalena. *(Pause)* I'm furious, thank you. *(Pause)* Some little pasta pusher has been using my name to push his pasta. *(Pause)* Then you've already seen it? *(Covering mouthpiece, aside to Mercanteggini)* He's already seen it! The whole world has probably seen it! *(Into phone again)* I've been compromised and humiliated! I want an immediate and precise retraction. *(Pause)* Of course there's no truth in it! Every claim was a lie! I did not diet. Vermicelli was not my physician. AND I NEVER EAT MACARONI! Forget about it? *(Pause)* How can you even suggest that I let it drop? Why, my public will think I'm selling my body for advertising purposes. *(Rises and paces)* Ah-hah. Ah-hah. Ah, ah. Mmm. Mmm. Oh. Oooh. Oooooh. Ah. Ah. Ooooh. Tsk, tsk, tsk. Nhhh. *(Somewhat appeased)* Sweet. No. No. *(Giggles, laughs)* Ah-hah? Yes. Ah-hah? Begin legal proceedings at once. Ciao. *(Hangs up)* I'll make them spit blood in court!

MERCANTEGGINI: You're magnificent.

GALAS: God will avenge me!

MERCANTEGGINI: Does your god always side with you?

GALAS *(Removing her glasses)*: He sees my sacrifices and my sufferings. He will defend me from my enemies.

(Bruna enters with puppy. The dog is a piece of fur which the actors manipulate like a puppet to give it the appearance of life. The tail should never stop wagging no matter who holds the dog.)

MERCANTEGGINI *(Rising, takes dog from Bruna and presents it to Galas)*: Magda, darling, I got you a little homecoming present.

GALAS: Oh, no! It's a puppy! *(Speaking baby talk to puppy)* Oh, is oo a widdle puppy? Yes oo is, yes, yes. Oh, he's adorable! We'll call him Baby 'cause he's our little baby!

(Doorbell rings. With grand operatic gesture, Bruna goes to answer the bell.)

BRUNA *(Reenters)*: Excuse me, madam and Commendatore Mercanteggini, there is a man from La Scala.

MERCANTEGGINI: Show him in, Bruna.

(She does so.)

FRITALINI: I am so sorry to call unannounced but this is a grave emergency *(Extending hand)* Fritalini.

(Dog snarls at him. Galas must also be a bit of a ventriloquist.)

GALAS: My little dog doesn't like you. Bruna, take him away. Go, go.

(Galas gives dog to Bruna. It snarls again and yaps as Bruna takes it out, managing a grand operatic gesture as she exits. Bruna also does ventriloquism.)

FRITALINI: Baldini is indisposed. We need a replacement for La Gioconda.

GALAS: When?

FRITALINI: Tomorrow night.

MERCANTEGGINI: But this is only twenty-four hours notice!

GALAS: Please sit down, Mr. Fritalini.

(They sit. Mercanteggini stands behind Galas.)

FRITALINI: You scored such a great success in this role last summer at the Verona Arena. We know you can do it.

GALAS *(To Mercanteggini)*: I can do it.

MERCANTEGGINI: This is so unexpected. I've been trying to get a reply from La Scala for months but there's never been an answer.

FRITALINI: Of course you will sing at La Scala. We shall give you a guest artist contract.

GALAS: I would like to be a full member of the company.

FRITALINI: I am afraid that is not possible at this time. Between us, it is Ghingheri. Every time he hears your name he says, "No! No! Not Galas! Not Galas, not that woman! Never!

Never! NEVER!" This is a golden opportunity. We have him over a barrel.

GALAS *(Looks to Mercanteggini, who shrugs, then swallowing her pride)*: Very well, I shall sing at La Scala. But I want you to understand one thing, Mr. Fritalini—someday I will be a member of that company and Ghingheri will pay for this for the rest of his life!

(Lights fade.)

SCENE 3

VILLA MERCANTEGGINI

MERCANTEGGINI: Magdalena, darling, wake up. Today is our audience with the pope.

(Galas enters. Her hair has returned to black.)

GALAS: I don't want to see the pope this morning. It's a gray day, it's going to rain, and wearing black would depress me. We'll go some other time.

MERCANTEGGINI: An appointment with the pope is different from an appointment with your dentist. This is a once in a lifetime opportunity.

(Phone is heard offstage. Mercanteggini answers it. Galas sits in a reclining chair reading the score of Tosca, *myopically. Mercanteggini's voice is heard from offstage having an animated conversation.)*

Pronto. Sì. Sì. Sì. Bellissimo. Sì. Bene. Aspettamo. Sì. Prego. Ciao. Prego.

GALAS *(Sings)*: Vissi d'arte . . .

(Mercanteggini enters.)

Vissi d'a—Who was that on the phone?

MERCANTEGGINI: This is really unbelievable. Ghingheri called. He wants you to sing at La Scala.

GALAS: Well! I hope you told him that never again will I sing at La Scala under a guest artist contract.

MERCANTEGGINI: They're not offering you a guest artist contract. This time you would be a full member of the company.

GALAS: Well well well well well! We certainly have changed our tune. When do they want to meet to discuss fees and repertoire?

MERCANTEGGINI: Apparently they're quite eager to have you. They want to come right over. I took the liberty of telling them we'd see them.

GALAS *(Leaping up and beginning to pace the garden exultantly)*: Aha! Oh this is too good to be true! It's too delicious! I have Ghingheri exactly where I want him. After I bailed them out and sang their Gioconda for them he didn't even thank me, oh no, he merely congratulated the rest of the company on being able to get through it without Baldini! After the way he's insulted me as an artist I'll make him crawl on his knees to me.

BRUNA *(Entering)*: Two men approach the temple. They wish to see the High Priestess. Norma frowns and a cloud passes over the moon.

GALAS: Send them in.

MERCANTEGGINI: Show them in, Bruna.

BRUNA: Let them not profane this sacred place. A goddess must not throw herself away for any man.

GALAS *(Murmurs)*: Bring them before me. Let them taste my justice.

(Bruna crosses her arms on her breast and exits with grand oper-atic gesture. She then shows in Ghingheri and Fritalini.)

Ah, welcome, Signore Ghingheri. This is my husband, Signore Mercanteggini.

GHINGHERI: Forgive our intrusion. But we have urgent business.

GALAS: Not at all. Would you gentlemen care for some tea?

GHINGHERI: That would be very nice, thank you.

GALAS: Bruna, bring some tea.

(Bruna exits with grand operatic gesture again.)

GHINGHERI: This is my associate, Signore Fritalini.

GALAS: I'm delighted to see you again, Signore Fritalini. I've tried
so often to reach you by phone. But you were never in . . . to
me.

GHINGHERI: Ah, business! Business!

MERCANTEGGINI: And you never answered our letters.

GHINGHERI: Of course we answered your letters. You mean they
never arrived?

MERCANTEGGINI: Never.

GHINGHERI *(To Fritalini)*: Did you hear that? They never got
our letters.

FRITALINI: We sent a Telex. It must have missed you.

GHINGHERI: Oh that's it. They must have missed it. There, that
explains it.

GALAS *(Exchanges a look with Mercanteggini)*: Ah, business!
Business!

GHINGHERI: Ah ha, yes, business. And speaking of business,
Madame Galas, I have brought along the contract for your
upcoming season at La Scala.

*(Fritalini hands Ghingheri two contracts after a frantic search
through all his pockets. Ghingheri presents a contract to Galas,
who looks at it myopically, then searches in vain for her glasses.
Mercanteggini has them ready for her. She blows him a kiss, puts
on the glasses and reads. Mercanteggini looks on.)*

Let us confirm then that you will open the season on
November seventh with *I Vespri Siciliani* and you will sing
four additional performances of this opera on the eighth,
ninth, tenth and eleventh. Then in January you will sing five
performances of *Norma*. New Year's Day on loan to the Rome
Opera, *(Galas looks at Mercanteggini, who quiets her with a
gesture)* and then on January eighth, sixteenth and twenty-
third at La Scala. Your fifth and final *Norma* of the season
will be on February second. In June you will appear in three
performances of *Don Carlo*. Let me say that we are very
pleased with this contract and we are especially delighted to
be able to invite you this time not as a guest artist but as a full
member of the company.

GALAS: In my unanswered letter to you I made it quite clear that I would only be interested in singing at La Scala if I could appear in *La Traviata*. I see no mention of this opera here.

(Ghingheri and Fritalini exchange an uneasy look.)

FRITALINI: The reason we did not include *La Traviata* is that we have already scheduled several performances of this opera with Baldini. She is closely identified with the role of Violetta. We felt that it would be inappropriate to have another soprano sing this role in the same season.

GALAS: Then that is your final decision?

GHINGHERI: Yes, we're sorry, but we already have a Violetta.

GALAS: Then there's nothing to be done?

GHINGHERI: Absolutely nothing. I'm sorry.

GALAS: I'm sorry, too. Because without *La Traviata* your offer doesn't interest me. Perhaps some other season?

(Ghingheri and Fritalini look thunderstruck. Bruna enters with tea.)

GHINGHERI *(Enraged)*: No soprano has ever turned down an offer from La Scala that includes an opportunity to open the season.

FRITALINI *(Hysterical)*: Not to mention the five hundred thousand lira and full membership in the company.

GALAS: No *Traviata*?

GHINGHERI AND FRITALINI: No *Traviata*!

GALAS: Gentlemen, let's drink our tea.

GHINGHERI *(Rising)*: No tea, thanks. I see we have wasted our time coming here.

GALAS: Unless you are willing to give me *La Traviata* I'm afraid you have.

GHINGHERI: That is impossible. We do not like Madame Galas's singing *that* much.

GALAS: Then I see, there's nothing further to discuss. *(Rises)* I do not wish to waste your precious time. The season is almost upon you and you must still find a soprano to sing your *Vespri*, *Norma* and *Don Carlo* for you. *(Returns the contracts to him)* Good day.

GHINGHERI: Good day. *(To Mercanteggini)* Good day.

MERCANTEGGINI: Good day.

FRITALINI *(To Galas)*: Good day.

GALAS: Good day.

FRITALINI *(To Mercanteggini)*: Good day.

MERCANTEGGINI: Good day.

(Ghingheri and Fritalini stand staring at Galas and Mercanteggini as if they expect them to change their minds at any moment.)

GALAS *(Finally breaks the silence with a very firm but polite)*: Good day!

(Ghingheri and Fritalini exit coldly, followed by Bruna with grand operatic gesture.)

MERCANTEGGINI: I think you made a mistake. They offered you most of what you wanted. This is the chance you've been waiting for. Who knows when it will come again?

GALAS: If I sing at La Scala it will be on my own terms or not at all. Ghingheri has to learn that every time he insults me he is going to pay for it. *(Kissing him on both cheeks)* Excuse me Giovanni. I'm going to take my bubble bath. *(Exits)*

(Bruna enters and clears the tea things. The bell is heard. She exits again with grand operatic gesture. A moment later Ghingheri and Fritalini stalk in.)

GHINGHERI *(With difficulty)*: We have reconsidered and we've decided that perhaps we could arrange for Madame Galas to sing *La Traviata*—if she wants to.

MERCANTEGGINI *(Surprised by their sudden turnabout)*: I'll tell her. *(Crosses to the side of the stage where Galas exited)* Magdalena, the gentlemen from La Scala have returned. They have reconsidered.

GALAS *(From offstage)*: Not for a million lira!

(Bubbles drift on.)

MERCANTEGGINI: You heard her, gentlemen.

(Ghingheri and Fritalini exchange an agonized look.)

GHINGHERI *(Obsequiously)*: We think that fee could be acceptable.

(Mercanteggini's mouth falls open.)

And now if you will please to sign the contract.

FRITALINI *(Giving the contracts to Mercanteggini)*: Please to sign.

GHINGHERI: You will be so kind as to make the emendations we discussed.

MERCANTEGGINI: It seems you like my wife's singing better now, eh?

GHINGHERI *(Contemptuously)*: Nonsense. She can't sing. But she can create a scandal and that is worth a fortune.

MERCANTEGGINI: My wife and I have a little superstition. We do not like to sign a contract until a month after we have reached an agreement.

GHINGHERI: Very well, then, but please sign the contract and return it to us as quickly as possible.

MERCANTEGGINI: We will return it to you as quickly as we can.

(Ghingheri and Fritalini bow and exit. Galas enters, drying her hair. Bubbles drift on with her.)

Magdalena, they have agreed to the million lira.

GALAS: How is that possible?

MERCANTEGGINI: You said, "Not for a million lira," and they agreed.

GALAS: But I didn't really mean a million lira. That was only a figure of speech. I used it merely to emphasize my point about *La Traviata*.

MERCANTEGGINI: Oh, they've agreed to *La Traviata*. But what's more important, I've stumbled on an amazing discovery. We can get virtually anything we ask for.

GALAS: Then it's all settled? You signed the contract?

MERCANTEGGINI: Not quite. I told him we were superstitious and need a grace period of about a month.

GALAS: But why did you wait? They might change their minds.

MERCANTEGGINI: It's a trick I learned in the brick business. They won't change their minds. On the contrary, they'll send out publicity, they'll make commitments, they'll sign a contract for your services to another theater all based on this agreement which has never been signed. By then we'll say your fee has gone up.

GALAS: Is that proper?

MERCANTEGGINI: Sure. It's business. This contract is no good, anyway. It doesn't include *La Traviata*. The whole thing has to be amended. *(Tosses the contract over his shoulder)*

GALAS: That's right.

MERCANTEGGINI: We'll get a million lira for the Rome *Norma* alone! Don't worry about a thing. You have me to handle your business affairs. And I'm doing a pretty good job, eh?

GALAS: You're brilliant. I don't know what I'd do without you. *(Embraces him)*

MERCANTEGGINI *(Stands behind Galas with his arms around her)*: Most managers are hungry. They're in a little too much of a hurry. So they end up selling their client cheap. I don't need the money. I can afford to wait until we get exactly what we want. *(Goes to kiss her neck)*

BRUNA *(Enters)*: The Vatican is on the phone.

(They break apart.)

MERCANTEGGINI: Oh my God! What am I going to say to them after we didn't show up for our audience? *(Exits)*

GALAS: Bruna, they want me at La Scala. Because I can sing Isolde and Norma they say I am a phenomenon.

BRUNA: Yes, you are a phenomenon. But you are stretching your voice in two different directions. Someday it will break in the middle.

GALAS: What should I do?

BRUNA: Limit your repertoire.

GALAS: But I can sing anything.

BRUNA: You only have so many Normas and each one is numbered. Make each one count.

GALAS: How many Normas do I have? *(Sits)*

BRUNA: Judging by your voice I would say eighty-six. But you must forget about Isolde.

GALAS: Why?

BRUNA: It isn't worth it. You kill yourself all evening and you have nothing in the end. Also drop Turandot from your repertoire, and never ever sing Salomé.

GALAS: But I can sing Turandot with no trouble at all.

BRUNA: Every Turandot will cost you a Norma. Think about it.

MERCANTEGGINI *(Enters)*: It seems we were missed. The pope wants to see us so they've made another appointment for Friday.

GALAS: All right, we'll go Friday.

MERCANTEGGINI: And the prelate specified that it would be formal.

GALAS: Bruna, put Commendatore Mercanteggini's tuxedo in the cleaners so that it will be back by Friday.

BRUNA: Yes, madam. *(Giving Galas a significant look, she exits with grand operatic gesture)*

MERCANTEGGINI *(Waving a magazine)*: Ah, here is another story circulating about your weight loss.

GALAS *(Wearily)*: What is it now?

MERCANTEGGINI: This one is really filthy.

GALAS *(Turns suddenly)*: What do you mean? Let me see that.

MERCANTEGGINI *(Keeping the magazine away from her)*: Ah, don't bother yourself with it.

GALAS: Now you really have my curiosity aroused. Let me see that. *(Pries magazine out of his hands and opens it)* Oh God, I've always hated that picture. *(Keeping her sense of humor)* What does it say? Tell me.

MERCANTEGGINI: They say you lost weight because you had a tapeworm.

GALAS *(Stricken with horror and revulsion, cries out)*: Aaagh! But it's not true. How could they lie about me like that? How could they lie? *(Flies into a rage)* It's horrible! It's too too horrible! *(She throws herself on Mercanteggini's knees and cries uncontrollably)*

MERCANTEGGINI *(Comforting her)*: They're just jealous, that's all.

GALAS: Why do they hate me? Why? Why? What have I ever done to them?

MERCANTEGGINI: They're all against you because you have the voice of the century.

GALAS: Why don't they love me for that?

MERCANTEGGINI: They feel you are a greater actress than any singer has the right to be.

GALAS *(Sobbing)*: I just can't understand deliberate cruelty.

MERCANTEGGINI: Great artists are acknowledged but never forgiven. We'll make no reply to this whatsoever. Rumors die out quickly if they go unsubstantiated. There, there, dry your eyes. I love you.

GALAS: You're the only person who ever has loved me. And you're the only person I've ever loved.

MERCANTEGGINI: I only want to protect you from the world and from your enemies.

GALAS: Oh my darling, oh my dear sweet wonderful, wonderful Baptista. I wish I could devote my whole life to you. If only I didn't have to work so hard.

MERCANTEGGINI: But you do. I understand that.

GALAS *(Gives a pained look at his incomprehension, then regaining her composure)*: I'm a little run-down. I'm not feeling up-to-date.

MERCANTEGGINI: Maybe you sacrifice yourself a little too much for your art. You should take a vacation once in a while.

GALAS: A vacation?

MERCANTEGGINI: It wouldn't hurt.

GALAS: When could I take a vacation? I have so many engagements.

MERCANTEGGINI: Let me check your appointment calendar. *(Gets a book and flips page after page as her hopes fade)* Next year you can do it.

GALAS: Next year?

MERCANTEGGINI: Yes, next year we will definitely take a vacation.

(Galas sinks with a look of weary resignation as the lights fade.)

SCENE 4

THE VATICAN

POPE: Deus benedicte tutti homine.

PRELATE: Forgive me, Your Holiness. It is very well to bless all men. But do you think you could expand your blessing to include women as well?

POPE: Deus benedicte tutti homine et tutti dame.

PRELATE: With your permission, Your Holiness. It would perhaps be better if you could make a more general and all-inclusive blessing.

POPE: Deus benedicte tutti homine, tutti dame et tutti fruitti.

PRELATE: Pardon me, Your Holiness. It is almost ten o'clock. It would be well if you withdrew and prepared for your audience.

POPE: Preparare pro audiencia?

PRELATE: So that Your Holiness might not miss the opportunity to make an entrance.

POPE: Bonus. *(Exits)*

PRELATE *(Showing in Mercanteggini, Bruna and Galas)*: If you will be so kind as to wait here His Holiness will be with you in a moment.

(Bruna weeps uncontrollably.)

MERCANTEGGINI: Bruna, why are you crying?

BRUNA: Because I'm so happy. *(Sobs loudly)*

(The Pope enters through a tiny door at the back. The music, lighting and his stately bearing inspire awe. He ascends the steps to his throne and sits. Far off boys' voices evoke heaven.

The Prelate signals for Mercanteggini, Bruna and Galas to go forward in turn and kiss the Pope's ring. The Pope blesses each of them. For this, Bruna removes her coat, revealing sackcloth and ashes, dons a crown of thorns and crawls to the Pope on her knees, flagellating herself with a flail she takes from her bag. When Galas goes forward proudly to kiss his ring he lowers it by degrees, forcing her to bow very low. She crosses herself with a gesture of contempt.)

POPE *(Rising and coming forward, he places his hand on Bruna's head)*: Let us bless the mother.

(Bruna falls to her knees as if she had just witnessed a miracle.)

(Touching Mercanteggini's forehead) And let us also bless Commendatore Mercanteggini and his wife *(Touches the forehead of Galas)*, whose musical art we know from having heard her on the radio. *(Smiles at Galas)* We heard you sing Wagner's *Parsifal* and were deeply moved. It is for that rea-

son that we wished to meet you. We only regret that you did not sing *Parsifal* in the original German. Wagner loses so much when translated into Italian.

GALAS: We were broadcasting for the Italian public. If we had sung in German only a very few would have understood us.

POPE: True. But Wagner's music should not be separated from his words. He wrote them both. They were born together and they are inseparable.

GALAS: I don't agree. Very little is lost in translation. In order to understand the depths of the music one must understand the sense of the words.

(The conversation becomes more animated.)

POPE: Your achievement in this opera is very great. All the greater perhaps because of all operas Wagner's are the most difficult to sing.

GALAS: Not really. The operas of the bel canto repertoire make far greater vocal demands. Wagner's operas are relatively easy.

POPE: But Wagner's operas were conceived on a far grander scale. His mythic heroes demand a greater emotional range.

GALAS: Nonsense. Why, there is more true feeling on any page of Donizetti, Rossini, Verdi or Bellini than there is in all the bombast and rhetoric of the *Ring*.

POPE: I have always found that—

GALAS *(Interrupting)*: Of course you can yell your head off in these operas *(Shaking a finger under the Pope's nose)* or you can sing them musically, which is quite a different matter . . .

(Pope is flabbergasted. Mercanteggini pulls Galas back, steps forward and changes the subject for fear that Galas might go too far.)

MERCANTEGGINI: Your Holiness, have you read the article about the new graffiti they've excavated beneath the Baths of Caracalla? Your Holiness probably doesn't bother to read the papers except for the most important articles that your aides prepare for you.

POPE: We read the papers from cover to cover. Nothing escapes us. Not even your legal battles with the Pastaciutta Mills. Our nephew is president of that company. The newspapers never tire of disporting themselves with the Pucelli name. We would be grateful if you would quickly settle this matter out of court so that the pope might be left in peace.

MERCANTEGGINI *(Nodding yes aside to Galas)*: Your Holiness, we will do everything in our power to arrive at a settlement as quickly as possible.

(Galas shakes her head no. Pope gives Bruna a rosary and offers his ring to be kissed, then gives Galas a rosary and offers hand. With the rosary, Galas lassoes his hand to prevent him from lowering it again, kisses the ring and steps back with hands clasped angelically in prayer.)

POPE: Have you brought umbrellas?

GALAS: No, why?

POPE: Because, if I may speak ex cathedra, it is going to rain.

(Pope dismisses them with a benediction and withdraws.)

GALAS *(To Mercanteggini)*: Now I want you to understand that it is you who promised the pope. I didn't promise the pope anything. Come Bruna.

MERCANTEGGINI: Now now, Magda.

(Bruna exits before them on her knees, managing a grand operatic gesture. Then Galas and Mercanteggini exit. They are shown out by the Prelate, who reenters.)

GALAS *(As Mercanteggini hustles her out)*: Besides this has absolutely nothing whatsoever to do with the pope.

(They are gone. Pope reenters.)

POPE: That woman is more fatiguing than a mission from Salt Lake City.

PRELATE *(Sending up his brows a little)*: Orthodox.

POPE: I'm not used to being flatly contradicted.

PRELATE: Where do you find the patience?

POPE: The martyrs are ever before me. Misericordia! This lawsuit could be the worst scandal since the fall of Innocent XVI. And this morning we have detected rat droppings among the papyrus plants.

PRELATE: They come up from the Tiber.
POPE: Are there any more audiences today?
PRELATE: That was the last.
POPE: Good. Disinfect our finger and the ring.

> (Prelate takes out a can of aerosol disinfectant and sprays the Pope's finger and ring as lights fade.)

SCENE 5

THE ROME OPERA

A view of an opera box as seen from behind the spectators. The box plays upstage and forms a kind of proscenium for the silhouetted figures of the spectators while the performance of the opera is in progress. Downstage of the box, the backstage scenes are played. During the scene change we hear Galas singing the "Casta Diva" and the final Act One duet between Pollione and Adalgisa is heard as the lights come up on the silhouetted tableau vivant of the spectators' backs in the box. There are incidental movements of fans, programs, opera glasses, egret feathers and the sparkle of jewels in the darkness. As the duet finishes and the curtain call is heard on tape, the people in the back mime applauding, as the light wipes vertically to indicate the rise and fall of the grand curtain. The people then assume the more casual attitudes of intermission, but do not move. As the last applause dies away, Galas flies onto the stage in her Norma costume, pursued by Mercanteggini and attended by Bruna in great consternation.

MERCANTEGGINI: But you must finish the performance!
GALAS: I can't! I wish to God I could. But I can't. The voice . . . the voice is slipping.
MERCANTEGGINI: Slipping?
GALAS: Yes, slipping! Slipping! The voice will not obey.
MERCANTEGGINI *(Growing more and more alarmed)*: How can that be?
GALAS: I told you, sometimes the voice obeys and sometimes it will not. Tonight it will not!
MERCANTEGGINI: You're speaking of your voice as though it had a will of its own.

GALAS *(With horror)*: It has! It does! Tonight it will not obey.

MERCANTEGGINI: You've got to get hold of yourself. It's your voice. You must command it.

GALAS *(In a hoarse whisper)*: It's no use.

MERCANTEGGINI: We demanded a million lira for this performance. You must go on.

GALAS *(Weeping)*: I can't! I can't! I can't!

BRUNA *(Quietly aside to Mercanteggini)*: Leave her alone. When the voice goes it is no use to call it back. Believe me, if she could finish the performance tonight, she would.

(There is a knock at the door.)

VOICE *(From offstage)*: Cinque minuti.

MERCANTEGGINI: What shall I tell them? That you don't want to risk being a flop?

GALAS: If I go back out there it will be worse than a flop. It will be a musical fiasco.

MERCANTEGGINI: Very well, I'll tell them to send on a replacement. *(Exits)*

GALAS: Where is my voice, Bruna? I call it and call it but it will not answer.

BRUNA: Only a happy bird can sing.

(A tumult of voices is heard off. Ghingheri, Fritalini and Mercanteggini enter arguing.)

GHINGHERI *(Ranting)*: This is impossible! Completely impossible! We have given *Norma* a thousand times and we never have this!

FRITALINI *(Echoing in falsetto)*: Impossible! Completely impossible!

MERCANTEGGINI: Well, there's a first time for everything. Send in the replacement.

GHINGHERI *(A note of hysteria creeping into the voice)*: That's just it! Don't you understand? There is no replacement!

MERCANTEGGINI: No replacement?

FRITALINI: No replacement!

MERCANTEGGINI: How is that possible? Why don't you have a replacement?

GHINGHERI *(Shrill and screaming)*: I don't know why we don't have a replacement! WE JUST DON'T HAVE A RE-PLACEMENT!

MERCANTEGGINI: Magdalena, they don't have a replacement.

GALAS: I heard him.

MERCANTEGGINI: What should we do?

GALAS: We'll have to cancel.

GHINGHERI: Have to cancel?

FRITALINI: Have to cancel?

GHINGHERI: Cancel is completely wrong! Cancel is impossible!

FRITALINI: Impossible!

(A tall tenor, Franco Cogliones, enters weeping in the Roman garb of Pollione.)

GHINGHERI: What's the matter with you?

COGLIONES *(Crying like a baby)*: She kicked me in the shins!

GALAS: Imagine me kicking a big strong man like you in the shins.

(Cogliones cries.)

GHINGHERI: Shut up, you idiot. *(To Galas)* The president of Italy is sitting out there. Do you want to ruin me, the Rome Opera, La Scala and your own career all in one stroke?

GALAS: I'm sorry. But I have no voice.

GHINGHERI *(Savagely)*: No voice? So what's new, Mrs. Galas? You never had a voice! But that never stopped you before.

GALAS: WHAT?

GHINGHERI: I know why you don't want to continue. You don't dare. You were lousy out there and everyone knew it.

GALAS: Lousy? You called my performance lousy?

GHINGHERI: There were boos after the "Casta Diva" and the stage crew found radishes among your roses. It appears your vanity is more important than your music.

GALAS: I'll fracture your skull you worm!

(Galas draws a dagger from her belt and attacks Ghingheri. Mercanteggini and Bruna prevent her. Fritalini screams and hides behind Ghingheri.)

I'll kill him! I'll kill him! I'LL KILL HIM!

(Bruna, with grand operatic gesture, drags Galas off amid the tumult.)

MERCANTEGGINI *(Mockingly to Ghingheri as he exits)*: Well, you have your scandal.

GHINGHERI: I should have known! I never wanted to let that woman sing in the first place. *(Gravely)* Give me a few minutes to inform the president personally and then go make the announcement. Tell them that Madame Galas has left the opera house.

(They exit at opposite doors. The announcement is heard in Italian over the public-address system. The crowd greets this news with an uproar of boos and jeers. The figures in the box at the rear stand and gesticulate. The gentlemen help the ladies on with their wraps as the house lights come up and Act One ends.
Curtain.)

Act Two

THE YACHT

At rise the sea chantey from the opening of Act Two of Ponchielli's La Gioconda *is sung severally and variously by sailors.*

SAILORS:
    Ho! He! Ho! He! Fissa il timone!
    Ho! He! Ho! He! Fissa! Fissa!
    Ho! He! Ho! He! Issa artimone!
    Issa!
    La ciurma ov'è?
    Ho! He! Ho! He!

OTHER SAILORS:
    Siam nel fondo più profondo
    Della nave, della cala,
    dove il vento furibondo
    spreca i fischi e infrange l'ala.
    Siam nel fondo più profondo. *(Etc.)*

BOYS:
    La, la, la, la *(Etc.)*
    Siam qui sui culmini, siam sulla borda.
    Siam sulle tremule scale di corda.

SAILORS: Ho! He! *(Etc.)*
OTHER SAILORS: Ah! *(Etc.)*
BOYS: Guardate gli agili mozzi saltar, guardate *(Etc.)*
SAILORS: Ho! He! *(Etc.)* La, la, la *(Etc.)*

OTHER SAILORS: Ah! *(Etc.)* La, la, la! *(Etc.)*

BOYS: Noi gli scoiattoli siamo del mar. Siam gli scoiattoli *(Etc.)* Ah!

SAILORS: Ho! He! Ho! Ah! *(Etc.)*

OTHER SAILORS: Ah! La, la, la *(Etc.)* Ah!

(Sailors exit. Bruna enters, as Greek chorus.)

BRUNA: Would that my mistress had never accepted the invitation to cruise on Odysseus's yacht. Would that she had never walked out on her performance at the Rome Opera. Would that she had not granted the press so many interviews. Better she had drowned in the wine-dark sea than that these things had come to pass.

ODYSSEUS *(From offstage)*: Poop deck!

(Galas enters laughing; Mercanteggini, Aristotle Odysseus and his wife, Athina.)

I hope you will enjoy cruising on my yacht as much as I do. Traveling this way, bounded only by the sea, the sky, the elements, imparts a godlike sense of freedom.

MERCANTEGGINI: Maybe so. But the immensity of it all restores one's sense of scale. We are reminded that Man and his endeavors are but a minute twitching in the infinite universe.

ODYSSEUS: We are all the more heroic for it. Every man struggles with an adversary knowing he must eventually lose.

GALAS: What adversary is that?

ODYSSEUS: Time.

GALAS: Ah, but we have this one great advantage. We know our foe; our foe does not know us. That is our triumph and our curse.

MERCANTEGGINI *(To Athina)*: I almost forgot. We brought our hostess a little gift.

ATHINA: You really shouldn't have.

MERCANTEGGINI: Ah, but we wanted to. *(Gives her a box)* Go ahead and open it.

ATHINA *(Looking inside the box)*: What is it?

MERCANTEGGINI: It's a necklace of shark's teeth. We bought it in the airport. Let's put it on.

(Athina does so.)

Very becoming. *(To Odysseus)* Don't you think?

ODYSSEUS: Exquisite. Shark's teeth are you, my dear. And before I forget, I have a little something for Magdalena.

(Odysseus takes out a jewelry box, opens it and removes a necklace of polished green stones. He places them around Galas's neck. She gasps.)

Cabochon emeralds. They were reputedly worn by Helene when she was abducted to Troy.

GALAS: They're lovely.

MERCANTEGGINI *(To Athina, pointing to her necklace)*: They're supposed to be sacred to pygmies. At least that's what the saleslady said. *(To Odysseus)* Do you have anything for seasickness?

ODYSSEUS: I have some Dramamine in my medicine chest. Come with me and I'll get you some. *(Then to Galas)* Ah, there on the starboard side. That little village, Ithaca. My namesake's birthplace and mine as well.

GALAS: I didn't know you were from Ithaca.

ODYSSEUS: This afternoon we'll drop anchor and go ashore. I want to show you the church where my parents were married. Come, my friend, and I'll get you some Dramamine. Look there! A flying fish! Did you see it? *(Odysseus laughs heartily and exits with Mercanteggini)*

GALAS: I am so looking forward to this little sightseeing trip. Perhaps it will give us a chance to get to know each other better.

ATHINA: I won't be going.

GALAS: Why not?

ATHINA: I've taken that tour before. Many times. I'm sorry.

GALAS: I'm disappointed. But I understand. If you've seen it all before. It will be the first time for me.

ATHINA: Yes, and I've heard all Soc's stories a thousand times over. Frankly I'm a little tired of them.

GALAS *(Taking her hand)*: I hope we'll be great friends.

ATHINA *(Looking her straight in the eye)*: Of course we will. Why shouldn't we be? *(Exits)*

GALAS: Bruna, what should I wear? Madame Blini designed me so many outfits I don't know where to start. I'll have to change ten times a day if I expect to wear them all. *(Starts off but pauses when she hears Bruna's foreboding tone)*

BRUNA: Sackcloth and modesty. Ashes and silence. Things that shadow and conceal. You should think of nothing else.

GALAS: Nonsense. A woman should always arrive last and wearing the least. *(Exits)*

BRUNA *(With grand operatic gesture, following her out)*: Do not go ashore today. Stay in. Hide yourself.

(Odysseus and Mercanteggini reenter.)

MERCANTEGGINI: Our family lost a lot of our factories during the war. But afterwards we built them up again. Bricks never go out of style. That's how we made our fortune.

ODYSSEUS *(Chuckling)*: I was completely wiped out in '29 and then again under the Germans. But every time I started again from scratch. It's easy to make millions—once you know how.

MERCANTEGGINI: But even with millions I still watch every penny. It's something that's ingrained in me.

ODYSSEUS: You don't mean to say you're penny-wise and pound-foolish?

MERCANTEGGINI: I wouldn't say that. But I am a man who husbands his wealth.

ODYSSEUS: Indeed you are. Your wife is a treasure.

MERCANTEGGINI: Ah yes, Magdalena is a great gal. My family practically disowned me when I married her. Eventually I gave up the family business to handle her career. Everything I knew about selling bricks I put into selling her voice. And it worked. Maria Magdalena Mercanteggini Galas is now the highest-paid singer in the world. Not to mention the most famous.

ODYSSEUS: Not to mention the best?

MERCANTEGGINI: That too. Of course, the best.

(Enter Ilka Winterhalter smoking a cigar.)

ILKA: Look at this, boys. Maria has really come out!

(Enter Galas. She has changed into a white silk jumpsuit with big roses printed all over it. Bruna looks on like a Fate.)

GALAS: How do you like it?

ODYSSEUS: Ravishing! Ravishing!

GALAS: Thank you. Giovanni, what do you think?

MERCANTEGGINI: Is this supposed to be a joke?

GALAS: What do you mean?

MERCANTEGGINI: Isn't it just a trifle vulgar?

GALAS: Madame Blini said it was perfect for sightseeing.

MERCANTEGGINI: You want to see the sights, not be a sight. You're not going to let people see you in that.

ILKA: Isn't she divine? Isn't she just ta-hoo ta-hoo divine? There's an aura about her.

MERCANTEGGINI *(Aside to Galas)*: Who is that horrible woman?

GALAS: Shh. That's Ilka Winterhalter. Be very nice to her. She's doing my profile for *Time* magazine.

ILKA: Magdalena, tell me, dear, how do you feel now that you've finally sung at La Scala?

GALAS: Oh, La Scala, wonderful theater, wonderful, but then, I am nearsighted, you see, all theaters look alike to me.

ILKA: Some of your critics say you have a wobbly voice.

GALAS *(Snarling)*: Well, it happens to be a trill!

ILKA: You're hypnotic. You're a priestess. A high priestess. Being in your presence is an almost mystic experience.

GALAS *(To Mercanteggini)*: Soc says I look ravished in it.

MERCANTEGGINI: Madame Blini should be shot.

ODYSSEUS: Drop the anchors! Let's disembark. Let's live, my friends. You want to live, don't you Magdalena?

GALAS: Yes, I do.

ODYSSEUS: I hope so, because I am only interested in people who want to live.

GALAS: I do want to live. I do want to live. I do.

ODYSSEUS: What about you, Baptista? Do you want to live?

MERCANTEGGINI: Aaaagh.

ODYSSEUS: Then since we are all in agreement, let's live!

97

(As they exit down the gangway, Odysseus's voice is heard trailing off.)

Let's live! Let's live! Let's live!

(Enter Athina and Hüre Von Hoyden.)

VON HOYDEN: I'm sure I don't know what you're talking about.

ATHINA: Do you think I'm blind? Do you think I can't see what's been going on under my very nose?

VON HOYDEN: You're mistaken. I don't like husbands. But I like wives even less. Here, take back these jewels he gave me. They were yours, I believe, and probably false. *(Drops a necklace, bracelet and ring into Athina's hand)*

ATHINA *(Flinging them into the sea)*: I don't want them.

VON HOYDEN *(Gasps)*: If I'd known you were going to fling them into the sea I never would have given them back. If you didn't want them you should have let me keep them. *(Looking over the side)* Oh well, there goes my old age insurance.

ATHINA: I want you to keep your hands off my husband.

VON HOYDEN: And what makes you think I've had my hands on your husband?

ATHINA: He took you ashore to show you the village where he was born, didn't he?

VON HOYDEN: Yes.

ATHINA: And you went to meet Krakitoukitifanipoulous, the hierophant of the island?

VON HOYDEN: Yes.

ATHINA: And you knelt before him to receive his blessing?

VON HOYDEN: Soc told you all this?

ATHINA: He didn't have to. It's the same routine with every woman he seduces. You got the treatment, honey. So I know the rest.

VON HOYDEN: He knows how to make a woman feel like a woman. But when he's through with you he throws you away like a used condom.

ATHINA: How dare you speak like that to me?

VON HOYDEN: I didn't mean you.

ATHINA: If you don't break off this affair with my husband I'm
going to sue him for divorce and name you as correspondent.

VON HOYDEN: You're wasting your time, being jealous of me.
He's already lost interest. It's the Greek opera singer who
fascinates him now.

ATHINA: Galas?

VON HOYDEN: They've gone ashore to meet Krapatoukifanny . . .
Krafticulo . . . Kooka tafi . . .

ATHINA: Krakitoukitifanipoulous?

VON HOYDEN: That guy. To receive his blessing. She's the one
you'd better watch out for.

ATHINA: I'm not worried. She's safely in the custody of her
husband.

(The Sailors' Chorus is heard again.)

Do you hear that? They're returning from the island. Go do
something with yourself before the soirée tonight. Perhaps
you can snag another victim.

VON HOYDEN: You know, you could open clams with that tongue
of yours.

ATHINA: If I see you anywhere near my husband tonight I'm
going to put you off this yacht.

VON HOYDEN: We'll be hundreds of knots out to sea.

ATHINA: Exactly.

*(Von Hoyden exits. Odysseus enters laughing; Mercanteggini
and Galas. Ilka and Bruna enter and exit holding hands.)*

GALAS *(To Odysseus)*: Thank you for a lovely afternoon.

ODYSSEUS: That was nothing, Magdalena. Tonight after we have
dined there will be a masquerade. We're all to come in costume.

GALAS: But what will I wear?

ODYSSEUS: Surprise me.

GALAS: But I didn't bring a costume.

ODYSSEUS: Improvise! Use your imagination. I'm sure you'll
come up with something.

ATHINA: Come, Soc. Hadn't we better leave our guests alone to
freshen up for dinner?

ODYSSEUS: But of course! I daresay tonight you will dine as you have never dined before. I have four chefs—one Greek, one French, one Italian and one Chinese.

MERCANTEGGINI: I have no appetite.

ODYSSEUS: An appetite for food is an appetite for life. You'll find something to tweak you. My cooks are as great artists in their own realm as our Magdalena is in hers. *(To Galas, kissing her hand and staring deeply into her eyes)* Until dinner then, divine one. *(Exits with Athina)*

MERCANTEGGINI: Now it's a masquerade! What next? Do these people do anything besides party morning, noon and night?

GALAS: Aren't you happy?

MERCANTEGGINI: Do you care?

GALAS: Of course I care. I want you to enjoy yourself.

MERCANTEGGINI: That's about all I *am* enjoying. You practically ignored me all afternoon.

GALAS: Did I? There were so many things to see and do I guess I just got carried away.

MERCANTEGGINI: And when we went to see that bishop or whatever he was . . .

GALAS *(Transported)*: Krakitoukitifanipoulous.

MERCANTEGGINI: It gave me a funny feeling the way the two of you knelt before him to receive his blessing. It was almost as if he were marrying you.

GALAS: You're not Greek. You don't understand these things. How could you?

MERCANTEGGINI: And then when we heard on the radio that the pope had died it was like an omen.

GALAS: The pope died? I didn't hear that.

MERCANTEGGINI: What do you mean you didn't hear it? I told you myself.

GALAS: Then it's really true? The pope is dead?

MERCANTEGGINI: Yes, the pope is dead.

GALAS: Good. Now you don't have to keep that promise you made him. We can go back to court.

MERCANTEGGINI: Really Magdalena, I'm surprised at you. Shouldn't you be thinking about the pope's death rather than your lawsuit?

GALAS: I don't care that much for the pope. *(Snaps her fingers)* Remember I am Greek Orthodox. To me he's just another bishop.

MERCANTEGGINI: But the bishop of Rome—

GALAS *(Interrupting)*: I do not recognize Rome and I do not recognize the pope.

MERCANTEGGINI: But think of your Italian public . . .

GALAS: My Italian public are a bunch of savages. Imagine, after that unfortunate Rome cancellation, smearing our entire villa with excrement!

MERCANTEGGINI: To them he's like God on earth. They consider him infallible.

GALAS: In matters of dogma he may be infallible, but in matters musical I found him quite fallible. Him and his Wagner! The pope should mind his own business and not go sticking his nose in my affairs.

MERCANTEGGINI: Magda, darling, I'm not a religious man, but really, what a way to speak of the pope!

GALAS: Well, really, whose side are you on anyway? Mine or the pope's?

MERCANTEGGINI: All right! All right! But I want you to know that this goes against everything I believe in. Squabbling in court is an utterly squalid and shabby way to conduct one's life. I don't see what you are trying to prove.

GALAS: It's the principle of the thing. Now please, let's go in to dinner.

MERCANTEGGINI: Very well, if you want to drag this sordid mess on and on, go ahead. We'll go back to court.

(He storms out. Galas follows dejectedly. Music.)

BRUNA *(Enters as before, to express foreboding)*: A little love is like a light breeze on a lovely day that fills the sails and moves the ship along. A lot of love is like a gale that hastens progress but rocks the boat. A great love is like a storm that tosses the vessel this way and that with no rhyme or reason until the passengers are ill and all capsize. Better a little love than a lot. Better a small love than a great. *(Exits with grand operatic gesture)*

(It is now evening. Latin music is heard. Japanese lanterns are lighted. Odysseus, Athina, Von Hoyden, Ilka and other guests enter dancing in a conga line in masquerade costumes. They break and dance in couples.)

ODYSSEUS *(Removing his mask)*: But where is La Galas and Mercanteggini?

(Galas reenters in gown, with vizard, followed by Mercanteggini.)

GALAS: Here I am.

ODYSSEUS: You look like a Greek goddess. But then, you are, after all, Greek.

GALAS: I thought Iphigenia.

ODYSSEUS: Iphigenia. Of course, Iphigenia. I will steer the yacht toward Tauris if you so desire.

GALAS: Don't go out of your way.

ODYSSEUS *(Noticing Mercanteggini standing alone looking over the rail)*: What's this? Baptista undisguised? You should know better than to be yourself at this kind of a gathering!

MERCANTEGGINI: If you don't mind I think I'll skip the costume party. I have a bit of a headache. I'll just stay up here on the deck and take the air.

ODYSSEUS: If you insist.

MERCANTEGGINI: I do.

ODYSSEUS: But here's a costume for you if you change your mind. *(Gives him a box)*

MERCANTEGGINI: How do you know it will fit?

ODYSSEUS: It's a one-size-fits-all affair. Magdalena, do you ever go in for popular music?

GALAS: Hot jazz, no. Rumbas, things like that, yes.

ODYSSEUS: We must go dancing. I will instruct the orchestra to play nothing but rumbas. And now friends, how about a little game of hide-and-seek? *(All cheer)* Athina, you're it.

ATHINA: But I was it last time.

(Guests laugh and scurry out different doors. Athina leans against the wall and covers her eyes and counts to one hundred. Mercanteggini sits upstage with his back to the audience and looks out to sea.)

MERCANTEGGINI: And these are supposed to be mature adults? It's as though they're in an endless childhood.

ATHINA: Ninety-seven, ninety-eight, ninety-nine, one hundred. Here I come, ready or not. *(Exits)*

(Guests cross and recross the stage as they play hide-and-seek in their masquerade costumes.)

ILKA *(Crossing with Odysseus)*: Isn't Galas divine? Isn't she just ta-hoo ta-hoo divine?

ODYSSEUS: I find her a suitable object for worship.

ILKA: Do you? Do you really? I'm doing a profile on her for *Time* magazine. I want to show the public what she's really like.

ODYSSEUS *(Chuckles)*: That's something I'd like to discover for myself.

ILKA: You too, eh? It looks like we may end up rivals.

(Ilka and Odysseus laugh and exit. Sounds of a rumba are heard off, mingled with the guests' laughter. Occasionally guests in masquerade costumes cross the stage. Two sailors wander on holding hands. Von Hoyden approaches the sailors and the three of them begin to make love.)

MERCANTEGGINI *(Watching, appalled)*: What is this, a masquerade or an orgy? I'd better go find Magdalena. *(Exits)*

SAILOR: I can't do it.

VON HOYDEN *(Drunkenly)*: What do you mean can't? You don't want to or you're too drunk?

ATHINA *(Enters, calling)*: Soc? Soc? Have any of you seen my husband?

SAILOR: No, ma'am.

VON HOYDEN: Don't look at me. I can't swim.

MERCANTEGGINI *(Enters in a state of great agitation, to Athina)*: Have you seen my wife? I can't find her anywhere.

ATHINA: No I haven't. Have you seen my husband?

MERCANTEGGINI: No, I'm sorry.

ATHINA *(Exiting)*: Soc? Soc?

MERCANTEGGINI *(Looking at Von Hoyden and sailors making it)*: These people are disgusting. They're like animals. I'm in a pigsty! *(Ilka crosses in a pig mask. A passenger in gorilla costume passes with cocktail in hand)* Excuse me, have you seen my wife? *(Ilka snorts and exits. To other guest)* Pardon, have you seen my wife?

(Each time he asks a guest this question they laugh a nightmarish laugh and exit. Weird laughter is heard coming from all sides. Enter Athina, nude, except for her hair which falls below her waist, partially covering her body. She is weeping.)

ATHINA: You have lost your Magdalena.

MERCANTEGGINI: What?

ATHINA: I came upon them in the dark. They had hidden in the lifeboat. I heard sounds and lifted up the tarp. And there the two great fishes lay, flopping in the net. Then twisting, turning head to tail, I heard her laugh and say, "It will open up my throat!" And then I heard her sing—a song such as I've never heard before. Her voice grew loud and mingled with the sound of wind and waves. It was as though a bird that had long been caged escaped and flew away. It soared and dipped and circled o'er these stinking fish.

MERCANTEGGINI *(Beside himself)*: It was dark. Are you sure it wasn't someone else?

ATHINA: I knew them by the wetness of their skin and the shimmer of her jewels. *(Exits wailing)*

MERCANTEGGINI *(To a sailor)*: Give me that bottle there. I need a drink. *(He drinks wildly, recklessly)* Let's have a party.

(He opens the box Odysseus gave him and takes out a Pagliacci costume. He puts it on, smears his face with clown white, muttering unintelligibly all the while. Then we hear Caruso's voice singing the aria "Vesti la Giubba" from Pagliacci. Mercanteggini lip-synchs the aria and gestures accordingly. Galas and Odysseus enter, drunk. They watch him through to the end of the aria.)

ODYSSEUS *(Applauding)*: Bravo! Bravo! It seems Giovanni Baptista has decided to join the party.

MERCANTEGGINI *(Glaring at him murderously)*: From what I've heard, it's you who've decided to join the party. *(Seizing Galas)* You, what have you done, huh? You pig, you're shit!

GALAS: You're drunk.

MERCANTEGGINI: Yeah? Well I'll be sober tomorrow. But you'll still be shit.

ODYSSEUS: You don't understand Magdalena. She's looking for a father figure.

MERCANTEGGINI: Who asked you, you rancid piece of pork?

ODYSSEUS: Well, if you're going to be a sore loser.

GALAS: Stop it! Stop it both of you!

MERCANTEGGINI: Now the sow is bellowing! That's what you are! You're a sow and you're a boar.

GALAS: Get away from me, you horrible old man. I hate you! I hate you! I hate you!

MERCANTEGGINI: I'll get a pistol and shoot you two Greeks dead.

GALAS: Well, I'll get a shotgun and kill you first!

ODYSSEUS: Come away, Magdalena. You don't need this.

MERCANTEGGINI: I built your career! You're nothing without me.

GALAS *(Laughs incredulously)*: Oh, ho ho!

ODYSSEUS: Yes, we have a word for a man who lives off his woman's earnings—pimp!

MERCANTEGGINI: I do not live off her career. I have millions of my own, *millions*!

ODYSSEUS: Magdalena means more to me than all the money in the world. I'll buy her from you. How much do you want for her? One million? Two million? Name your price. I'll write you a check.

MERCANTEGGINI: Will you know what to do with her? I doubt it.

(The following three speeches are spoken together, three times in a round, meant to evoke an operatic trio.)

MERCANTEGGINI: I'm the one who built your career. You were nothing before me and you'll be nothing after me . . .

GALAS: Twelve years, twelve years. You must let me go. I want to live! . . .

ODYSSEUS: She wants to live! Let her live! . . .

MERCANTEGGINI: All these years, I have lived only to expand her fame and her prestige. I never thought of myself.

ODYSSEUS: Ah, go back to your bricks. That was more your line. I am only interested in buoyant things, things that float.

Come, Magdalena. In the future, man will travel at the speed of light and this great ass will be sitting there on his pile of bricks. *(He exits)*

(Galas goes to follow him.)

MERCANTEGGINI: So you're really leaving me for that repulsive pile of putrescent flesh?
GALAS *(Turns back)*: Yes.
MERCANTEGGINI: Then there's nothing else to say, is there?
GALAS: Only . . .
MERCANTEGGINI: Yes?
GALAS: Will you still be my business manager?
MERCANTEGGINI *(With disbelief)*: What?!!
GALAS: Will you still handle my career?
MERCANTEGGINI: Your career is over as far as I'm concerned.

(Galas stalks off. Music. Mercanteggini weeps, sits. Ilka enters.)

ILKA *(Seeing him weeping)*: Is something wrong?
MERCANTEGGINI: I have just received word that someone I loved has died.
ILKA: Oh, that's too bad. I'm sorry you're not feeling better. I was kinda hoping you could help me with something.
MERCANTEGGINI: What do you want?
ILKA: Well, I'm writing a profile on Magdalena for *Time* magazine. I'd like to help my readers distinguish the real Magdalena from the legends that spring up about her. We all know Magdalena the artist. But what about Magdalena, the woman.
MERCANTEGGINI: What do you want to know?
ILKA: Well, her spectacular weight loss, for example. She went, if you'll pardon my saying so, from two hundred and fifteen pounds to one hundred and thirty-five in a little over a year. I'm sure every woman in America would like to know how she did it.
MERCANTEGGINI: She swallowed a tapeworm.
ILKA *(Shocked)*: A tapeworm?
MERCANTEGGINI: Yes, she took a tapeworm. Didn't you know that?

ILKA: Well, I heard rumors of course, but I was never certain . . .

MERCANTEGGINI: Well, you know she always had an enormous appetite. She could never control it.

ILKA: Really?

MERCANTEGGINI: Sure. Why, in Greece during the war she even sang to the soldiers for food. And she'd eat it all herself.

ILKA *(Writing more and more furiously)*: Really? It was that bad, huh?

MERCANTEGGINI: Oh terrible, terrible. With an appetite like that, dieting is just no use. So she went to a doctor who gave her the egg of a tapeworm. He got it out of the ass of an infected patient.

ILKA: That's incredible! Are you sure?

MERCANTEGGINI: I ought to know. I'm her husband.

(Blackout.)

SCENE 2

GALAS'S APARTMENT, PARIS

Galas stands silhouetted against the window with her back to the audience, looking out. Enter Bruna.

GALAS: Has the postman arrived yet, Bruna?

BRUNA: You know he hasn't. You've done nothing but stand and look out that window all afternoon.

GALAS: Do you smell tar?

BRUNA *(Sniffs)*: No, madam.

GALAS: It's very strange, I smell tar. That postman comes later and later every day.

BRUNA: There's a new man on. He needs time to learn his route.

(Doorbell rings.)

GALAS: There's the bell. Bruna, see who it is.

(Bruna exits with grand operatic gesture.)

BRUNA *(Returning)*: Miss Von Hoyden to see you. *(Exits again with grand operatic gesture)*

(Von Hoyden enters wearing a sari.)

GALAS *(Embracing her and kissing both cheeks)*: Hüre!

VON HOYDEN: Magda, sweetie, long time no see.

GALAS: It is a long time, isn't it? Where have you been?

VON HOYDEN *(Throwing herself into a chair)*: Oh Indya, Indya!

GALAS: Have you heard from Soc?

VON HOYDEN: God, no. I have a maharaja now. How have you been?

GALAS: Ah, well, you know, I'm never really well.

VON HOYDEN: What's wrong?

GALAS: Nothing's wrong, really. It's just that nothing's right, if you understand me.

VON HOYDEN: Aren't you happy?

GALAS: Happy? Now that's too much to ask. I live on—that's about it.

VON HOYDEN: But you've had it all. Think of how many other people live and have nothing.

GALAS: To have nothing isn't so bad. To have everything and lose it—now that isn't funny.

VON HOYDEN: Do you know what I think, Maggie? I think you take men too seriously.

GALAS: In what way?

VON HOYDEN: Well, you know, most men can't help themselves.

GALAS: What do you mean?

VON HOYDEN: I mean they're men and there's very little that can be done about it.

GALAS: To me a man has always been a thing apart. To love is akin to worship.

VON HOYDEN: But one must keep one's eyes wide open about the reasons one is loved in return.

GALAS: Reasons? There are always so many reasons for everything. People are always so fast to invent reasons, especially where they do not exist. So many reasons.

VON HOYDEN: Soc, for instance, loves fame.

GALAS: Fame?

VON HOYDEN: No woman could ever be famous enough for him. That's why he remarried.

GALAS: I gave up my career for him.

VON HOYDEN: That was the very thing he loved.

GALAS: Then you think I've lost him?

VON HOYDEN: Not if you learn how to play the other woman.

GALAS: I'm afraid that role is not in my repertoire.

VON HOYDEN: And why not? All women are actresses at heart.

GALAS: I have always wanted to be loved completely and for myself alone. I could never play second fiddle. I must be the first woman. That, I believe, is the true meaning of the term, prima donna.

VON HOYDEN: Ah, but the other woman has certain advantages.

GALAS: What possible advantages could she have?

VON HOYDEN: For one thing, the wife is always jealous of the other woman, because she feels the other woman is getting the best part of the man. But the other woman is never jealous of the wife. All you have to do is learn to wait.

GALAS: But what do I do from morning to night while I'm waiting for him to call?

VON HOYDEN: Amuse yourself. Play cards. Gossip. Spend money on clothes. Accept dinner invitations. You're a lady of leisure and that's a luxury.

GALAS: I go crazy when I'm not working.

VON HOYDEN: Now take my maharaja for instance. Don't you dare. He has nine wives. That's enough to form an all-wife baseball team. *(Galas laughs)* But he prefers to spend his time with me. But I have to be patient. My turn doesn't come around that often. But when it does it's a great relief to him. I enjoy my freedom.

GALAS *(Her face turns into a tragic mask)*: That's it. I hate freedom. First I belonged to my mother, then I belonged to my husband, then I belonged to my art and now I don't belong to anyone.

VON HOYDEN: It's time to belong to yourself. Well, I'm off. Shopping, then lunch with the girls.

GALAS *(Quietly)*: Hell.

VON HOYDEN: What was that?

GALAS: Oh, nothing.

VON HOYDEN: Good-bye, sweetie, and remember you're a free woman. Cheer up. How about a little smile? *(Galas forces a smile)* That's the Magdalena I like to see. Au revoir, chérie.

GALAS *(Embracing her)*: Good-bye.

(Von Hoyden exits.)

(Galas sniffs the air) There's that tar again. *(She returns to her vigil at the window. Bruna reenters)* Has the postman arrived yet, Bruna?

BRUNA: There's some good news for you.

GALAS *(Eagerly)*: Good news? What is it? Quickly!

BRUNA: You've won your lawsuit against the Pastaciutta Mills.

GALAS *(Suddenly morose)*: Is that all?

BRUNA: And there's an invitation to a dinner party at the Finzi-Continis tonight.

GALAS: Short notice.

BRUNA: They sent it to the Villa Mercanteggini by mistake. Commendatore Mercanteggini forwarded it.

GALAS: Thoughtful of him.

BRUNA: There's still time to go if you want to.

GALAS: You know I've never been able to stand the Finzi-Continis.

BRUNA: It might do you good to go out for a change.

GALAS: Do you think?

BRUNA: A little conversation and admiration might be just the thing you need to put the roses in your cheeks.

GALAS: "The roses in my cheeks." Where do you pick up expressions like that?

BRUNA *(Going off into a spasm)*: I don't know. I suppose my mother used to say it. Didn't your mother have any little expressions like that?

GALAS: I don't know. *(Comforting Bruna)* I suppose she did. *(Glancing in the mirror)* "Gilding the lily."

BRUNA: What's that?

GALAS: She used to say, "Gilding the lily." I remember once when I was a little girl I went into my mother's room and I saw her standing before the mirror applying mascara with a tiny brush. I said, "Mamma, what are you doing?" and she said,

"I'm gilding the lily, dear, gilding the lily." For years I thought applying mascara was *called* gilding the lily. You know even today I never apply mascara that I don't think, I'm gilding the lily.

BRUNA: If you want to go to that dinner party tonight there's still time to gild the lily.

GALAS: What if Soc calls?

BRUNA *(As if on the phone)*: I'm sorry, madam is not at home. May I take a message, please?

GALAS: Perhaps it would be better not to seem to be always waiting.

BRUNA: Shall I lay out your silk moiré?

GALAS: Where was I last seen in it? Check the file.

BRUNA *(Consulting the file)*: Winston Churchill, Prince Rainier and Grace, Ilka Winterhalter.

GALAS: It's safe. They're all either dead or in Monte Carlo.

BRUNA: Tonight you will appear in public and show the world you do not care what your rivals may say about you.

GALAS: Rivals? I have no rivals. Thank heaven I have not. When other singers sing the roles that I sing the way I sing them, when they appear as I appear, do as I do, act as I act—then they can call themselves my rivals, and not until then.

BRUNA: Yes, madam. I know you do not fear any rivals.

GALAS: No, I do not fear them. Because I haven't any, you see.

BRUNA: Yes, madam, of course.

GALAS *(Becoming more insistent)*: On the contrary. I can sing the roles they sing. I have sung them. These so-called rivals of mine say that they sing a lot of operas, but what I see is that they sing a very few. *(With a weary tone)* They sing *Aïda*, they sing *La Boheme*, they sing *Carmen*. And they sing these same operas over and over again, year in and year out. I do not take it easy. *(Dressing herself behind a screen)* I work hard, and I work a lot, bringing to life a Medea, an Anna Bolena, an I Puritani, and when one develops a new role—new! I mean they are new to the public. They are really very old. As I was saying—when one develops a new role, one loses months of work, months of money, months of time. Because I cannot accept another job—pardon me for using the vulgar expression, "job," but you know I do not gain any salary while I'm preparing a new work. And when one brings to life a new role, one also runs the risk of being a flop. Aha! Yes! Believe me, I could go out there and yell my head off in *Aïda*, but to sing a work musically, note by note, no more, no less, according to the composer's intentions, that is quite a different matter. So, it may sound a bit immodest. I hope you will understand me when I say that I have no rivals. Many enemies *(Coming out from behind the screen fully dressed in a formal gown)*, but no rivals. Have I forgotten anything?

BRUNA: No, madam.

(Galas goes to the mirror and plays with her stole before it. Each different way she arranges her stole suggests a different role in her repertoire.)

GALAS: Don't wait up for me tonight, Bruna. Here I go. *(She reaches the door, stops dead in her tracks and stands there frozen for a long moment)* I can't face it. I can't, oh no, I can't face it. Bruna, are you doing anything tonight?

BRUNA: I was planning to go to the cinema.

GALAS: Are you going with someone?

BRUNA: No, I'm going alone.

GALAS: Oh, stay with me tonight, Bruna, we'll have a nice game of cards.

BRUNA: But tonight is my only night off, madam.

GALAS: Oh stay with me. Oh, what fun we'll have! I'll bet there's something nice on television.

BRUNA: But there is a new James Bond picture, madam, and I have a little crush on Sean Connery.

GALAS: Please stay with me tonight, Bruna. *(Bruna still isn't convinced)* I'm afraid to be alone tonight. *(Seizing her arm)* I'm feeling a little depressed.

BRUNA: Very well, madam.

GALAS: Thank you, Bruna; and Bruna, would you call me Magdalena?

BRUNA: No, madam, I am sorry. I wouldn't feel right doing that. *(Exits with grand operatic gesture)*

GALAS: Oh, what fun we'll have tonight, Bruna. I need some good news.

BRUNA *(Reenters with the dog)*: Madam, your dog is dead.

GALAS: Ah Toy, poor Toy. My baby, my baby. *(Takes the dog)* How many moonlight rendezvous you saw. How many jet planes you peed on. How many pairs of expensive pumps you chewed up and destroyed. Oh, the secrets you knew. *(She lays down the dog on her vanity and withdraws her hand suddenly in horror)* I used to replace them when they got old or died. Wouldn't it be wonderful if we could do that with people? When Soc remarried I saw no future for myself anymore. But even later, when he grew tired of the widow of the American president, and came back to me, it was never the same. I have always wanted to be loved completely, and for myself alone.

BRUNA: Your public loves you.

GALAS: The public, the public. When I sing well they applaud, and when I do not they boo and jeer. That's the public. Pah! You know, it's very strange, but there are certain nights when the public thinks that I am giving a great performance, but I do not feel that way at all. On such nights all compliments embarrass me. And yet there are certain other nights when I feel that the performance is going particularly well, and that I have attained a kind of perfection, but then the public does not agree. This is what haunts me.

BRUNA: A great artist is acknowledged but never understood. The voice is like the juice of a fruit: they squeeze it and throw the skin away.

(Phone rings. With grand operatic gesture, Bruna goes to answer it.)

GALAS: Oh well, there are singers and then there are artists, and you see I speak deliberately of both. The singer sings notes, but the artist makes manifest what lies behind the notes, behind the gestures. That is the difference.

BRUNA *(Reenters)*: Madam, it is a call from Ithaca. Aristotle Plato Socrates Odysseus is dead.

GALAS *(Stricken, assumes a posture of Greek tragedy)*: Tell them I'm not at home. I don't even want to speak to them. *(Looks about the room as though she does not recognize the place)* Well, it seems I must find my joy in my music again. To live is to suffer, to endure pain. Anyone who says differently is a liar. People should tell their children that! *(Exits behind screen, laughing wildly)* Oh well, I was never really popular. I really wanted to be a dentist. What difference would it have made? Life is the same for every human being on this earth. The only difference is the weapons used against one and the weapons one uses in turn. What you want and what you're willing to do to get it, that is personality. Personality plus circumstance equals fate. *(She reenters in a kimono. The pose and gestures suggest Madame Butterfly. Bruna ties the obi)* Bruna, do you know where I put the fan that was given to me by the female impersonator of the Kabuki theater?

(With grand operatic gesture, Bruna goes to fetch the fan. Galas enters more fully into the character of Butterfly. Bruna reenters, looks on horrified at Galas's mad behavior.)

BRUNA: Here it is, madam.
GALAS: You see, the fan *(Snaps open the fan)* conceals a knife *(Draws knife from fan)* —the perfect weapon for a female impersonator. Bruna?
BRUNA: Yes, madam?
GALAS: Would you sing the "Vissi d'arte" to me?

(She blindfolds Bruna with a glove. Bruna moves her lips hesitatingly and sings the "Vissi d'arte." We hear the full orchestra. Galas kneels in prayer.)

What do I do from morning to night if I don't have my career? I have no family, I have no husband, I have no babies, I have no lover, I have no dog, I have no voice and there's nothing good on television tonight. What do I do, what do I do from morning to night? I can't just sit around and play cards or gossip—I'm not the type.

(Suddenly her gaze falls on the fan. She looks to heaven as if for permission, smiles, takes fan, rises, opens fan and exits toward the screen. Before she disappears behind the screen, she looks

back at Bruna and smiles in affirmation. She throws a scarf over the screen, then raises her hand with the dagger.)

Grazie, Bruna.

(Her hand comes down with great force. As the last notes of the "Vissi d'arte" fade away, the scarf is dragged down behind the screen. Pounding on the door is heard, and then the sound of the door being broken down. Mercanteggini rushes onto the stage, sees Bruna blindfolded, looks behind the screen and cries out.)

MERCANTEGGINI: Magdalena? What has happened here?

(Tableau vivant as the lights fade slowly.)

CURTAIN

STAGE
BLOOD

1974

Stage Blood was first presented by The Ridiculous Theatrical Company at the Evergreen Theatre in New York City on November 11, 1974. Scenic design was by Bobjack Callejo, costume design was by Arthur Brady and lighting design was by Richard Currie. It was directed by Charles Ludlam. The cast was as follows:

CARLTON STONE, SR.	Jack Mallory
CARLTON STONE, JR.	Charles Ludlam
HELGA VAIN	Lola Pashalinski
JENKINS	John D. Brockmeyer
EDMUND DUNDREARY	Bill Vehr
ELFIE FEY	Black-Eyed Susan
GILBERT FEY	Jack Mallory
GHOST	? ? ?

⌒ Characters ⌒

CARLTON STONE, SR., an elderly player

CARLTON STONE, JR., an actor-manager, his son

HELGA VAIN, a mature actress,
Carlton, Sr.'s wife, Carlton, Jr.'s mother

JENKINS, the stage manager

EDMUND DUNDREARY, thespian

ELFIE FEY, a stagestruck, small-town girl

GILBERT FEY, Elfie's father

GHOST

⌒ *Act One*

A theater with the curtain closed.

After the audience is seated, the curtains part, revealing a bare stage, riggings and the glare of a work light. Enter Carlton Stone, Sr. (Stone) and Carlton Stone, Jr. (Carl). They are having a heated argument. Stone is obviously drunk.

CARL: Pop, please! Lay off that booze!

STONE: Don't nag me! You're worse than your mother.

CARL: We've got a show to do and you're no good half in the bag.

STONE: Son, I'm nervous.

CARL: You are nervous. What are you nervous about?

STONE: I'm nervous about being nervous. It's Mudville,* you know. Tonight is Mudville.

CARL: Pop, you should be glad we're playing your hometown.

STONE: I didn't want to take this booking.

CARL: We needed the money . . .

STONE: I've got flopsweat! *(Drinks from a bottle)*

CARL: Pop, put that stuff away! *(Grabs bottle and empties it)*

STONE *(Incensed, threatening with cane)*: Are you crazy? That's good liquor! . . . *(Carl returns bottle)* I used to be Hamlet.

CARL: Pop, don't . . .

STONE: Now I'm just the ghost. Poetic justice. I'm a ghost of my former self.

CARL: Pop, you're making me feel guilty. I never wanted to play Hamlet. It was your idea.

---

*Or the name of the town in which *Stage Blood* is played.

STONE: Someone had to play it. You don't want the Caucasian
Theatrical Company to take its final bow, do you?

CARL: No, Pop, of course not.

STONE: What else would you do if you didn't act?

CARL: I don't know, Pop. I never thought about it.

HELGA *(From offstage)*: Where is it?

JENKINS *(From offstage)*: This way.

CARL: This is it.

*(A door at the back of the theater opens and three somewhat weary
and bedraggled theater people—Helga, Edmund and Jenkins—
enter, dragging some trunks with them down the aisle.)*

HELGA: There's something about an empty theater.

EDMUND: Especially on opening night.

HELGA: Don't be sarcastic, Edmund. We were lucky to get a booking at all.

JENKINS: We'll be lucky to give a performance at all with no
Ophelia.

CARL: Aargh, don't remind me!

JENKINS: Somebody's got to remind you. We need a new Ophelia
by tonight and you've got to find one.

CARL: Don't look at me.

EDMUND: Jenkins is right, Carl. It's your responsibility.

CARL: But it was Pop's fault that she quit.

JENKINS: Yes, Carlton got us into this mess.

STONE *(Quietly)*: She was unprofessional.

JENKINS *(Defensively)*: She never missed a performance.

STONE: What do you call this?

JENKINS: Why, you old reprobate. You didn't understand her acting because she was Stanislavski-trained. She works honestly
and truthfully.

STONE: What do you know of honesty and truth? I call it lies and
deception. Deceiving the audience into believing in surface
reality, illusion. The great actor gives you a glimpse beneath
the surface. Something that lies beyond your honesty and
truth.

HELGA: Darlings, we don't need honesty and truth. We need an
ingenue.

EDMUND: Maybe you should ask your Ouija board for the answer.

HELGA *(Enigmatically)*: Of course. Ouija never lies.

JENKINS *(Exasperated)*: Ouija! Ouija! Ouija! Karen is gone and all you can talk about is your goddamn Ouija board!

HELGA: In every theatrical company, there is always one damn fool who's in love.

EDMUND *(Mockingly dramatic)*: Ah, the agony. *(Calling)* Karen! Karen!

JENKINS: That's enough.

(All laugh.)

(Beside himself) I said that's enough! *(Turning on Stone with sinister intensity)* I'll get even with you, Carlton Stone. If it's the last thing I do, I'll get even with you! *(Exits)*

HELGA: Now, now, Jenkins!

CARL: Leave him alone; he'll get over it.

EDMUND: I hope he doesn't go in the prop room and sulk for hours. The set's got to go up. We play tonight, you know.

STONE: Where are the dressing rooms?

CARL: I don't know. Let's find them. Take a break for lunch, everybody, and we'll have a dry run-through at one . . . if that's all right with you, Mother.

(Helga grunts in acknowledgment. All exit except Helga and Edmund.)

HELGA *(Looking up from her Ouija board)*: "Something is rotten in the State of Denmark."

EDMUND: What's that?

HELGA: "Something is rotten in the State of Denmark." That's the line that's going to be flubbed tonight. Ouija says so.

EDMUND *(Peeved)*: But that's *my* line.

HELGA: And according to Ouija, you're going to blow it tonight.

EDMUND *(Helplessly)*: Oh, for God's sake!

HELGA: Ouija never lies.

EDMUND *(Pensively)*: "Something is rotten in the State of Denmark." I've said that line hundreds of times and I've never gone up in it once.

HELGA *(Darkly)*: Well, you will tonight. Mark my words.

STONE *(Reentering with Carl)*: You may humbug the town as a tragedian, but comedy is a serious thing, my boy, so don't try that just yet.

CARL: But, Pop, couldn't you give me a few pointers? How do you play Hamlet?

STONE *(Taking a recorder from his breast pocket)*: Will you play upon this pipe?

CARL: But, Pop, I don't know how.

STONE: I pray you.

CARL: Believe me, I can't.

STONE: It's quite simple, you blow at this end and cover the holes with your fingers and thumb.

CARL: I knew that much. But I couldn't play a tune. The result would be mere cacophony.

STONE: Son, I can't tell you how to play Hamlet any more than I can tell you how to play this flute. In order to play Hamlet, you have to have *been* Hamlet. Why, look you now, how unworthy a thing you make of Hamlet! You would play Hamlet; you would seem to know his stops. You would pluck the heart of his mystery. You would sound him from his lowest note to the top of his compass; and there is much music, excellent voice, in this little organ, yet you cannot make it speak. 'Sblood, do you think Hamlet is easier to be played on than a pipe? Call Hamlet what instrument you will, though you can fret over him, you cannot play him.

EDMUND: I'd like to do a murder mystery.

STONE: Why, *Hamlet*'s the greatest murder mystery of all time.

EDMUND: What about *Oedipus Rex*?

CARL: Ah, yes, a great gimmick. The detective discovers his own guilt.

HELGA: The detective done it, huh?

EDMUND: Just like *The Mousetrap*.

JENKINS *(Entering)*: A man could make a fortune who could write a better *Mousetrap*.

STONE: But that's my point. *Hamlet* gave to the mystery story the one quality it had formerly lacked, the quality without which it could never attain greatness . . . a streak of the irrational.

HELGA: You mean the Ghost?

STONE: Exactly. Hamlet was not even sure that a crime had been committed, let alone who committed it.

HELGA *(Enthralled)*: A streak of the irrational!

EDMUND: Ah, yes, it seems today we had a streak of the irrational and it has left us without an Ophelia.

HELGA: Will the show go on?

STONE: Of course the show will go on. The show *must* go on! I will play Ophelia myself if necessary.

CARL: I don't know about that, Pop. We're doubling as it is!

HELGA: Why must the show go on? I've always wondered.

STONE: Actors must eat, and in my company, a day you don't act is a day you don't eat.

HELGA: I've never missed a performance. Be a darling, Jenkins, and hand me a sandwich, will you?

JENKINS: I'll see if the sandwiches have arrived. *(Exits)*

STONE: Now you're talking about potboilers, not Shakespeare.

EDMUND: Shakespeare wrote shameless potboilers. That's why he called them *As You Like It, Much Ado About Nothing* and *What You Will.*

STONE: Pshaw! Can you imagine a play entitled *As You Don't Like It?*

EDMUND: My point exactly. It wouldn't sell.

STONE: Are you denying the genius of Shakespeare?

EDMUND: No, I am only saying that in the theater, genius is often wedded to a mountebank.

STONE: This is outrageous!

EDMUND: Come now, Carlton, great actor though you are, can you deny that you have ever stooped to monkeyshines?

STONE: How dare you! What you do to Shakespeare shouldn't happen to John Simon!

HELGA: Which brings us back to potboilers.

EDMUND: And the irrational.

JENKINS *(Entering)*: And murder mysteries. Here are the sandwiches.

STONE: Faugh!

CARL *(Grabbing the bag of sandwiches from Jenkins)*: Well, what'll it be, Mother . . . ham or turkey?

HELGA: I'll take turkey.

CARL: I don't think turkey's good luck on opening night, Mother.

HELGA: Better give me ham.

CARL: You've got it. And don't eat the bread.

HELGA: Carl, I've only had two pieces of bread today—not more than eight hundred calories . . .

CARL *(Consulting a small notebook)*: Mother, if my memory serves me, you have had exactly *twelve* hundred calories today.

HELGA: Impossible!

CARL: Salad dressing, Roquefort cheese . . . goose-liver pâté! Admit the pâté.

HELGA: I admit the pâté.

CARL *(Incredulous)*: Banana Surprise!

HELGA: I wasn't surprised, I was appalled.

CARL: Mother, I'm afraid that if you eat those two slices of bread, you'll have gone over your limit. And you know what that means; no frozen skim milk later.

HELGA: Oh! *(Struggling with her conscience)* Very well. No bread.

CARL: Oh, I'm proud of you, and because you were so disciplined, I'll see to it that you get strawberry.

GIRL *(From the back of the house)*: Excuse me, Mr. Stone, but I know the role of Ophelia.

CARL AND STONE: You do?

GIRL *(Still from the back of the house)*: I know every line of it. I can do the "mad scene" for you, if you don't believe me. *(Entering down the aisle)* "Where is the beauteous Majesty of Denmark?"

(Carl nudges Helga with his elbow.)

HELGA: Huh?

CARL *(In a whisper)*: Give her the cue.

HELGA: Oh, the cue . . . "How now, Ophelia?"

GIRL *(Sings)*:

How should I your true love know
From another one?—
By his cockle hat and staff,
And his sandal shoon.

HELGA: Alas, sweet lady, what imports this song?

GIRL *(Going to Edmund)*: There's rosemary, that's for remembrance—pray you, love, remember. And there is pansies, that's for thoughts.

EDMUND: A document in madness: thoughts and remembrance fitted.

GIRL: There's fennel for you, and columbines. There's rue for you. And here's some for me. We may call it herb of grace o' Sundays. O, you must wear your rue with a difference. There's a daisy. I would give you some violets, but they withered all when my father died. They say 'a made a good end. *(Sings:)*

For bonny sweet Robin is all my joy.

EDMUND:
Thought and affliction, passion, hell itself,
She turns to favor and to prettiness.

GIRL *(Sings)*:
And will 'a not come again?
And will 'a not come again?
No, no, he is dead,
Go to thy deathbed! *(Points to Stone)*
He never will come again.

His beard was as white as snow,
All flaxen was his poll.
He is gone, he is gone,
And we cast away moan.
God 'a' mercy on his soul!

And of all Christian souls, I pray God. Good-bye you. *(Exits)*

STONE: Follow her close; give her good watch, I pray you.

(Carl goes after the Girl.)

O, this is the poison of deep grief: it springs
All from her father's death. *(Turning to Helga)* O Gertrude, Gertrude,
When sorrows come, they come not single spies,
But in battalions! First, her father slain;
Next—

HELGA: Will somebody stuff this ham with cloves? This is our lunch break, and I don't want to rehearse. I want to enjoy my lunch in peace.

GIRL *(Peeking out from the wings)*: Well?

(All stand dumbfounded for a moment and then Stone applauds. Carl, who is behind the Girl, pushes her onto the stage. Everyone joins in the ovation.)

STONE: Brava! Brava! My child, you can act! Can't she, Carl?

CARL *(Nodding)*: Yesiree.

EDMUND *(Kneeling before the Girl)*: Please accept this rose.

(It is a trick rose and it squirts the Girl in the face.)

STONE *(To Edmund)*: You damn practical joker! *(To the Girl)* Your words came down on wings of inspiration, as if not learned by rote but like the very beating of your heart. *(Turning to Carl very excitedly)* Carl, you must let her. You really must. She will play Ophelia! She must! Zounds! A talent like this comes along once in a lifetime. Oh, I'm out of breath. *(Gasping)* Ah! Ah! Ah!

CARL: Jenkins! Don't just stand there. Get Pop's oxygen!

STONE: Ah, the excitement! Ah! Ah! *(He clasps the Girl's hands)* How fortunate, how very fortunate that you found us, that we found you. Oh! Ah! Ah! Ah! *(Gasping for breath)*

JENKINS: Carlton, you're getting all excited. Calm down.

STONE *(Icily)*: You take a morbid interest in my health, Jenkins. I think you envy me my role.

JENKINS: You're paranoid.

STONE: Even paranoids have real enemies. I know you've been slowly tightening my armor.

JENKINS: You've been putting on weight, that's what it is.

STONE *(Beating his forehead with his fist dramatically)*: Aagh, what a curse it is to have the stage manager against you!

JENKINS: It's a good thing you don't have any food props or you'd think I was poisoning you.

(Helga starts and looks suspiciously at her hero sandwich.)

STONE *(Spitting dramatically)*: "The funeral baked meats will coldly furnish forth the marriage tables."

HELGA: What do you mean by that?

STONE: If you want me, Carl, I will be in my dressing room. *(Exits grandly)*

GIRL: May I play tonight, Mr. Stone? Oh, may I?

CARL: What's your name, sweetheart?

GIRL: Elfie Fey.

CARL: Not a bad stage name. What does your Ouija board say, Mother?

HELGA *(At the Ouija board)*: "Something is rotten in the State of Denmark."

EDMUND *(Vaingloriously)*: I won't go up in my lines tonight, I won't! *(Stalks out)*

ELFIE: What do you think, Mr. Stone? Do I have what it takes to be an actress?

CARL: Can you starve, Elfie? *(Turning to Jenkins, who has been muttering under his breath)* What's the matter now, Jenkins?

JENKINS: When I talk, people won't listen to me.

CARL: If you would just . . .

JENKINS: Not get so emotional?

CARL: Try to talk a little more dispassionately.

JENKINS: I'm in charge. They gotta listen to me.

STONE *(Reentering)*: The other day you told me to shut up and when I did, you walked out of the room and didn't even say what you had to say.

JENKINS: If I said to you, "Carlton, shut the fuck up . . ."

EDMUND: They'd probably applaud. There's a conflict of power.

CARL: I don't think so. Pop doesn't want to be responsible for the stage management, would you?

STONE *(To Jenkins)*: Last night we were supposed to start at seven. But you didn't show up till seven. Everybody was ready to go.

EDMUND: Nobody thought we'd start at seven.

HELGA: I thought you said we'd start at eight-thirty.

CARL: It was never made clear whether we were supposed to be here at seven or begin at seven.

JENKINS: That should be made clear next time.

STONE: The reason I was late is that while on the telephone, I discovered that I had crabs.

HELGA: Echt!

CARL: I discovered my first crabs on the phone, too.

EDMUND: Like father, like son.

STONE: These were hardly my first! Twenty minutes before the dress rehearsal . . . I didn't want to infest my costumes because they wouldn't be cleaned for another week. Wearing those costumes every night, I knew I'd never get rid of them. So I went out and got some A-200 and all my makeup and went home and treated myself.

HELGA: Where did you get crabs?

STONE: Oh, Helga!

JENKINS: I think the show's in trouble.

CARL: But you thought the last show was in trouble.

JENKINS: Your old man should let me do my play. Can't you talk him into it?

CARL: All eighteen hundred pages of it? It would take weeks to perform. That plot isn't your tightest.

JENKINS *(Showing a glimpse of an enormous script)*: This is the tightest plot that has been constructed in the last four hundred years . . . No! . . . In the whole history of drama. Someday some poor sucker will be writing his doctoral thesis on the relationship between my writings and my bowel movements.

EDMUND: I had a psychiatrist who was very interested in my bowel movements.

STONE *(To Edmund)*: That reminds me. You've got a dislocated diphthong. Instead of saying "I'm," you're saying "aum" or "om" or "ahm" or something. I find it jarring. *(Sticks his fingers in Edmund's mouth as he tries to say "I'm")*

EDMUND *(Almost strangling)*: I'm. I'm. I'm. *(Bites Stone's fingers)*

STONE *(Screams with pain)*: Ouch!

EDMUND: I'll go over all my "I'ms" in the first act! *(Exits)*

CARL: Pop, Jenkins wants you to do his play.

STONE *(Heartily)*: I would, if he'd cut it.

JENKINS *(Pressing the script to his breast like a mother protecting her child)*: Never!

STONE: In my boyhood days, I had enough of good reviews and empty houses. The story is everything.

HELGA: That's what we owe our success to. Your father and I could always pick a story.

JENKINS: It would be a crime to cut this play. Besides, it's impossible. You can't cut one word. My plot is tightly woven like a hand-knit sweater; you cut one thread and the whole thing ravels. Why, this plot is tighter than Ibsen! Tighter than Scribe!

STONE: Tighter than a bull's ass in fly season?

JENKINS: Every new form seems formless at first . . . someday you'll see . . . Ah! What's the sense of talking to you!

STONE *(Laughing heartily)*: Talk! Talk! I'm listening.

JENKINS: What's the use?

ELFIE: What's the name of your play?

JENKINS: *Fossil Fuel.*

ELFIE *(Venturing an opinion timidly but ever for the underdog)*: I don't think anyone understands your work.

JENKINS: If they did, they'd hang me!

HELGA *(Looking up from her Ouija board suspiciously)*: What do you mean by that?

STONE: I am in the same predicament as almost all theater managers throughout history. Actors of genius greatly outnumber playwrights of genius. Good actors abound; good playwrights are far to seek. The best actors of every generation have been forced to lean heavily on the classics and revivals of recent successes.

HELGA: A good melodrama!

JENKINS: Faugh!

STONE: But I prefer fustian, my boy, I do!

JENKINS: Mere bombast.

STONE: What's mere about bombast?

EDMUND: I always found Shakespeare too long and windy.

STONE: Yes, you wouldn't want to break your wind! *(Sits on a "farting cushion," which Edmund has placed unbeknownst to the others)* A pooh-pooh cushion! *(Throws it at Edmund)* You damn practical joker!

(Everyone laughs uproariously.)

HELGA: Tut tut! Falstaff farts in Shakespeare.

JENKINS: There were many playwrights in Shakespeare's own time—give or take a generation—who were far better than Shakespeare. Marlowe's mighty line, for instance, "And sooner shall the sun fall from its sphere, than Tamberlaine be slain or overcome." What of the forbidden love of John Webster's *Duchess of Malfi,* not to mention his invention of echo effects in the fifth act. Or Middleton and Rowley's *The Changeling!* Many scholars acknowledge these to be unique masterpieces, each one a distillation of an entire literary gift. These men wrote only a few plays. I have put everything into one!

EDMUND: In other words, it's your first play!

JENKINS: Well, I've got news for all of you.

ALL: !!!!!!!

JENKINS: The plays of Shakespeare were, in fact, never written by Shakespeare.

HELGA: Really?!

JENKINS: They were written by another playwright of the same name!

HELGA: Now that's a cue if I ever heard one.

CARL: That's my exit cue. *(Exits)*

JENKINS: There's nothing as safe as Shakespeare if you do it straight.

EDMUND: But that's pure bardolatry.

JENKINS: Bardolatry leads to bardicide.

HELGA: Bard is box, darlings. It's as simple as that.

JENKINS *(With disgust)*: Box office! That's all you ever think of.

HELGA: Frankly, I think his box is bigger than his bite.

EDMUND: I'm for a good story with a message you can take home with you. And I'm sure that everyone in this company will back me up on it.

JENKINS: Of course, of course! Everyone will agree. But that's the M.D.R, baby, Minimum Daily Requirement: a good story that raises an issue. But what then, huh? Repeat the old forms? Never! *(Shouting like Lear)* Recycle! Waste nothing! Do you hear what I'm saying? Cling to the Now through which all Future plunges to the Past!!!

(Suddenly everyone is silent for a long moment. Jenkins becomes self-conscious.)

EDMUND *(Applauding)*: Well played! Bravo, Jenkins! I say, quite a performance!

HELGA: Almost a Lear!

EDMUND: Yes, not quite a Lear.

JENKINS: You're all fools, fools! How long do you intend to go on hacking it in Shakespeare? Dishing up culture with a capital *K*! How can you go on pretending that there is a validity to monarchy, and that the high-born speak sublime blank verse, while the poor and laboring classes speak prose and doggerel?

EDMUND *(Very bored and condescending)*: Is that communism you're espousing, Jenkins?

JENKINS: Oh, what's the use? Anything left of stage center would look like communism to you!

EDMUND: I don't like politics. The theater is like a religion to me.

JENKINS: Ah, yes. The art-religion . . . Out of the frying pan into the fire.

STONE: That *Hamlet* exists at all is a miracle!

JENKINS: It's a miracle we don't dissolve when we take a bath. *(To Stone)* This show's in trouble and you're the only one who can do anything about it. The theater needs new blood.

STONE *(Scornfully)*: There's blood enough in *Hamlet*, my boy. Blood enough for anyone.

EDMUND: It's getting quite late. Hadn't the set better go up?

JENKINS *(Belligerently)*: All right, all right! That's all I'm good for around here!

HELGA: Now, now, Jenkins.

EDMUND: For God's sake, let him alone, don't coddle him!

(Jenkins, Helga and Edmund gather up their belongings and exit.)

ELFIE: Well, Mr. Stone, what do you say?

STONE: Oh, you'll play Ophelia, all right. There's no time to rehearse you, so you'll have to use common sense.

(Calls to Carl, who enters in Hamlet's "customary suit of solemn black" and blond wig.)

Carl, run through your scene with her, will you? The blocking is a little complicated. If you need me, Carl, I will be in my dressing room. *(Exits)*

ELFIE: What's blocking?

CARL: It's the plan of all the actors' movements and positions on the stage. Let's run through it. There isn't much time and I have got to get a cup of coffee before the performance tonight. Jenkins, would you run out and get us a couple of cups of coffee?

JENKINS *(Carrying a ladder across the stage)*: Do you want the set to go up or don't you? It's bad enough that I have to go out on a rum run for your old man. I ain't goin' out for coffee, too. *(Exits)*

CARL: Sorry I asked.

ELFIE: That fellow's got a chip on his shoulder, hasn't he?

CARL: Never mind the coffee, let's run the scene.

JENKINS *(Reentering apologetically)*: You can have some from my thermos, though.

(Elfie and Carl exchange a look of surprise.)

CARL: Why, thank you, Jenkins.

JENKINS *(Pouring hot coffee into a red thermos cup, which they share)*: I haven't got any sugar, though.

CARL AND ELFIE: That's all right, I don't take sugar. *(They exchange a look. Then in unison)* Neither do I.

CARL *(To Elfie)*: Neither do I.

JENKINS: And it's a good thing you don't. Sugar causes cancer.

CARL: Still eating those health foods, eh Jenkins?

JENKINS: I swear by vegetable juices.

CARL *(To Elfie)*: Jenkins is a vegetarian.

JENKINS: It's just that I can't stand butchers and butchery. *(Exits)*

ELFIE: You meet so many interesting people in the theater.

CARL: Yes.

ELFIE: Oh, this is so exciting! You must love the theater.

CARL: I am attracted by the theater, but frankly, I'm repelled by it. I would never have tried to go into the theater if my parents hadn't been actors. I always wanted to be a marine biologist. The people in the theater are so insincere, they don't seem to know where the play leaves off and real life begins. And besides, it's not a healthy life. You get a lot of exercise, but at night. I guess that's why acting is called the world's second oldest profession.

ELFIE: Yes, you're cut off from the solar energy. But night is a very intuitive time, don't you think?

CARL *(Lost in thought, but suddenly coming back to himself)*: What? . . . Oh, yes, intuitive.

ELFIE *(Elbowing him)*: Shall we rehearse?

CARL: Oh, we'll be all right but we won't run the risk of getting stale, will we?

ELFIE: Your zeal is only matched by your indifference.

CARL: Your iambics are only surpassed by your pentameters.

ELFIE: Listen, there's one thing about Ophelia I don't feel, ya know what I mean?

CARL: What do you mean?

ELFIE: Is Hamlet mad or only pretending to be?

CARL: He's only pretending.

ELFIE: I don't believe it. If he loves Ophelia, why would he pretend? No, I think he really was mad.

CARL: He wanted to get her out of the way. He was afraid she might get hurt.

ELFIE: And besides, if she really loved him, she would have known that he was not sincere. She would have . . . sensed it.

CARL: Listen, I have watched my father play Hamlet over five hundred times, and I don't know if I'm mad or only pretending to be.

ELFIE: When you act, do you really become the character?

CARL *(Emphatically)*: No, that would be dangerous. Acting is the art of seeming, not being. For instance, I will play Hamlet here tonight. I will seem to be Hamlet. Now, suppose I took a part in another play where I played a character who's playing Hamlet. I would seem to be Hamlet in that play, too. That would be just as good as playing Hamlet, don't you think? Only better. Whatever role we play, we construct it out of our own personalities anyway. We can never be anything other than what we are, so I say to seem is better than to be.

ELFIE: I see. To be an actress or not to be an actress . . . to ruin one's life before a room full of people. What fun!

CARL *(Rashly)*: Besides, Hamlet was a great actor.

ELFIE: And she was just a green ingenue.

CARL: A green ingenue . . . sounds like a sauce.

ELFIE: Listen. There's something I've always wanted to know about acting. When you have to cry on stage, actually produce real tears, night after night, how do you do it? Do you provoke the pain externally by pinching yourself where nobody can see? Or do you endow the situation with sense memory? Once I read in Uta Hagen's book that instead of concentrating on producing real tears, which would make you lose the value of the scene, what you should do is invoke a poetic image that would bring tears to your eyes, like a lonely, frail, delicate tree in the middle of a vast, windy prairie.

CARL: Throughout the great ages of the theater, the greatest actors of every generation have, well, uh . . . my mother always did it this way. *(Grabs a Kleenex from the dressing table and begins to cry violently)*

ELFIE *(Amazed)*: Real tears!

CARL: Would you like to try it?

ELFIE: Yes!

CARL: Take this onion, take this handkerchief. Now, holding the handkerchief in the right hand and the onion in the left (of course, if you're facing in the other direction, it's all reversed, but we'll get to that). Now, the handkerchief is like a little stage curtain, concealing the onion from the audience's view. It goes up and comes down, see? Up and down. Of course the great Berma was reputed to have been able to hold both the onion and the handkerchief in one hand, but I think that's too advanced for you. We'll just take it one step at a time. Forget the play, the scene, the character, just go for the external thing; go for the emotion. Work yourself up.

(Elfie begins to cry.)

CARL *(Coaching her on)*: Get upset . . . get more upset. Lower your head . . . Squeeze a little onion juice in your eye. That's it. *(Pointing to a tear on her cheek)* There it is! A little one, but it's a beginning. You were beautiful. You were . . . beautiful! You may keep the onion if you wish.

ELFIE: I'll treasure it always. I wish I could be right for you. I wish I could be thirty-five, have my hair bleached and say sophisticated things.

CARL: Promise me something, Elfie.

ELFIE: What?

CARL: That you'll never say sophisticated things, never have your hair bleached and never ever be thirty-five.

(They kiss.)

JENKINS *(Interrupting)*: Do you know that half hour was called fifteen minutes ago? *(Exits)*

CARL: Come. On to the dressing room. I hope you're the type that can wear any size.

ELFIE: What shall I take as a stage name?

CARL: How about Irving?

STONE *(Overhearing as he enters in Ghost costume)*: Ah, yes, Irving. I used to fetch his ale when I was pump boy at the Old Beefsteak Club Room.

CARL: Pop is a member . . .

STONE: In good standing . . .

CARL: In good standing of the Sublime Society of Beefsteaks!

STONE: Of which Sheridan was a member. I want you to understand one thing, Miss Fey. Our company may be small, but it's pretentious.

JENKINS *(Entering)*: Will you three please get off the stage? It's time to let the audience in.

STONE: This is going to be a great performance. I feel inspired. Miss Fey, you have inspired me.

(Exeunt omnes. There is a change of light and the sounds of an audience heard over Elizabethan music. The curtain rises on Act I,

Scene 1 of the Caucasian Theatrical Company's production of Hamlet. *Elsinore. Fog on the battlements. A banshee wails.)*

EDMUND: Who's there?

HELGA: Nay, answer me. Stand and unfold yourself.

EDMUND: Long live the King!

HELGA: Bernardo?

EDMUND: He.

HELGA: You come most carefully upon your hour.

(They shake hands. Edmund has a buzzer concealed in his palm and gives Helga a shock.)

(Under her breath) You damn practical joker!

EDMUND: 'Tis now struck twelve. Get thee to bed, Francisco.

HELGA: For this relief much thanks. 'Tis bitter cold, and I am sick at heart.

EDMUND: Have you had quiet guard?

HELGA: Not a mouse stirring.

EDMUND:
Well, good night.
If you do meet Hamlet and Horatio,
The rivals of my watch, bid them make haste.

(Carl and Jenkins enter.)

HELGA: I think I hear them. Stand, ho! Who is there?

JENKINS: Friends to this ground.

CARL: And liegemen to the Dane.

HELGA: Give you good night.

JENKINS: O, farewell, honest soldier, who hath relieved you?

HELGA: Bernardo hath my place. Give you good night. *(Exits)*

CARL: The air bites shrewdly, it is very cold.

JENKINS: It is a nipping and an eager air.

CARL: What hour now?

JENKINS: I think it lacks of twelve.

EDMUND: No, it is struck.

JENKINS:
Indeed? I heard it not. It then draws near the season
Wherein the spirit held his wont to walk.

(Ghost enters.)

Look, my lord, it comes.

CARL:

Angels and ministers of grace defend us!
Be thou a spirit of health or goblin damned,
Bring with thee airs from heaven or blasts from bell,
Be thy intents wicked or charitable,
Thou com'st in such a questionable shape
That I will speak to thee. I'll call thee Hamlet,
King, father, royal Dane. O, answer me.
Let me not burst in ignorance, but tell
Why thy canonized bones, hearsed in death,
Have burst their cerements, why the sepulchre
Wherein we saw thee quietly interred
Hath oped his ponderous and marble jaws
To cast thee up again. What may this mean,
That thou, dead corpse, again in complete steel,
Revisits thus the glimpses of the moon,
Making night hideous, and we fools of nature
So horridly to shake our disposition *(They all shake)*
With thoughts beyond the reaches of our souls?
Say why is this? Wherefore? What should we do?

(Ghost beckons.)

JENKINS:

It beckons you to go away with it,
As if it some impartment did desire
To you alone.

EDMUND:

Look with what courteous action
It waves you to a more removéd ground.
But do not go with it.

JENKINS: No, by no means.

CARL: It will not speak. Then will I follow it.

JENKINS: Do not, my lord.

CARL:

> Why, what should be the fear?
> I do not set my life at a pin's fee,
> And for my soul, what can it do to that,
> Being a thing immortal as itself?
> It waves me forth again. I'll follow it.

JENKINS:

> What if it tempt you toward the flood, my lord,
> Or to the dreadful summit of the cliff
> That beetles o'er his base into the sea,
> And there assume some other horrible form
> Which might deprive your sovereignty of reason
> And draw you into madness? Think of it.
> The very place puts toys of desperation,
> Without more motive, into every brain
> That looks so many fathoms to the sea
> And hears it roar beneath.

CARL:

> It waves me still.
> Go on. I'll follow thee.

EDMUND: You shall not go, my lord.

CARL: Hold off your hands.

JENKINS: Be ruled. You shall not go.

CARL:

> My fate cries out
> And makes each petty artery in this body
> As hardy as the Nemean lion's nerve.
> Still am I called. Unhand me, gentlemen.
> By heaven, I'll make a ghost of him that lets me.
> I say, away! Go on. I'll follow thee.

(Ghost and Hamlet exit.)

JENKINS: He waxes desperate with imagination.

EDMUND: Let's follow. 'Tis not fit thus to obey him.

JENKINS: Have after. To what issue will this come?

EDMUND: Something is denten in the State of Rotmark. O, shit!

(A bloodcurdling scream is heard. All run into the dressing room. Helga stands with blood on her hand, screaming. Stone lies dead, his head in the toilet, blood issuing from his ear.)

CARL *(Coming in)*: What is it? What's happened? Omigod, it's Pop!

HELGA *(In shock)*: At first I thought it was real. Then I saw it was only stage blood!

CARL: He's dead.

HELGA: It isn't real. It's stage blood, I tell you! Stage blood!

(Curtain.)

⌒ *Act Two*

Same as in Act One.

Helga sits at the dressing table removing her makeup. Edmund is seated on the toilet, upstage.

EDMUND *(Reading* Variety*)*: Pap, pap, nothing but pap. *(Tears the page he's reading and cleans himself with it, attempts to flush)* This damn toilet never works.

HELGA: I'll have Carl take a look at it. He's real good with the W.C.

EDMUND *(Begins to shave)*: What does your Ouija board say now, Helga?

HELGA: All that is, I see.

EDMUND: You're going to go up in your lines tonight?

HELGA: Yeah, Ouija doesn't play favorites. *(She opens a jar of cold cream and a snake jumps out at her. She screams. Affectionately:)* You damn practical joker.

EDMUND *(Referring to Ouija board)*: Why don't you ask it who killed the old man?

HELGA: Who do you think killed him?

EDMUND: I think you did it.

HELGA *(Laughing gaily)*: Of course I did it . . . to get the company for you, my baby.

(Helga embraces and kisses Edmund, whose face is covered with shaving cream.)

EDMUND: Oh, come on, right here!

HELGA: No!

EDMUND: There's plenty of time . . . I've been a bad boy today, Mamma.

HELGA: Edmund's been a bad boy.

(He drops his pants. She playfully whips him with his belt.)

EDMUND: I'm gonna get you, Mamma.

HELGA: He's after me!

EDMUND *(Grabs her fur coat and throws it over them)*: Venus in furs!

CARL *(Calling from offstage)*: Mother! Mother!

HELGA *(Startled)*: Oh, my God, it's Carl! He'll be here any minute.

(They jump up. Edmund grabs his clothes and tries to put on his pants.)

EDMUND: Tell him you've had enough. You're fed up. Lay down the law. Do you want *him* to manage this company or *me*?

HELGA: You, of course, darling. *(Kisses him)*

EDMUND: What are you going to tell him?

CARL *(Off)*: Mother?

HELGA: Don't worry about me. Hide. He'll be here any minute.

(Edmund hides behind the arras. Carl enters, goes to the toilet to urinate.)

CARL: Toilet not working?

HELGA: Yeah. Would you have a look at it?

CARL: I'll fix it. *(Does so)*

HELGA: Now, Carl, what's the matter?

CARL: I want to run some lines from the closet scene.

HELGA: Must we? This day has just exhausted me.

CARL: It seems so cold-blooded. This morning we buried Pop, this afternoon we've replaced him and tonight we're going on.

HELGA: We must perform. There is no posthumous fame for actors.

JENKINS *(Poking in his head)*: Carl, there's a man out front who wants to see you.

CARL: Who is it?

JENKINS: He looks like a mortician's bill collector, if you ask me.

HELGA: You can't get much lower than that.

CARL *(To Helga)*: All right, we won't rehearse. *(To Jenkins)* Send him in.

(Jenkins exits.)

HELGA: I'm going to see about supper.

CARL: Mother, there's something I want to discuss with you.

HELGA: What is it?

CARL: Mother, I think Pop was murdered.

HELGA: Carl, I don't want to talk about this. It was suicide. He was all washed up. He couldn't take the humiliation of playing his hometown.

CARL: Someone we know did it. Someone in this company.

HELGA: Carl, you're frightening me.

CARL: Perhaps a little fear would do you good. Someone in this company killed my father and I'm not going to rest until I find out who it is.

HELGA: You look tired.

CARL: I can't think about that now. There's the performance tonight, and later I've got to go over all the books. Pop always took care of the business end, and I guess now it's up to me. There are a lot of bills to be paid; death is expensive.

HELGA: Carl, I think you're working too hard. You shouldn't have to think about money. You need to concentrate on playing Hamlet just now. Why don't we get someone else to take care of the dull business end of it? Then you'd have more time to think about your art—

(A small crash is heard offstage.)

CARL *(Suddenly starting to his feet, draws prop sword)*: "What's that! A rat!" *(Stabs sword through the costume rack, as if it were the arras in the closet scene of* Hamlet*)* "Dead for a ducat! Dead!"

HELGA *(Shrieks)*: Don't!

CARL *(Diving through the costume rack)*: There's no one there!

(The door to the dressing room, stage left, opens and Edmund falls in dead, with a dagger stuck in his back. Helga and Carl turn and gasp. Edmund jumps up laughing, and pulls the dagger out of his back.)

EDMUND: Ha! Ha! Ha! Cute trick, don't you think? I had Jenkins order it.

CARL: *You* had Jenkins order it?!

EDMUND: Yes, the blade retracts into the handle. We should try it out tonight, don't you think?

HELGA: Carl, Edmund has a lot of ideas about how we can improve the company.

EDMUND: Yes, Carl, I'm going to handle the management from now on.

CARL: You? *(Laughing)* Mother, did you hear that?

HELGA: It's true, Carl. Edmund and I are going to be married.

CARL *(Retching)*: Mother! "A beast that wants discourse of reason would have mourned longer."

HELGA: Now, Carl, don't get all excited. It'll just spoil your performance.

CARL: It didn't hurt your performance *(Makes obscene gestures)* did it, Edmund?

EDMUND: Your sense of humor and mine differ.

CARL: Well, if you don't like it, get out of my dressing room, motherfucker!

(They go to fight. Helga comes between them.)

GILBERT *(Entering)*: Oh, excuse me, I'm interrupting.

HELGA: Not at all. We were just leaving. *(Pushes Edmund through the door and, following, turns to Carl)* Carl, try to understand. *(Then looking Gilbert up and down)* Exactly like a mortician's bill collector. *(Exits)*

GILBERT: You don't know me, Mr. Stone. My name is Fey, Gilbert Fey. I'm Elfie's father.

CARL: What can I do for you?

GILBERT: Prevent my daughter from going on the stage.

CARL: Isn't that up to her?

GILBERT: It most certainly is not. She's underage. If she leaves with you on tour, I'll slap you with statutory rape.

CARL: Your threats don't frighten me, Mr. Fey. She's your daughter; you control her.

GILBERT: If only I could. She's strong-willed and once they get a taste of the theater, there's no reasoning with them.

CARL: Your daughter is an inspired actress.

GILBERT: I know that I may be wasting my time appealing to the honor of an immoral actor, but I do appeal to that honor in the hope that it exists. Please help me.

CARL: As you just pointed out, you have the law on your side. What do you need me for?

GILBERT: Ah, if only it were as simple as that.

CARL: You see this bottle?

GILBERT: Stage blood?

CARL: Yeah, stage blood. It's not real blood; it's the blood we use on stage. That's what your daughter has in her veins.

GILBERT: You are an actor; disillusion her. She must not go the way Carlton went.

CARL: Carlton? What do you know about my father?

GILBERT: I'll make a deal with you. Stop my daughter's career and I'll tell you who killed your father.

CARL: It's a deal. On one condition: that you let her finish the performance tonight. You see, we don't have an Ophelia.

GILBERT: Ah, that sounds dangerous.

CARL: Mr. Fey . . . a moment ago you called me an immoral actor. Frankly, I was shocked. Now I see that perhaps what you say may be true. The theater is my church. To act my experience of God. But I only have one scruple: to get the play onto the stage. Because I sacrifice myself to that end, I do not flinch at sacrificing others. Let your daughter play Ophelia tonight, and I promise that I will send her back to you, a little shaken perhaps, but cured of the theater forever.

GILBERT: Thank you.

CARL: But I warn you, I shall have to hurt her. Perhaps even subject her to some humiliation.

GILBERT: Yes, hurt her, if you must. But cure her of this thing, this stage blood.

CARL: Consider her cured.

GILBERT (Starts to go, stops and turns): What if she doesn't believe you?

CARL: Don't worry about that, Mr. Fey. Those of us who make our livings at make-believe are the most easily taken in by it.

GILBERT *(Smiling an oily smile and taking his wallet out of his inside jacket pocket)*: May I offer some remuneration for what may be your greatest performance?

CARL *(Snatching the money)*: Now get out before I throw you out!

(Gilbert beats a hasty retreat. Jenkins enters with a toilet brush and scrubs toilet bowl, whistling while he cleans.)

(To Jenkins) You're going to have to play the Ghost tonight. I don't know what you're going to do for armor.

JENKINS *(Still scrubbing bloody toilet)*: I just happen to have a suit that fits me.

CARL: That fits you???

JENKINS *(In cold blood)*: Yeah, I always had a feeling I was going to play that part someday.

CARL: But you knew Pop would only let you play it over his dead body.

(Pregnant pause.)

JENKINS: It wasn't me. But I think I do know who killed your old man. *(Starts to leave, then turning and coming toward Carl)* And I'm going to tell you after tonight's performance.

(A sandbag falls from the flies just outside of the door and crashes to the floor of the stage, missing Jenkins by inches.)

CARL: A sandbag! Jenkins, if I've told you once, I've told you a thousand times, never whistle in the dressing room. It's bad luck! Unless you say a line from *Hamlet* immediately afterward. Now go get into costume. And Jenkins, when you hear that call—"Places"—you know that you're going on because if you're not, you're in the wrong business. We've got a performance to give, and you're on in the first act. Now go on . . . and Jenkins, break a leg.

(Jenkins exits hurriedly, trips over the sandbag and falls.)

JENKINS: "He smote the sledded Polacks on the ice."

CARL: Are you sure that's from *Hamlet?*

JENKINS: Yes, it's from Horatio's first ghost scene. They always cut it.

CARL: No wonder. I never thought that Shakespeare would stoop to a Polish joke!

(Jenkins exits.)

(Alone, changing from Carl to Hamlet) A father is a necessary evil. Shakespeare must have written *Hamlet* in the months following his father's death. Fatherhood in the sense of conscious begetting is entirely unknown to man. From only begetter to only begotten. For all we know, fatherhood may be a legal fiction. Who is the father of any son that any son should love him? The son unborn mars his mother's beauty; born he brings pain, divides affection, increases care. He is a male: his growth his father's decline, his youth his father's envy, his friend his father's enemy. *(Regarding his nude body in the mirror)* Oh, that this too too solid flesh would melt.

JENKINS *(From offstage)*: Hamlet, I am thy father's spirit.

CARL *(Startled)*: Oh, it's Jenkins rehearsing.

STONE'S VOICE: You are the dispossessed son; I am the murdered father; your mother is the guilty queen.

(Ghost enters as in Hamlet. *He speaks in Stone's voice.)*

CARL: I can't believe my eyes.

GHOST:
　　To my son I speak. The son of my soul.
　　The son of my body.
　　My son! and what's a son?
　　A thing begot within a pair of minutes, thereabout;
　　A lump bred up in darkness, and doth serve
　　To balance those light creatures we call women;
　　And at the nine months' end creeps forth to light.
　　What is there yet in a son,
　　To make a father dote, rave or run mad?
　　Being born, it pouts, cries and breeds teeth.
　　What is there yet in a son?
　　He must be fed, be taught to go, and speak.
　　Ay, or yet? Why might not a man love a calf as well?
　　Or melt in passion o'er a frisking kid, as for a son?
　　Methinks a young bacon,

Or a fine little smooth horse colt,
Should move a man as much as doth a son;
For one of these, in very little time,
Will grow to some good use; whereas a son,
The more he grows in stature and in years,
The more unsquared, unlevel'd he appears;
Reckons his parents among the rank of fools,
Strikes cares upon their heads with his mad riots,
Makes them look old before they meet with age:
This is a son.

CARL: Art thou there, truepenny?

GHOST: I died so that my namesake may live forever. My brother didn't do it. My brother didn't do it.

CARL: I never thought he did!

GHOST: Man at ten is any animal, at twenty a lunatic, at thirty a failure, at forty a fraud, at fifty a criminal. Damn good gin that was!

CARL *(Applauds)*: Father! A masterly rendition.

(The Ghost disappears.)

HELGA *(From offstage)*: Carl . . . Carl. *(Enters)* Carl, you're not dressed yet . . . and you're on in five minutes!

(She frantically helps him dress.)

CARL: All these hooks and eyes . . . I'll never make it . . . Why can't we get any tights that fit?

HELGA: You're not in New York now, darling, this is Mudville. Carl, why don't you get one of your tricks to do your sewing for you?

CARL: It's so hard to meet anyone on the road, Mother.

HELGA: Tell me about it.

CARL: It could be worse, Mother. We could be in Vienna.

HELGA: Carl, I told you never to mention Vienna to me again.

CARL: Slowly I turn and inch by inch, step by step . . .

HELGA: Ah, Vienna, the city of my nightmares. The only town we played where we had to go back to our hotel rooms to take a piss.

CARL: What about the night that Edmund Dundreary was discovered in his hotel room forcing a load of shit down the sink with his thumb? He couldn't find the key to the W.C. in the middle of the night.

HELGA: Jenkins never got over it.

CARL: I never got over it.

HELGA: Vienna never got over it. Carl, haven't you forgotten something?

CARL: Oh, yes, the locket.

HELGA (*Holds up wig*): Carl . . .

CARL: No! Not the wig.

HELGA: Carl, you've got to wear the wig.

CARL: Mother, if I've told you once I've told you a hundred times: I hate that wig!

HELGA: Carl, you have to wear the wig!

CARL: People laugh at me when I come on stage in that wig.

HELGA: Go with it, go with it! Carl, please, you cannot play Hamlet without being blond. It's never been done in theater before.

CARL: Well, why not? Some Danes have black hair.

HELGA: Name five. Please, Carl, wear the wig. (*In baby talk*) Wear the wiggie, wiggie, wiggie. (*Carl resists*) Please, Carl, don't make me beg. (*She begins crying*)

(*He gives in and takes the wig.*)

Thank you. And tonight could you true up the "To be or not to be" speech? It's been a little too two-dimensional. Try to mean what you are saying. No wooden Hamlets. Not even in the sticks. (*Exits*)

CARL: Yes, Mother. Why, I know the "To be or not to be" speech so well that I could say it backwards. "Question the is that; be to not or, be To." (*He enters the playing area as Hamlet and begins the "To be or not to be" speech*)

To be or not to be . . .
(*Whispers*) Line!
That is the question.
Whether 'tis nobler in the mind to suffer

The slings and arrows of outrageous fortune,
Or to take arms against a sea of troubles
And, by opposing, end them. To die—to sleep,
No more; and by a sleep to say we end
The heartache and the thousand natural shocks
That flesh is heir to: 'tis a consummation
Devoutly to be wished. To die, to sleep,
To sleep—perchance to dream. Aye, there's the rub:
For in that sleep of death what dreams may come
When we have shuffled off this mortal coil,
Must give us pause—there's the respect
That makes calamity of so long life.
For who would bear the whips and scorns of time,
The oppressor's wrong, the proud man's contumely,
The pangs of despised love, the law's delay,
The insolence of office and the spurns
That patient merit of the unworthy takes,
When he himself might his quietus make
With a bare bodkin? Who would fardels bear,
To grunt and sweat under a weary life,
But that the dread of something after death,
The undiscovered country, from whose bourn
No traveler returns, puzzles the will,
And makes us rather bear those ills we have
Than fly to others that we know not of?
Thus conscience does make cowards of us all,
And thus the native hue of resolution
Is sicklied o'er with the pale cast of thought,
And enterprises of great pitch and moment
With this regard their currents turn awry
And lose the name of action—Soft you now,
The fair Ophelia! Nymph, in thy orisons
Be all my sins remembered.

(Enter Elfie as Ophelia.)

ELFIE:

Good my lord,
How does your honor for this many a day?

CARL: I humbly thank you, well, well, well.

ELFIE:

My lord, I have remembrances of yours
That I have long-ed longed long to redeliver.
I pray you now receive them.

CARL:

No, not I,
I never gave you aught.

ELFIE:

My honored lord, you know right well you did,
And with them words of so sweet breath composed
As made the things more rich. Their perfume lost,
Take these again, for to the noble mind
Rich gifts wax poor when givers prove unkind.
There, my lord.

CARL: Are you honest?

ELFIE: My lord?

CARL: Are you fair?

ELFIE: What means your lordship?

CARL: That if you be honest and fair, your honesty should admit
no discourse to your beauty.

ELFIE: Could beauty, my lord, have better commerce than with
honesty?

CARL: Ay, truly, for the power of beauty will sooner transform
honesty from what it is to a bawd than the force of honesty
can translate beauty into his likeness. This was sometime a
paradox, but now the time gives it proof.

*(Helga and Edmund enter watching from the wings, dressed as
Gertrude and Claudius.)*

EDMUND *(To Helga)*: We almost muffed it in that last little scene.

HELGA: I'm afraid that Carl is going to be trouble.

EDMUND: You can handle him. Use a little psychology.

HELGA: That's underhanded, Edmund. I wouldn't stoop to using
psychology.

(Elfie and Carl continue the performance of Hamlet.*)*

CARL: I did love you once.

ELFIE: Indeed, my lord, you made me believe so.

CARL *(Seeing his mother and Edmund kissing in the wings)*: You should not have believed me, for virtue cannot so inoculate our old stock but we shall relish of it. I loved you not.

ELFIE: I was the more deceived.

CARL: Get thee to a nunnery. Why wouldst thou be a breeder of sinners? I am myself indifferent honest, but yet I could accuse me of such things that it were better my mother had not borne me: I am very proud, revengeful, ambitious, with more offenses at my beck than I have thoughts to put them in, imagination to give them shape, or time to act them in. What should such fellows as I do crawling between earth and heaven? We are arrant knaves all; believe none of us. Go thy ways to a nunnery.

ELFIE: O, help him, you sweet heavens.

EDMUND: She's good, really good.

HELGA: She even makes *him* look good.

CARL *(As Hamlet)*: I have heard of your paintings too, well enough. God hath given you one face and you make yourselves another. You jig, you amble, and you lisp; you nickname God's creatures and make your wantonness your ignorance. Go to, I'll no more on't, it hath made me mad. I say we will have no more marriages. Those that are married—all but one—shall live. The rest shall keep as they are. To a nunnery, go.

(Applause is heard. Carl exits from the stage through the arras to the dressing room. We hear Elfie as Ophelia finishing the scene with her lament through the curtain.)

ELFIE:
O, what a noble mind is here o'erthrown!
The courtier's, soldier's, scholar's, eye, tongue, sword,
Th'expectancy and rose of the fair state,
The glass of fashion and the mould of form,
Th'observed of all observers, quite, quite down!
And I, of ladies most deject and wretched,
That sucked the honey of his musicked vows,
Now see that noble and most sovereign reason

Like sweet bells jangled, out of time and harsh,
That unmatched form and feature of blown youth
Blasted with ecstasy. O, woe is me
T'have seen what I have seen, see what I see!

(During Elfie's speech, Jenkins and Carl are in the dressing room.)

JENKINS *(Handing Carl a half full whiskey bottle)*: Here's the
whiskey bottle you wanted. I found it in the prop room.
CARL: I'll empty it. Do you have some tea?
JENKINS: That's tea in it now. I know you don't drink.
CARL *(Sniffs it)*: Tea!
JENKINS: Rose hip . . . organic . . . vitamin C.
CARL: Thank you, Jenkins, you're my right arm.
JENKINS: But, tell me, what scene are you going to use it in?
CARL: In a little scene I'm going to play right now. *(Both listening
to last of Elfie's speech)* Leave me alone with her.
JENKINS: What are you going to do?
CARL: That's between the Father, the Son and the Holy Ghost.
JENKINS: P.U. All religion stinks to . . .
CARL: High heaven? Yes, I know.

*(Jenkins heaves a sigh and exits. Elfie enters the dressing room.
Carl is sitting at the dressing table drinking.)*

ELFIE: Carl, is something wrong?
CARL: Why do you ask?
ELFIE *(Troubled, perhaps even haunted)*: There was something
about your eyes . . . I don't know. Maybe it was just my imagination, but you looked as though you were going to tear my
clothes off me. It frightened me.
CARL: Tear your clothes off you? *(He drinks from the bottle)*
ELFIE *(Shocked)*: Carl, you're not drinking? *(Trying to reason with
him)* You should smoke grass, dear. That stuff will ruin your
liver.
CARL *(Brash, almost obnoxious)*: Of course, I'm drinking. I'm an
actor, not a goddamn hippie! The drama originated as a fes-
tival of Dionysus. *(Ranting)* Grapes! Wine! Intoxication!
ELFIE: Please stop drinking! You have a performance to give.

CARL: That's one of the highly guarded secrets of our profession. All actors are better drunk. *(Belches)*

ELFIE: That's disgusting!

CARL: What's disgusting about it? It's more constructive than what most people do when they're drunk.

ELFIE: Here, take back your rabbit's foot.

CARL: I never gave that to you.

ELFIE: You did, but take it back. For to the noble mind, rich gifts wax poor when givers prove unkind.

CARL *(Sarcastically)*: I saw the movie.

ELFIE: Carl, I know that you're going through something terrible about your father. But I'll stand by you. I'd do anything for you.

CARL *(Rubbing her face with his hand)*: What's that on your face?

ELFIE: Makeup. I'm an actress now.

CARL: What do you need makeup for? What's wrong with your own face?

(He splashes her face with water and wipes it clean. Then he kisses her.)

ELFIE *(Aroused)*: Carl, do you know how you make me feel?

CARL *(Shocked at her willingness)*: No, I don't know how I make you feel, but I know how you look—like a whore! *(Spanks her)*

ELFIE *(Outraged)*: I hate you and I hate the theater! I'll do Jenkins's studio performance tonight but, after that, I never want to see you or the inside of a theater again. *(Exits)*

CARL: Don't slam the door. *(Sound of door slamming and applause)*

(Gilbert enters.)

GILBERT: Well played, Mr. Stone. You've kept your part of the bargain.

CARL: And now, Mr. Fey, you keep your part of the bargain. Who did it, Mr. Fey? Who was the dirty rat who killed my father?

GILBERT: I killed him.

CARL: You!!!

GILBERT: Look at my face . . . over here in the light.

CARL: Omigod!

GILBERT: You see a resemblance? Yes, I killed Carlton and I impersonated the Ghost . . . We were twins, Carlton and I, and we were both stagestruck.

CARL: Then you're my . . .

GILBERT: Yes, I'm your Uncle Gilbert.

CARL: You killed your own brother to indulge a petty jealousy?

GILBERT: Yes, yes. It should be easy for you to understand. It's in my veins too—this stage blood.

CARL: You killed your own brother to play his role for one night?!

GILBERT: You'd let me fry for that, wouldn't you? But there's more to it than that, believe me. Hear me out. Percy and me . . . yes, that was your old man's name before he changed it for the stage—Percy Fey . . .

CARL (Shocked): You mean my name isn't Stone?

GILBERT: No, it's Fey, Raymond Fey.

CARL: Ray Fey! Omigod! It's horrible!

GILBERT: Percy got a local girl in trouble, and she bore his baby in a woodshed. Percy didn't want the little bastard to saddle him with responsibility, so he seized the child and tried to drown it in a drunken scene. I beat on him and saved the child. He ran away that night with a road show and never came back. I made that girl an honest woman, and raised his child . . . Elfie Fey.

CARL: Then she's my sister!

GILBERT: She's your half-sister.

CARL: He might have killed Elfie. Still, revenge cannot be justified.

GILBERT: Then you mean you'll let me fry, after all? But whatever course of action you choose to take, never let her know that that foul, old, drunken piece of human garbage . . . God rest his soul . . . was her father.

CARL: Uncle Gilbert, you'll find that blood is thicker than water, especially stage blood . . . Uncle Gilbert, do you think you could memorize a short speech of about twenty lines? You see, Elfie and I are doing a scene from Jenkins's experimental drama, *Fossil Fuel*. We're trying to convince Mother that it might be profitable to add an avant-garde play to the repertoire. And I think we might just have a part in it for you.

GILBERT: Oh, I'd be honored to play with you, Mr. Stone.

CARL: Come back tonight after the performance, and I'll have the whole thing written out for you.

GILBERT: Aye, my lord. *(Exits)*

EDMUND *(Entering dressing room)*: Carl, your mother wants to see you.

CARL: You say my mother?

EDMUND: She wants to speak with you in her dressing room before the closet scene.

CARL: Tell her I'll obey. Were she ten times our mother!

(Carl puts on a wig and enters the Hamlet *stage where Helga as Gertrude awaits him. Gilbert sneaks into the dressing room during the following scene; he snoops around, takes a sip from the fake bottle of booze, spits it out, then eavesdrops by the arras.)*

CARL: Now, Mother, what's the matter?

HELGA: Hamlet, thou hast thy father much offended.

CARL: Mother, you have my father much offended.

HELGA: Come, come, you answer with an idle tongue.

CARL: Go, go, you question with a wicked tongue.

HELGA: Why, how now, Hamlet?

CARL: What's the matter now?

HELGA: Have you forgot me? *(Weeps. An onion drops from her handkerchief)*

CARL:
No, by the rood, not so!
You are the Queen, your husband's brother's wife,
And, would it were not so, you are my mother.

HELGA: Nay, then I'll set those to you that can speak.

CARL:
Come, come, and sit you down. You shall not budge.
You go not till I set you up a glass
Where you may see the inmost part of you.

HELGA: What wilt thou do? Thou wilt not murder me?
Help, ho!

GILBERT: What, ho! Help!

CARL *(Draws)*: What's that? A rat? Dead for a ducat, dead!
(Makes a pass through the arras)
GILBERT: O, I am slain.
HELGA: O me, what hast thou done?
CARL: Nay, I know not. Is it the King?
HELGA: O what a rash and bloody deed is this!
CARL: A bloody deed. Almost as bad, good mother,
As kill a king, and marry with his brother.
HELGA: As kill a king?
CARL: Ay, lady, it was my word. — *(Lifts up the arras and sees that he has accidentally killed Gilbert)*

Uncle Gilbert?
Thou wretched, rash, intruding fool, farewell!
I took thee for thy better. Take thy fortune.
Thou find'st to be too busy is some danger. —
Leave wringing of your hands. Peace, sit you down,
And let me wring your heart; for so I shall
If it be made of penetrable stuff.
If damned custom have not brazed it so,
That it be proof and bulwark against sense.
HELGA:
What have I done, that thou dar'st wag thy tongue
In noise so rude against me?
CARL:
Look here upon this picture, and on this,
The counterfeit presentment of two brothers.
This was your husband. Look you now what follows.
HELGA:
O Hamlet, speak no more.
Thou turn'st mine eyes into my very soul,
And there I see such black and grainéd spots
As will not leave their tinct.
CARL:
Nay, but to live
In the rank sweat of an enseaméd bed,
Stewed in corruption, honeying and making love
Over the nasty sty—

HELGA:

>O speak to me no more.
>These words like daggers enter in mine ears.
>No more, sweet Hamlet.

CARL:

>A murderer and a villain,
>A slave that is not twentieth part the tithe
>Of your precedent lord, a vice of kings,
>A cutpurse of the empire and the rule,
>That from a shelf the precious diadem stole
>And put it in his pocket—

HELGA: No more.

(Ghost enters.)

CARL:

>A king of shreds and patches—
>Save me and hover o'er me with your wings,
>You heavenly guards? What would your gracious figure?

HELGA: Alas, he's mad.

CARL:

>Do you not come your tardy son to chide,
>That lapsed in time and passion, lets go by
>Th'important acting of your dread command?
>O, say.

GHOST:

>Do not forget. This visitation
>Is but to whet thy almost blunted purpose.
>But look, amazement on thy mother sits.
>O, step between her and her fighting soul.
>Conceit in weakest bodies strongest works.
>Speak to her, Hamlet.

CARL: How is it with you, lady?

HELGA:

>Alas, how is't with you,
>That you do bend your eye on vacancy,
>And with th'incorporal air do hold discourse?
>Forth at your eyes your spirits wildly peep,
>And as the sleeping soldiers in th'alarm

Your bedded hairs like life in excrements,
Start up and stand on end. O gentle son,
Upon the heat and flame of thy distemper
Sprinkle cool patience. Whereon do you look?

CARL:

On him, on him! Look you, how pale he glares!
His form and cause conjoined, preaching to stones,
Would make them capable. —Do not look upon me,
Lest with this piteous action you convert
My stern effects. Then what I have to do
Will want true color; tears perchance for blood.

(A second Ghost enters, pushes the first off the edge of the stage, and exits hurriedly pursued by the first.)

HELGA: To whom do you speak this?
CARL: Do you see nothing there?
HELGA: Nothing at all; yet all that is I see.
CARL: Nor did you nothing hear?
HELGA: No, nothing but ourselves.
CARL:

Why, look you there, look how it steals away!
My father, in his habit as he lived!
Look where he goes even now out at the portal!

(Carl exits, chasing the Ghosts out of the theater.)

HELGA:

This is the very coinage of your brain.
This bodiless creation ecstasy
Is very cunning in.

CARL: Ecstasy!!!

(Blackout. All the characters in the play grope about the stage in the darkness, carrying lighted candles.)

JENKINS *(Announcing)*: Ladies and gentlemen, please stand by. Remain seated. A fuse has blown.
HELGA *(Voice in the dark)*: What's the matter?
JENKINS: There's a short circuit.

HELGA: Call wardrobe and have it lengthened. *(If the audience moans, Helga says, "Did you people come here for entertainment or revenge?")*

VOICE OF OPHELIA: Alas, he's mad!

HELGA: Behind the arras, hearing something stir, whips out his rapier, and cries, "A rat, a rat," and in his brainish apprehension kills the unseen, good old man.

EDMUND: O, heavy deed!

HELGA: Your wisdom best shall think.

EDMUND: It shall be so. Madness in great ones must not unwatched go.

(Suddenly the lights come up on Carl.)

CARL: Jenkins, Jenkins!

JENKINS *(Entering)*: Carl! I dug up this skull in the prop room last night. It's real!

CARL *(Taking the skull)*: Alas! Poor Urine. He pissed his life away.

JENKINS: Carl, that skull belonged to the stage manager of the Walnut Street Theater.

CARL: In Philadelphia?

JENKINS: Yeah. He had seen Edwin Booth play Hamlet countless times, so, when he died, he willed his skull to the theater, to be scraped out and bleached and used in productions of *Hamlet*.

CARL: Jenkins, why don't you do that?

JENKINS: I've donated my body to science, but I guess they could send over the head.

CARL: Jenkins, what did you say this stage manager's name was?

JENKINS: Bernard . . .

CARL: Not Bernard Waxberger?

JENKINS: Bernard Waxberger!

CARL: I knew him, Jenkins! Why, you'd never know to look at him now, but he had quite a sense of humor. Many a time while Pop was trampling the boards as Hamlet, he'd carry me piggyback through the flies. You know, he knew all the minor roles in Shakespeare's plays.

JENKINS: They're the most difficult.

CARL: Of course. Everybody knows that. Whenever a road company came in with a skeletal cast, he'd just fill in. He was reputed to have been the greatest Osric who ever lived . . . Jenkins, I read your play last night. All eighteen hundred pages of it. It's good! Really good. You've got something there.

JENKINS: You read it?

CARL: That scene where the woman is tied to a railroad track is really suspenseful.

JENKINS: That may not be good. I want to keep the emotional tone low-key. An author must look on murder and mutilation with a dispassionate eye. You see, I cannot show the inner workings of the murderer's mind. I must not. For the identity of the murderer is kept hidden until the end of the play . . . Carl, I've thought it ever since this morning. Karen killed your father. It was a simple case of revenge.

CARL: No, Jenkins, no. Karen didn't do it. *They* did it to him. They made him play the same role night after night, year in and year out. To a true artist that deadly repetition can lead to only one of two things: alcoholism or madness. My father was a consummate artist, Jenkins . . . He resorted to both of them!

JENKINS: You mean . . .

CARL: Year in and year out, Carlton Stone played on like a shadow. He was a perfectionist.

JENKINS: Great Scott!

CARL: Yes, Jenkins. My father died to perfect the role of the Ghost!

(Blackout.)

⌒ Act Three

Same as Acts One and Two.

Elfie and Carl are warming up for Jenkins's studio performance.

CARL: There's just one thing I don't understand, Elfie. If Grotowski calls his book *Towards a Poor Theatre*, why does the book cost fifteen dollars?

ELFIE: Let's exercise.

CARL: I'll watch.

ELFIE: Carl, what do you do for exercise?

CARL: I act.

ELFIE: That's not enough. If you want to be a great actor, you must hone your body. Yoga is designed to unite the body with the soul. A lot of people think that the brain is the most important organ of the body. It simply isn't true. The Japanese have a saying: "If the liver is not in good condition, neither is the disposition."

CARL: What do you think is the most important organ of the body, Elfie?

ELFIE: The heart. What do you think is the most important organ?

CARL *(Pause)*: Let's exercise.

ELFIE: OK. Let's start with the Salute to the Sun. *(Carl gives an army salute)* Oh, Carl, try being serious. And remember to inhale and exhale.

CARL: I will try to keep that in mind.

ELFIE: OK, so start in a prayer position, and follow me.

(She goes through the exercise smoothly. Carl tries, but cannot bend to the floor. Elfie continues exercising.)

Grab your ankles, put your head to your knees, with the palms of your hands to the floor . . .

CARL: Elfie, I can't get my hands to the floor.

ELFIE: Why not?

CARL: I don't know. I think my pants are too tight.

ELFIE: Continue.

(Elfie finishes the exercise. Carl continues to try to reach the floor, and by heavy breathing finally makes it. He gasps with relief.)

CARL: I see. You breathe in. And then you breathe out.

HELGA *(Entering with Edmund and Jenkins)*: . . . and when I was at the Yale Drama School, the students stood on the back of the chairs and applauded for twenty minutes. They couldn't get enough of me.

(Pause.)

They've been rehearsing for days.

EDMUND: Rehearsing?

HELGA: Yes, it's Jenkins's play—what was it called? *Dinosaur Dung*, wasn't it?

EDMUND *(Laughing)*: *Fossil Fuel,* my dear. But then you're joking, aren't you?

HELGA *(In a loud whisper)*: Don't make me laugh. It's supposed to be a tragedy.

(They take seats in the theater.)

(Calling affectionately) Carl! *(With difficulty)* Son. How are you doing?

CARL: It's not how I'm doing, but what I'm doing that I keep asking myself.

HELGA: I mean the play. How is it going?

JENKINS *(In a temper)*: It's a joke! All a big joke.

HELGA: A joke?

CARL: Don't pay any attention to him. *(Aside)* It's going brilliantly. He's nervous, that's all.

EDMUND *(Condescending)*: Opening night jitters? Stage fright? I have no sympathy for actors trembling in the wings. If you want to go on the stage, then get on with it.

HELGA: Carl, what kind of character do you play?

CARL: Well, there aren't really any characters in the play.

HELGA: No characters? Then how do you tell the story?

CARL: It doesn't have a story, either. In a way it's all the stories that ever were, rolled into one . . . and there are these images . . .

JENKINS: Carl, please, you shouldn't be out front. You should be in your place. You're spoiling the whole illusion.

CARL: Excuse me.

HELGA *(To Carl, half humorously)*: Break a leg! *(To Edmund)* Aren't they cute?

EDMUND: I hope this won't take too long.

HELGA: I think they're ready to begin.

EDMUND: I mean the performance.

JENKINS: Ladies and gentlemen . . .

HELGA *(To Edmund)*: Shhh, they're beginning.

GILBERT *(Entering obtrusively in spite of himself, with script in hand)*: "Pardon me for living, but . . ." *(Realizes that the performance has begun)* Oh . . . dear me . . . I'm interrupting . . . I mean I'm late. *(Exits)*

HELGA *(Aside, incredulously, to Edmund)*: Did you hear what he said? "Pardon me for living!"

EDMUND: Some things are unpardonable.

JENKINS: I'll begin all over again. Where was I?

EDMUND: You were saying, "Ladies and gentlemen."

JENKINS: Oh, yes. Ladies and gentlemen, *Fossil Fuel* by James Jenkins. Starring . . . Elfie Fey as the Allmother and Carlton Stone, Jr. as her son.

HELGA *(Under her breath)*: There's something decadent about this.

CARL *(From the side, imploring her)*: Mother, please!

HELGA: Carl, this reminds me of the time I played Arkadina in *The Seagull.* "O Hamlet, thou hast cleft my heart in twain."

CARL: "Throw away the worser part and live the better with the other half."

HELGA: Did I tell you about the time I appeared at the Yale Drama School . . .

EDMUND *(Applauding)*: Brava, Helga, brava!

CARL: Sit down, Mother.

(The curtain opens revealing Elfie wrapped in white sheets sitting on a phony-looking stage rock.)

JENKINS: The action of the play is set nine thousand nine hundred and ninety-nine years in the future after the ecological disaster. All life has been blotted out, all is empty, all is null, all is void.

HELGA: She's not wearing any makeup.

(During the following, Jenkins periodically yells "Cue!" and a bell rings. Carl attaches strings to Elfie and the set.)

ELFIE: OOOOOOOOOOMMMMMMMau! OMMMMMMMMM-MMMMMMau! Ommmmmmmmmmmmmau! *(Screams)* OOOOOOOOOOOMMMMMMMMMMAU! OOOO-mmmmmAAAAAuuuuu! Haya HeeYah Haya HeeeYah Hayaheeeyah. *(Grunts)* My wooommmmb! Nunga nunga nunga nunga nunga nunga. *(Then she breaks out of the scene and says matter-of-factly:)* Rebirth. *(She then lies on her back and enacts ritual labor pains)* Labor Ritual/May Day— Unyin Square. *(Screams experimentally)*

HELGA: This is either pure madness or pure genius. But I can't tell which.

GILBERT *(Poking his head in)*: There's such a thin line, I think.

HELGA *(Whispering hoarsely to Edmund)*: Who is that man!

EDMUND: Why don't you ask him?

ELFIE: Mankind, man unkind, mankind, man unkind, mankind, man unkind.

HELGA: The lady doth protest too much, methinks!

ELFIE *(Screaming in labor)*: EEEEEEEYow! EEEEEEEYOW! EEEEEEEYOW!

HELGA: Oh, for God's sake, is that caterwauling starting up again?

(Smoke bombs go off. Carl crawls out from between Elfie's legs, and is wailing like a baby.)

HELGA: I smell sulphur. Is that necessary?

JENKINS: Yes, it's intentional.

HELGA *(Laughing)*: Oh, it's a stage effect! I like that.

EDMUND: It smells like the devil! If you wanted fog, why didn't you use the fog machine? At least dry ice doesn't smell.

JENKINS: I didn't want fog. I wanted smoke!

EDMUND: Well, what's the difference? *(Aside to Helga)* They want to work in the theater, but they don't want to know its effects!

HELGA: The theater is chilly tonight.

JENKINS *(Flaring up, loudly)*: That does it! The play is over! That's enough! Curtain!

CARL: But we haven't finished.

JENKINS: Enough! Curtain! *(Stamping his foot)* Bring down the curtain! *(Finally lowers it himself)* You must forgive me. I forgot that only the chosen few can write plays and act in them. I have infringed on a monopoly! My life . . . The theater . . . Oh, what's the use! *(He makes a helpless gesture and exits)*

HELGA: What's the matter with him?

CARL: You hurt his feelings.

HELGA: What did I say? The theater *is* chilly tonight. He said himself it was going to be a joke. Now he wants to be taken seriously! I know what's behind all of this. He's trying to make us feel guilty that we're doing the classics. He's jealous of the classics. I'll bet he just wishes he could write a play as good as . . . as good as *Hamlet!* But no! He'll never admit to any feelings of inferiority. He covers up with his ravings about new forms. I think what he calls new forms are nothing but bad manners!

ELFIE: We meant to give you pleasure.

HELGA: Really? Then why don't you do the usual sort of play and not make us listen to your obscene noises.

(Elfie stalks off. Carl follows.)

GILBERT *(Entering behind Helga and Edmund, dressed as the Ghost)*: You shouldn't wound young people's pride like that.

HELGA *(Turning)*: Sir, I'll thank you to mind your own business! *(She turns back with a horror-stricken look on her face)* OMIGOD!

EDMUND: What is it?

HELGA: It can't be . . .

EDMUND: What?

HELGA: For a moment I thought it was Carlton!

EDMUND: Calm yourself, my dear. You're imagining it.

HELGA: If you think I'm imagining it: look!

EDMUND *(Turns, looks at Gilbert and screams)*: Give me some light!

(There is a blackout. Applause. Lights come up on Helga and Edmund in their Hamlet *costumes, bowing. They try to steal an extra bow, but the applause dies suddenly, stopping them in their tracks. Flustered, they exit into the dressing room.)*

HELGA: Did you know about this meeting?

EDMUND: Carl told Jenkins to pass it around.

HELGA: What do you expect?

EDMUND: Either a pathetic abdication speech or a power grab. I'm ready for either.

HELGA: Is our protégée, Elfie Fey, going to be at this meeting?

JENKINS: No, she's not.

HELGA: Oh, she didn't take her call.

CARL *(Entering)*: Mother. Mr. Dundreary. Where's Jenkins?

JENKINS: Here I am.

CARL: Is Elfie here?

JENKINS *(Darkly)*: No Carl, she's not. She said she was going down to the river.

CARL: Omigod!

EDMUND: Now, Carl, I know you murdered Gilbert Fey.

CARL: It was an accident. It wasn't a real rapier. The blade retracts into the handle—like you said.

EDMUND: Who would believe it? He had just told you that he killed your father.

CARL: How did you know that?

EDMUND *(Pointing to the keyhole)*: The keyhole.

CARL: This is blackmail.

EDMUND: That's one word for it. I call it the simple economics of discretion.

CARL: What do you want?

EDMUND: Your company, your role, your mother and your name.

CARL: My name?

EDMUND: Yes, the name Stone is a theatrical trademark. *(Brandishing a contract)* And you're going to sell it to me for the legal sum of one dollar—and agree to act only in London.

CARL: Why in London?

EDMUND: 'Twill not be noticed there. The acting there is as bad as yours. Sign on the dotted line.

JENKINS: Don't sign, Carl. Don't give anything to that sleazy son of a bitch.

EDMUND: Sign, or I'll blab to the police.

CARL: They have me where they want me. *(Signs)* Uncle Gilbert didn't do it. Are you people blind? Can't you see that he was shielding someone? It was Elfie—Elfie killed my father!

HELGA: What was her motive?

CARL: He tried to drown her when she was a little child, left her to be raised by the petty bourgeoisie. Then, as her artistic aspirations grew and were thwarted, so did her resentment, and now . . . now she's gone down to the river!

ELFIE *(Entering in a wet swimsuit)*: Of course I went down to the river. I always take a swim after a performance.

JENKINS: Elfie didn't do it, Carl. It was Edmund and your mother. They are . . . they have been . . .

HELGA: There's no need for delicacy, Jenkins. You're trying to say that Edmund and I had a "special relationship." Well, it's true and Carl knows all about it.

JENKINS: Then you admit it?

HELGA: I admit to having a lover, but not to being a murderess. I told you, Carl, it was suicide.

CARL: Pop was discovered poisoned by the dread hebenon poured into the porches of his ear. I think that's a rather unlikely way to commit suicide.

EDMUND: Really, people wouldn't believe this if it were acted upon the stage!

CARL: Someone in this company killed my father *(To the audience)* and we're not leaving this theater until we find out who it is. Each of you had a motive. If only one of you didn't, then we could suspect the least likely person.

ELFIE: You're just like Hamlet, seeking to avenge your father's death.

CARL: That would be neat, Elfie. But it wouldn't quite be true. How can I seek revenge for something I have done myself so often in my dreams? I know I should be horrified by all this. I know I should seek the murderer out of moral indignation or revenge. But the truth is that the situation in the abstract has so taken hold of me that I have come to regard the actors in it as merely pieces in a puzzle, baffling and fascinating to the point of monomania.

GILBERT *(Entering)*: So you thought you could get away from me, did you, you little slut! You're coming home with me!

CARL: Uncle Gilbert!

GILBERT: You swore to me!

CARL: And I swear now.

ELFIE: There's no need to swear, Carl. *(To Gilbert)* I heard everything, Uncle Gilbert. Did you think that anything could keep me away from the theater? I would defy you forever. *(To Carl)* Carl, I'm convinced of your greatness as an actor now. You were able to convince me that you didn't love me.

CARL: But Elfie, Carlton was my father, too . . . That makes you my sister.

HELGA: That's where you're wrong, son. Your father was no actor. You were the son of a plumber. That accounts for your knack in fixing the W.C., and why you're not blond.

CARL *(To Elfie)*: Now there's nothing standing in our way . . . Tell me, all of you, who was the greatest actor that ever lived?

EDMUND: Sir Johnston Forbes-Robertson.

HELGA: Modjeska.

ELFIE: Eleonora Duse.

JENKINS: Chaucey Allcott.

CARL: Henry Irving.

GILBERT: The greatest actor who ever lived was Carlton Stone, Senior!

CARL: You say that, Uncle Gilbert? After all he put you through? Really, I think you're being more than generous. Oh, Pop was a great personality, it's true, but an actor in the true sense? Not really. Why, Pop never heard of Grotowski! He never did his yoga. Why, his idea of a great play was a play with a good part in it for him! A great speech was a speech he could give with bombast. No, I think Pop was little more than a ham.

GILBERT: Carl, how could you?

CARL (*Shamed*): Perhaps I'm being a little harsh on Pop. He did have perfect timing. Why, even his death was so perfectly timed that it revealed his friend's secret ambition, his wife's adultery, and loyalty in a man he thought was his enemy. In all of his career, Pop only stepped out of character once: when he took exception to his son's assertion that Irving was anything to compare with his old man!! (*Removes Gilbert's disguise, revealing him to be Stone*)

ALL: Carlton!

STONE: Carl, when did you guess?

CARL: Well, Pop, you didn't give yourself away until the play within the play scene. I saw you come on as the Ghost, and I remembered something you said, "In order to play Carlton, you have to have been Carlton." . . . There's just one thing I can't figure out, Pop: who is Elfie Fey?

STONE: My mistress, young man, my mistress.

HELGA: Well!

ELFIE: I'm sorry, Carl. You're just too immature for me.

STONE: Sorry to cut you out of the action, son.

CARL: That's all right, you two. I'm having a rather interesting "experimental" relationship: with Jenkins!

HELGA: It's a mother's dream come true. To have a son who's gay!

EDMUND: Helga, you told me you did it.

HELGA: I wanted to do something to make you admire me.

EDMUND: A remark like that could cost me my job.

STONE: Edmund, you're a scoundrel. But I like a good scoundrel, so I'm giving you a raise. That's not bad coming from a man who knows you're fucking his wife, is it?

EDMUND (*Beaming*): You're one in a million.

CARL: That's my Pop!

HELGA (*Indignant*): Yesterday I felt positively wanton. Now I'm beginning to feel a little hemmed in.

STONE: By the way, Edmund, I hear you bought my name. That name was, in fact, Raymond Fey. And that's the name you're going to be acting under from now on: Ray Fey! Here's your itching powder, Ray *(Opens paper and blows powder on Edmund)*; and all along I thought I had crabs. *(To Carl)* You see, my boy, all this was contrived . . .

CARL: It certainly was.

STONE: . . . to teach you a little lesson.

EDMUND: Don't make hangmen of your superiors.

HELGA: That although there is only one way of being born, there are many ways of getting killed.

JENKINS: Never suspend your disbelief.

ELFIE: And that the important thing in life is not to tell the truth, but to perfect the mask!

STONE: Ah, yes, we all learned something along the way. But I just wanted to teach you that in order to play Hamlet, you have to have been Hamlet. And from what I see in these reviews, you *were* Hamlet out there tonight.

ALL: Reviews!!!!

(Stone hands out newspapers to all present.)

EDMUND: "The costumes were beautiful." *Women's Wear Daily.*

HELGA: "An unmasculine Hamlet." *New York Post.*

ELFIE: "Exhilarating." *New York Times.*

JENKINS: "Stones Hone Bard's Bones." *Variety.*

ELFIE: "A *Hamlet* with a happy ending!"

HELGA: "Very hedonistic!"

EDMUND *(In the voice of Eric Blore)*: "Very eighteenth century!"

JENKINS: "And very advanced dramaturgically."

CARL: Gee, Dad, the rest is silence?

STONE: Is there any music to compare with it? *(Hands recorder to Carl, who miraculously begins to play "Greensleeves")*

(Stone and Elfie exit, while Carl plays the recorder.)

CARL *(Suddenly very excited)*: Jenkins, I'm going to do your play!

JENKINS: *Fossil Fuel?*

CARL: Well, that's the only play you've written, isn't it?

JENKINS: Yes.

CARL: Until we do that one, you'll never get on to the next.

JENKINS: Oh, no!

CARL: What is it now, Jenkins?

JENKINS: If people are beginning to like my work, there must be something wrong with it.

EDMUND *(Shocked)*: Jenkins, you're a snob. And here all along I thought you were a communist.

(Edmund gives Helga a jewel case, which she opens; a mouse pops out. They exit laughing.)

CARL: Jim, there's just one thing I can't figure out. Pop was playing dead in the dressing room, but we saw him go on as the Ghost. How could he be in two places at the same time!

JENKINS: Beats me.

STONE *(Reentering)*: Jenkins, are you going hunting tomorrow?

JENKINS: Hunting?!

STONE: For props.

JENKINS: Yes.

STONE: I've just remembered. We've run out of stage blood.

(The Ghost enters, reading Variety.*)*

END

CAMILLE

A TEARJERKER

A Travesty on
La Dame aux Camélias
by Alexandre Dumas Fils

1973

⟶ *Production History* ⟞

Camille (A Tearjerker): A Travesty on La Dame aux Camélias was
first performed in 1973. The play was remounted by The Ridiculous Theatrical Company at the Charles Ludlam Theater in New
York City in August 1990. Scenic design was by Mark Beard, costume design was by Elizabeth Michal Fried, lighting design was by
Terry Alan Smith and sound design was by Mark Bennett. It was
directed by Everett Quinton. The cast was as follows:

BARON DE VARVILLE	H. M. Koutoukas
NANINE	Stephen Pell
MARGUERITE GAUTIER	Everett Quinton
JOSEPH	Kevin Scullin
NICHETTE FONDUE	Carl Clayborn
OLYMPE DE TAVERNÉ	Cheryl Reeves
SAINT GAUDENS	Bobby Reed
PRUDENCE DUVERNOY	Eureka
GASTON ROUÉ	Jim Lamb
ARMAND DUVAL	Georg Osterman
DUVAL, SR.	Jean-Claude Vasseux
MOLNIK	James Eckerle

⟶ *Characters* ⟵

BARON DE VARVILLE, Armand's rival

NANINE, the maid

MARGUERITE GAUTIER, a courtesan

JOSEPH, the butler

NICHETTE FONDUE, a childhood friend of Marguerite

OLYMPE DE TAVERNÉ, Saint Gaudens's mistress

SAINT GAUDENS, a roué

PRUDENCE DUVERNOY, a milliner

GASTON ROUÉ, a playboy

ARMAND DUVAL, Marguerite's lover

DUVAL, SR., Armand's father

MOLNIK, Olympe's butler

⌒ Act One

Marguerite's drawing room, Paris, 1848.

VARVILLE *(Pacing up and down with a bouquet of flowers)*: Will she see me?

NANINE: Madame says she wants to be alone.

VARVILLE: So, she's playing cat and mouse, eh? Well, I hope she finds him amusing, whoever he is.

NANINE: Madame is alone. She has seen no one for three days. She's been ill again. It's a pathetic story . . .

VARVILLE: Oh, yes, that is a pathetic story. Only unfortunately . . .

NANINE: Unfortunately?

VARVILLE: Unfortunately, I don't believe it.

NANINE: There are enough true things that can be said about Madame, so there's no use your telling things that aren't true. Madame never tells lies.

VARVILLE *(Laughs)*: Of course not.

NANINE: During her long illness, Madame accumulated over fifty thousand francs' worth of debts, and that's no lie.

VARVILLE: Bring Madame these flowers and tell her I am offering to pay her debts. Is it my fault I love her?

NANINE *(Taking the flowers)*: I don't know. It may be better to owe money to some people than gratitude to others. *(She exits into Marguerite's room with the flowers. From offstage)* Marguerite, the Baron de Varville is still waiting. He says he is willing to pay all your debts if you will only see him. And he sends these flowers.

VARVILLE: Birds of paradise and aspidistra.

MARGUERITE *(From offstage)*: Aagh, get them away from me! Get those flowers away from me!

(The bouquet of flowers comes flying out of the door.)

VARVILLE *(Picking them up)*: You don't care for them?
MARGUERITE *(Off)*: What do they call me?
VARVILLE: Why ... er ... ah ... you are called many things that one would hesitate to repeat.
MARGUERITE *(Off)*: I mean my name. What is my name?
VARVILLE: Marguerite Gautier.
MARGUERITE *(Off)*: No, no, you fool. I mean by what name am I known in the Bohemian quarter?
VARVILLE: The Lady of the Camellias.
MARGUERITE *(Enters)*: Why?
VARVILLE: Because you wear no other flowers?
MARGUERITE: And I can bear no other flowers. Their scent makes me ill. *(Coughs)* Now take your birds of paradise and get your aspidistra out of here.

(Varville does not move.)

You're not going?
VARVILLE: No.
MARGUERITE: Then, for God's sake, play the piano, dahling. Your music is your only saving grace.
VARVILLE *(Obeying)*: Is it my fault I love you? *(Begins playing)*

(Nanine enters, begins setting the table.)

MARGUERITE: If I were to listen to everyone who's in love with me, I would have no time for dinner. *(To Nanine)* Did you order dinner?
NANINE: Yes, Madame.
MARGUERITE *(To Varville)*: I let you call on me when I'm in and wait for me when I'm out. But if you insist on talking of nothing but your love, I will withdraw my friendship.
VARVILLE: What have you got against love?
MARGUERITE: I have nothing against love. It just makes such dull conversation.

VARVILLE: And yet, last year at Marienbad you did give me some hope.

MARGUERITE: My dear, that was last year, that was Marienbad. I was ill; I was bored. But this is Paris and I'm very much better, and not at all bored.

NANINE: Marguerite, the doctor called again this morning.

MARGUERITE: What did he say?

NANINE: He said you are to rest as much as possible.

MARGUERITE: Dear doctor, always giving me good advice. *(To Varville)* What's that you're playing?

VARVILLE: A rhapsody by Rauschenberg.

MARGUERITE: It's charming.

VARVILLE: Listen, Marguerite, I have eighty thousand francs.

MARGUERITE: How nice. I have a hundred thousand.

VARVILLE: Your indifference to me is like a camellia, no scent and no thorns.

MARGUERITE *(Aside to Nanine)*: He is the most persistent man in Paris. He insists on loving me.

NANINE *(Confidentially)*: He has eighty thousand francs.

MARGUERITE: How he bores me with his eighty thousand francs.

(The bell rings. Butler goes to the door.)

BUTLER *(Announcing)*: Nichette Fondue.

NICHETTE: Marguerite!

MARGUERITE: Nichette!

NICHETTE: You're looking well.

MARGUERITE: I always look well when I'm near death. Will you stay for supper?

NICHETTE: I can't. Gustave is waiting downstairs.

MARGUERITE: Oh, Nichette, you're still seeing that Gustave?

NICHETTE: Yes. He's been promoted to comptroller!

MARGUERITE: Oh, Nichette, you can do much better than a comptroller!

NICHETTE: But I never want to do better than Gustave. I love him.

MARGUERITE: Nichette, you're a very pretty girl, but a very bad businesswoman.

NICHETTE: You'll see, Marguerite. One of these days you'll fall like a ton of bricks.

MARGUERITE: Me, fall in love? No, no, Nichette!

NICHETTE: Toodle-oo, Marguerite. *(Exits)*

MARGUERITE: Ta-ta, Nichette.

(Bell rings.)

BUTLER *(Announcing)*: Madame Olympe de Taverné. Monsieur Saint Gaudens.

MARGUERITE: At last, Olympe. I thought you weren't coming.

OLYMPE: Blame it on Saint Gaudens. It's his fault.

SAINT GAUDENS: It's always my fault. Good evening, Marguerite. Good evening, Varville.

OLYMPE: I just found out today that Saint Gaudens is of Polish extraction.

MARGUERITE: No.

OLYMPE: His dentist is Polish. *(Aside to Marguerite)* Did you invite Gaylord?

MARGUERITE: I thought you would bring him.

OLYMPE: With Saint Gaudens? You know how jealous he is.

MARGUERITE: I thought you had him trained.

OLYMPE: You can't teach an old dog new tricks.

MARGUERITE: I like older men. They're so . . . grateful.

OLYMPE: And they have so much poise.

SAINT GAUDENS: Is Varville staying for supper?

MARGUERITE: No, he isn't. He's being punished for bringing me the wrong flowers.

SAINT GAUDENS: Didn't he bring camellias?

MARGUERITE: No, he didn't.

OLYMPE: How gauche *(Pronounces it gwäsh)* of him. He committed a real false pah!

SAINT GAUDENS: Varville's in the doghouse.

MARGUERITE *(At the window)*: Prudence!

PRUDENCE *(From offstage)*: What do you want?

MARGUERITE: I want you to come over here at once.

PRUDENCE *(Off)*: Why?

MARGUERITE: Because it's my birthday and the Baron de Varville is still here, and he's boring me to death.

PRUDENCE *(Off)*: I have two young gentlemen here who have asked me out to supper.

MARGUERITE: Well, bring them over here to supper. Anything is better than the Baron. Who are they?

PRUDENCE *(Off)*: You know one of them, Gaston Roué.

MARGUERITE: Of course I know him. And the other?

PRUDENCE *(Off)*: A friend of his.

MARGUERITE: Come on over, dahlings, there's plenty of food here.

OLYMPE: It's so convenient to have Prudence living just across the courtyard.

MARGUERITE: Yes, she delivers my gossip fresh every morning.

SAINT GAUDENS: Who is this Prudence?

OLYMPE: She was once a kept woman who tried to go on the stage and failed. So, relying on her acquaintance with fashionable people, she opened a milliner's shop.

MARGUERITE: And nobody buys her hats but me.

OLYMPE: But you never wear them.

MARGUERITE: Dahling, they're beastly. I wouldn't wear one to a dogfight. But I adore Prudence, and she is hard up. *(Coughs a little)* It's cold this evening.

(Bell rings.)

BUTLER *(At the door)*: Madame Prudence Duvernoy, Monsieur Gaston Roué and Monsieur Armand Duval.

PRUDENCE *(Barges in wearing a big hat)*: The classy way they announce people here! I knew this party was going to be piss elegant!

GASTON *(To Marguerite, kissing her hand)*: I trust you are well, Madame.

MARGUERITE: Quite well, thank you. And you?

PRUDENCE: Gee, the classy way they talk here! Marguerite, I want to present to you Monsieur Armand Duval, the man who is more in love with you than any man in Paris.

MARGUERITE: Nanine, set two more places. I hope his great passion hasn't spoiled Monsieur Duval's appetite.

ARMAND: Please accept this book as a remembrance of your birthday.

MARGUERITE: *Manon Lescaut?*

ARMAND: Yes. The story of a woman who brightened her wit with champagne, and her eyes with tears.

MARGUERITE: It's not a sad story, is it? I don't like sad thoughts.

ARMAND: It has a sad ending.

MARGUERITE: Well, I'll read it, but I won't read the ending.

SAINT GAUDENS: My dear Gaston, I'm so glad to see you!

GASTON: Saint Gaudens . . . as young as ever!

SAINT GAUDENS: Younger. Only my teeth are aging.

GASTON: And your love affairs—prospering?

SAINT GAUDENS: Well, there's Olympe here.

GASTON: So, you've taken up with this little trollop, eh?

OLYMPE: Watch who you call little.

MARGUERITE *(To Nanine, who is setting the table)*: Not the Melmac, Nanine, the Limoges.

GASTON: Whatever became of Beatrice?

SAINT GAUDENS: I gave her up. Her lover was a banker but she loved me for myself alone. But, still, the affair required a lot of hiding in cupboards, prowling about the back stairs, and waiting in the street.

GASTON: Which gave you rheumatism.

SAINT GAUDENS: Not a bit, but times change. We none of us grows any younger.

GASTON *(To Marguerite)*: Isn't he wonderful?

MARGUERITE: We are all growing old at exactly the same rate so there will be no sympathy for anyone, do you hear? *(To Armand)* Are you following me?

ARMAND: Yes.

SAINT GAUDENS *(To Armand)*: Are you related to Monsieur Duval, the receiver general?

ARMAND: Yes, sir, he is my father. Do you know him?

SAINT GAUDENS: I met him years ago at the Marchioness Fanzee-panzee's summer house, with your mother whom I remember as a very beautiful and charming fairy of a woman. You take after your mother.

ARMAND: My mother died three years ago.

SAINT GAUDENS: Forgive me.

ARMAND: I am always glad to be reminded of my mother.

SAINT GAUDENS: Are you an only son?

ARMAND: I have one sister . . .

(Armand, Saint Gaudens and Olympe join Varville at the piano.)

MARGUERITE *(Aside to Gaston)*: I think your friend is charming.

GASTON: He is and, what's more, he adores you. Doesn't he, Prudence?

PRUDENCE: What?

GASTON: I was telling Marguerite that Armand is madly in love with her.

PRUDENCE: He's got it bad and that ain't good. Ah, l'amour, l'amour!

GASTON: He loves you so much, my dear, that he doesn't dare tell you about it.

MARGUERITE: Varville, please, please!

VARVILLE: You told me to keep on playing the piano.

MARGUERITE: When I am alone with you, not when I have friends.

PRUDENCE: He's loved you for two years.

MARGUERITE: Quite an old story, then.

GASTON: Armand simply lives at Gustave's and Nichette's to hear them talk about you.

PRUDENCE: I want something to drink.

OLYMPE: Look, I found some champagne.

(Prudence, Gaston and Olympe get involved in opening the bottle of champagne.)

NANINE *(Taking Marguerite aside)*: Marguerite, when you were ill a year ago, remember I told you of a young man who called to inquire after you every day but wouldn't leave his name?

MARGUERITE: I remember.

NANINE *(Pointing discreetly)*: That's him. Armand Duval.

MARGUERITE: How nice of him. *(Calling across the room)* Monsieur Duval, do you know what I have just been hearing? That you called to inquire after me every day when I was ill.

ARMAND: It's quite true.

MARGUERITE: Then the least I can do is thank you. Did you hear that, Varville? *You* never did that for me, did you?

VARVILLE: I have only known you for a year.

MARGUERITE: Don't be ridiculous, this young gentleman has only known me for five minutes.

BUTLER *(Enters with boar's head on platter)*: Dinner is served. *(Exits)*

PRUDENCE: Here is supper. I'm famished.

VARVILLE: I have no luck. Good-bye, Marguerite Gautier, Lady of the Camellias. *(Kisses her hand)*

MARGUERITE: Good-bye. When shall we see you again?

VARVILLE: Whenever you wish. *(Bowing)* Gentlemen. *(Exits)*

SAINT GAUDENS: Good-bye, Varville, old boy. Better luck next time.

(Varville exits. They watch him leave. When he completes his exit:)

MARGUERITE: Let's eat!

(They rush madly to the table.)

PRUDENCE: You really are too hard on the Baron, dear. You could end up a baroness if you played your cards right. We're none of us getting any younger, and it's time you settled something about your future—while you still have one!

OLYMPE: I simply adore the Baron. He's rich, handsome, wealthy, talented and he's got money! Do you know that he's just written a book?

MARGUERITE: Really?

GASTON: Ah, yes, his memoirs are considered the breviary of The Decadence.

PRUDENCE: And he's got eighty thousand francs.

MARGUERITE: How he bores me with his eighty thousand francs.

OLYMPE: Eighty thousand francs! I wish someone would offer to bore me that way! Do you know what Saint Gaudens gave me for my birthday? A coupé! But he didn't give me any horses to go with it!

PRUDENCE: Still, a coupé is a coupé is a coupé!

ALL *(Clinking glasses simultaneously)*: Touché!

SAINT GAUDENS: I'm ruined. Why can't I be loved for myself alone?

OLYMPE *(Shrieking with laughter)*: The idea!

MARGUERITE: Oh, come on Saint Gaudens, come and get your MDA.

SAINT GAUDENS: What's MDA?

MARGUERITE: Monsieur, don't ask.

PRUDENCE: What are those little fellows?

GASTON: Partridges.

PRUDENCE *(To Butler)*: You can put some on my plate.

GASTON: Some? Partridges aren't oysters, you know.

PRUDENCE: Well, they're not much bigger than oysters.

GASTON: What a birdlike appetite. Now we know who ruined Saint Gaudens . . . she did!

PRUDENCE: She! She! Is that any way to talk of a lady? Why in my day . . .

GASTON: We needn't go back to Louis the Fifteenth! Marguerite, fill Armand's glass. He's looking sad.

SAINT GAUDENS: This dinner is delicious.

PRUDENCE: I want another drink.

MARGUERITE: Gaston, play the piano. Come on, Saint Gaudens, sing us a song.

SAINT GAUDENS: How can I sing when I'm having my supper?

MARGUERITE: Sing for your supper.

PRUDENCE: I want another drink!

(Saint Gaudens begins to sing "Plaisir d'Amour.")

MARGUERITE: No, no, not that one! Let's have something gay, dahling.

(Saint Gaudens sings "Frère Jacques" and all join him, singing in rounds.)

ALL: Bravo! Bravo! *(Tap glasses with silverware)* Toast!

GASTON *(Making a toast)*: Ah, life is short and sweet and Prudence is short and fat.

(All clink their glasses together and drink.)

PRUDENCE *(Quite drunk)*: I want another drink!

OLYMPE: Fat, fair and forty!

PRUDENCE: All right, smart-ass, how old do you think I am? *(Everyone leans forward)* I'm . . . thirty-six!

(Riotous laughter.)

GASTON: But you don't look a day over forty!

PRUDENCE: I've been told I have the skin of a twelve year old.

GASTON: Well you better give it back, you're getting it wrinkled.

(*More riotous laughter*)

(*Prudence hits Gaston over the head with a partridge. Saint Gaudens whispers in Olympe's ear.*)

OLYMPE (*Shrieking with laughter*): That's the funniest story I've ever heard in my life!

PRUDENCE: Tell me! Tell me! (*Motioning to Saint Gaudens*) Whisper in my ear.

MARGUERITE: That isn't fair. Tell us all. We want to hear it too.

PRUDENCE (*Laughing almost uncontrollably*): I know what's coming, but do go on.

MARGUERITE: I want to hear it too.

SAINT GAUDENS: You tell her, Gaston.

GASTON: Ah, but you tell it so much better than I do.

SAINT GAUDENS: But it's your story.

GASTON: But I like to hear you tell it.

MARGUERITE (*Shouts in a masculine voice*): Let's have the story, man. Out with it!

OLYMPE: If Saint Gaudens won't tell it, *I* will.

SAINT GAUDENS (*Cupping his hand over her mouth*): I'll tell it! I'll tell it! Well, you remember that awful divorce last year of Odile de Lille and that stockbroker of hers. Well, last week I saw her at the Ballet Gala at the Opera. They were doing *Zinnia, the Mute Girl of Cincinnati*. And who should arrive in the next box but Odile's ex! And he leaned over and said in a very loud voice, "Odile, my dear, how does your new husband like that worn-out twat of yours?" And she said—

OLYMPE (*Breaking loose and interrupting*): "He likes it fine, once he gets past the worn-out part!"

(*Everyone laughs uproariously except Armand.*)

MARGUERITE: Monsieur Duval, you're not laughing. Don't you like Gaston's jokes?

ARMAND: I have heard Gaston's jokes. In fact, he learned some of them from me. But I would rather they were not repeated in your presence.

MARGUERITE: Come now, I'm not a colonel's daughter just out of the convent.

SAINT GAUDENS: Who hasn't been deceived? One's friends and one's mistresses are always deceiving one.

PRUDENCE: Ah yes, just as in *Bérénice* by Racine . . .

(Prudence takes center stage, gesturing madly and emitting Gallic gutturals. The others look at her in wonderment.)

MARGUERITE: Oh, she's acting.

PRUDENCE: Oh, mon pauvre chevrolet. J'aime le chateaubriand. Oh, le coq au vin, le coq au vin, sur le table avec les pommes frites.

(Standing at the table, she leans back on top of it, in a kind of reverie. Gaston throws a pie in her face. Everyone laughs.)

MARGUERITE: Bravo, Saint Gaudens. You are a hero and we are all in love with you. All those madly in love with Saint Gaudens hold up your hands. *(To Saint Gaudens)* Well, hold up your hand, dahling. Unanimous. Prudence, my dear, you really ought to stick to Maeterlinck. You will always be remembered for your *Joyzelle*. Gaston, play something for Saint Gaudens to dance to.

GASTON: I don't know anything but St. Vitus's Dance.

MARGUERITE: Then we'll have St. Vitus's Dance. Come on, Saint Gaudens . . . Armand, move the table.

PRUDENCE: But I haven't finished.

OLYMPE: Do I have to dance with Saint Gaudens?

MARGUERITE: No, I'm going to. Come along, little Saint Gaudens.

ARMAND: Aren't you afraid that you're not well enough to dance?

MARGUERITE: I'm not afraid of anything except being bored.

OLYMPE: Come, Armand.

SAINT GAUDENS: Your hollandaise was divine, my dear.

MARGUERITE: It's especially good around the Jewish hollandaise.

(All dance to the music that Gaston plays. Marguerite coughs. The music stops. All look to her.)

SAINT GAUDENS: What's the matter?

MARGUERITE: Nothing. I lost my breath.

ARMAND *(Going to her)*: Are you all right?

MARGUERITE: Yes. It's nothing. Don't stop. *(Starts to dance again and then falls)*

ARMAND: Stop, Gaston.

PRUDENCE: Marguerite is ill.

MARGUERITE: It's nothing. *(Falls again)*

ARMAND *(Catching her)*: The party's over.

PRUDENCE: She's always ill just when everybody is having a good time.

OLYMPE: You can never have any fun here.

PRUDENCE: Let's go somewhere else. Let's go to my place. Wait a minute! I'm just beginning to get hungry again! Bring the food with us. Forward . . . march!

GASTON *(To Armand)*: She's been laughing too much and she's spitting up blood. It's nothing. It happens to her every day.

(All exit with the food except Marguerite and Armand.)

MARGUERITE *(Looking in a mirror)*: How pale I look!

ARMAND: You're killing yourself.

MARGUERITE *(Startled that he's still there)*: If I am, you're the only one who objects. The others don't worry about me.

ARMAND: The others don't love you as I do.

MARGUERITE: Ah yes, I had forgotten that great love of yours.

ARMAND: You laugh at it.

MARGUERITE: I've heard it too many times to laugh anymore. It's an old joke and the joke is on me.

ARMAND: Promise.

MARGUERITE: What?

ARMAND: To take care of yourself.

MARGUERITE: My good man, if I were to begin to take care of myself, I would die. Don't you see that it is only the fever-ish life I live that keeps me alive? The moment that I am no longer amusing to people, they leave me, and the long days are followed by longer nights. I know, I was in bed for two months and after three weeks, no one came near me.

ARMAND: Those people are horrible.

MARGUERITE: They're the only friends I have and I'm no better than they are.

ARMAND: Don't say that. Let me take you away from all this. We could go to the country where I would take care of you like a brother. I'd never leave you and I would cure you. Then, when you were strong again, you could return to this life if you wished, but I don't think you would want to.

MARGUERITE: How depressing. I don't like sad thoughts.

ARMAND: Have you no heart, Marguerite?

MARGUERITE: I'm traveling light, no heart.

ARMAND: Have you never been in love with anyone?

MARGUERITE: Never!

ARMAND: Thank God!

MARGUERITE: You're a strange boy. You've drunk too much wine and that has made you sentimental. Tomorrow it will be a different story.

ARMAND: Was it wine that brought me here every day when you were ill?

MARGUERITE: No, that couldn't have been wine. But why didn't you come up?

ARMAND: What right had I?

MARGUERITE: Since when are men so formal with women like me?

ARMAND: And I was afraid.

MARGUERITE: Afraid?

ARMAND: Afraid that you would grant me too promptly that which I wanted to win through long suffering and great sacrifice. Imagination lends too much poetry to the senses, and the desires of the body make concessions to the dreams of the soul. I would rather die for your love than pay fifty francs for it.

MARGUERITE: So, it's as bad as that! And you would look after me?

ARMAND: Yes.

MARGUERITE: You would stay with me all day long?

ARMAND: Yes.

MARGUERITE: And even all night?

ARMAND: As long as I didn't weary you.

MARGUERITE: And what does this great devotion come from?

ARMAND: The irresistible sympathy which I have for you.

MARGUERITE: So you are in love with me too. Why don't you just say it? It's much more simple.

ARMAND: If I say it, it will not be today.

MARGUERITE: Never say it.

ARMAND: Why?

MARGUERITE: Because only two things can come of it. Either I shall not accept—then you will have a grudge against me—or I shall accept, and you will have a mistress who is sad or gay with a gaiety sadder than grief, who spits up blood and spends a hundred thousand francs a year. That is all very well for a rich old man like the Baron, but it is very bad for a young man like you . . . If what you say is true, go away at once. Love me a little less or understand me a little better. I'm not worth much. You're too young and sensitive to live in a world like ours. Love some other woman and marry . . . I'm trying to be honest with you.

ARMAND: What if I were to tell you that I've spent whole nights beneath your windows and that for two months I've treasured a glove you dropped.

MARGUERITE: I should not believe you.

ARMAND: You're right to laugh at me. I'm a fool. There's nothing else to do but laugh at me.

MARGUERITE: Armand, can't we just be friends?

ARMAND: That's too much, and not enough. Don't you believe in love, Marguerite?

MARGUERITE: I don't know what it is. It's hard to believe in it if you've never had it.

ARMAND *(Crushing her in his embrace)*: Let me make you believe. We'll rent a country house. Fresh air and good food will make you well in no time.

MARGUERITE: But that takes money.

ARMAND: I have money.

MARGUERITE: How much?

ARMAND: I have seven thousand francs a year.

MARGUERITE *(Pulling away from him and laughing)*: I spend more than that in a week. And I've never been too particular where it came from, as I guess you know.

ARMAND: Don't talk like that!

MARGUERITE: It's true. The hard cold facts are we need hard cold cash. Why, the rental of a country house, horses and a carriage to get around, to get us there and back . . . Enough for the table, even simple food costs money . . . No servants except for Nanine . . . *(Handing him a pen and paper)* Oh, I'm no good at arithmetic. You figure it out.

(Armand sits down at the desk and begins figuring. A knock at the door. Nanine enters with an enormous bouquet of red camellias.)

NANINE *(Aside to Marguerite)*: The Baron de Varville sent these. Looks like he's learned his lesson. They're camellias this time.

ARMAND *(Finishing the sum)*: Eighty thousand francs.

NANINE: He's waiting downstairs.

MARGUERITE: What did you say?

ARMAND: I said we'll need eighty thousand francs.

NANINE: I said the Baron de Varville is waiting downstairs.

ARMAND: But don't worry, darling, I'll get it somewhere.

MARGUERITE: Eighty thousand francs. *(Nanine exits. Armand tries to take Marguerite in his arms but she resists)* Take this camellia and bring it back to me when it dies.

(She hands Armand a flower and he kisses it.)

ARMAND: When will that be?

MARGUERITE: How long does it take a flower to wither? A morning, an evening. Tomorrow night.

ARMAND *(Crushing the flower in his hand)*: Here, it's dead already.

MARGUERITE: No, no, impossible. I wear red camellias when I've got the rag on . . . when the moon is not favorable to pleasure. I'll be wearing white ones tomorrow.

ARMAND: I can't wait. Let me sleep here tonight beside you like your brother or at the foot of your bed like your dog. But let me wait here until the camellias turn white.

MARGUERITE: You put tears on my hand. Yes. Yes. No! Yes!

ARMAND *(Overjoyed)*: You'll take me? Like this, at a moment's notice?

MARGUERITE: Does it seem strange to you? *(Taking his hand and placing it on her heart)* Feel my heart beating. I shall not live as long as others so I have promised myself to live more quickly.

ARMAND: Don't talk like that, I beg of you.

MARGUERITE: But however short a time I have to live, I shall yet live longer than your love.

ARMAND: I thought you didn't like sad thoughts.

MARGUERITE: I don't. But they come sometimes.

(Bell rings.)

NANINE *(Enters whispering)*: Madame, the Baron is waiting. Shall I send him away?

MARGUERITE *(Aside to Nanine)*: Tell him to wait. *(To Armand)* Armand, would you run out and get me some marrons glacés? I suddenly have the maddest craving for marrons glacés.

ARMAND: Aren't there any in the house?

MARGUERITE: No, and nothing but marrons glacés will do. Please go out and get me some.

ARMAND: Marguerite, is something wrong? I feel you're trying to get rid of me.

MARGUERITE: Now what on earth gave you that idea? Come back at midnight, and I'll be waiting for you.

ARMAND: How do I know you'll let me in when I come back?

MARGUERITE *(Giving him a key)*: I'll give you the key and you can let yourself in. Now go, quickly.

(Armand starts out the door. Marguerite blocks his way and shows him another.)

No, this way.

(Armand rushes out. There is a pause. Armand rushes in again.)

ARMAND: I love you. *(Exits)*

MARGUERITE *(To Nanine)*: Is it possible that he does love me? Or can I even be sure that I love him, I who have never loved? Show the Baron in, Nanine.

NANINE: I shall pray for you, Madame.

MARGUERITE: Why?

NANINE: Because you are in danger.

MARGUERITE: Oh pooh. Lying keeps my teeth white. Send the
Baron in, Nanine.

(Varville enters carrying a large leather bag.)

Baron!

VARVILLE: You kept me waiting long enough.

MARGUERITE: Hello, you. I have just been putting my account
books in order. *(Showing him the book)* See?

VARVILLE: Lovely.

MARGUERITE: But, look at all these bills. I have eighty thousand
francs' worth of debts. Will you lend me the money?

VARVILLE: No.

MARGUERITE: What will I do?

VARVILLE: Come with me to Siberia *(Marguerite coughs)* and I'll
give you all the money you want.

MARGUERITE: If you are my friend, why won't you give it to me
now?

VARVILLE: Because if I do, you may no longer have any use for
me. It has been months since we've as much as spent a night
together. *(Varville plants a kiss on Marguerite's arm. Lipstick
is left. She wipes it off and sprays it with an atomizer)* Until we
do, your bills will go unpaid.

*(Marguerite sits down at the piano and begins to play Chopin.
Varville looks over the papers on the desk. He finds the sheet on
which Armand was doing the sum and picks it up.)*

What's this? "House: thirty thousand francs; horses and
carriage: twenty thousand . . . Nanine, Marguerite and
myself . . . thirty thousand." Who is this "myself"?

MARGUERITE *(Still playing)*: Myself, of course. My doctor insists
that I go to the country this summer for my health. That's
why I asked you for the eighty thousand francs. I'm afraid of
getting sick again. I know how it bores you.

VARVILLE: This note says, "Nanine, Marguerite *and myself* . . ."
A summer in the country, away from the glamour of Paris,

living quietly with the cows and the chickens sounds very unlike you, my dear.

MARGUERITE: But, it's true.

VARVILLE: You can't fool me. I know you've found a playmate for this rustic holiday.

MARGUERITE *(Stops playing suddenly)*: Damn Chopin and all his sharps and flats!

VARVILLE: I'm afraid your mind isn't on it, my dear.

MARGUERITE: You know quite well that I could never play it.

VARVILLE: Let me spend the night and you can have all the money you need.

MARGUERITE: Only if you will play the piano for me. *(Rings a hand bell for Nanine)*

VARVILLE *(Bitterly)*: My one merit. *(Begins to play)*

(Nanine enters.)

MARGUERITE *(Aside to Nanine)*: Bolt the door and don't answer it, no matter what happens.

NANINE: Yes, Madame. *(Exits)*

VARVILLE: Are you two through whispering over there?

MARGUERITE: I was just giving some last minute orders to Nanine.

VARVILLE: Yes, I'm sure you were. *(Continues playing. The door-bell rings)* Someday I'm going to get temperamental and complain when doorbells ring while I am trying to play.

(Marguerite grabs items from bag as needed.)

MARGUERITE *(Pulling out whip and masks of black leather)*: Did the doorbell ring? I didn't hear it.

VARVILLE *(Continuing to play)*: Does my music shut out the world for you, my dear?

MARGUERITE: You play beautifully. *(Puts on mask)*

VARVILLE: You lie beautifully.

(Doorbell rings again.)

MARGUERITE *(Masking Varville)*: Thank you, that's more than I deserve.

VARVILLE: Oh, no, it's not half as much as you deserve.

(They laugh. Doorbell. The clock begins striking twelve.)

I wonder who it could be at this hour.

MARGUERITE *(Handcuffing Varville to the piano)*: If I told you, you wouldn't believe me.

VARVILLE: Try me *(She pulls a dildo out of the bag and gets rid of it fast)*.

MARGUERITE *(Whipping him)*: I could say that someone has found the wrong door. *(Laughs)*

VARVILLE: The great romance of your life! *(Laughs)*

MARGUERITE: That might have been! *(Starts to whip piano)*

(They both laugh—she ironically, he bitterly—as the curtain falls.)

⌐ Act Two

SCENE I

A country house at Auteuil. A room looking out on a garden.

ARMAND: Where is Marguerite?

PRUDENCE: She is in the garden picking strawberries with Nichette, who has come to spend the day with her. I'm just going to join them.

ARMAND: One moment, Prudence. A week ago, Marguerite gave you some diamond bracelets to have reset. What has become of them?

PRUDENCE: Well, that's a long story. I . . . er . . . I . . . ah . . .

ARMAND: Come, tell me frankly. Where are Marguerite's bracelets?

PRUDENCE: Do you want the truth?

ARMAND: Of course I want the truth.

PRUDENCE: Sold.

ARMAND: Her gowns?

PRUDENCE: Sold.

ARMAND: Her horses and her jewels?

PRUDENCE: Sold and pawned.

ARMAND: Who has sold and pawned them?

PRUDENCE: I did.

ARMAND: Why did you not tell me?

PRUDENCE: Marguerite made me promise not to.

ARMAND: And where has all the money gone?

PRUDENCE: In payments. Ah, my dear fellow, she didn't want to tell you. Marguerite's creditors went to the Baron de Varville to settle, and he had them thrown out of his house. They wanted their money. I gave them part payment out of the few thousand francs you gave me. But, someone told them that Marguerite had been abandoned by the Baron and was living with a penniless young man. They stormed her house and ripped off all of her goods. Marguerite wanted to sell everything, but it was too late. So rather than ask you for the money, she sold her horses, her carriage, her gowns and her jewels. Here are the receipts and the pawn tickets. *(Gives him the receipts)*

ARMAND: How much money is needed?

PRUDENCE: Fifty thousand francs. Ah, I hate to say I told you so. You think it is enough to be in love, and go to the country, and live on air. You'll soon find out that someone has to pay the rent on your pastoral dream! Ah, l'amour, l'amour. Toujours l'amour! Yecch.

ARMAND: Ask our creditors for a fortnight's grace. I will pay.

PRUDENCE: Are you going to borrow the money?

ARMAND: Yes. I suspected something of the kind and have written to my solicitor.

PRUDENCE: No, Armand, you'll only quarrel with your father and ruin your whole future.

ARMAND: Hush, she's coming. *(Marguerite enters wearing wooden shoes)* I want you to scold Prudence for me, dearest!

MARGUERITE: Why?

ARMAND: She forgot to bring me my mail, so I shall have to go to Paris to get it myself. I didn't give anyone our address here because I wanted to be left in peace. I'll be gone only a couple of hours.

MARGUERITE: Yes, go dear, but do come back quickly.

ARMAND: I shall drive in and be back in an hour.

MARGUERITE: And take care of yourself.

ARMAND: And you too. Take care of her, Prudence.

MARGUERITE: Each moment will be an eternity.

PRUDENCE: For God's sake, he's not going to war! He's just going to get his mail.

NICHETTE *(Entering)*: Oh, what a happy couple!

ARMAND: Hello, Nichette. I'm just leaving. I'm sure you girls have a lot to talk over. *(Exits with Prudence)*

MARGUERITE: You see, this is where we have been living for the last three months. Salon, bedroom, anteroom and kitchen. Furnished in a way that would divert a hypochondriac. Was I right?

NICHETTE: Are you happy?

MARGUERITE: Very happy.

(Picks up hand bell, rings it with abandon. Nanine enters with tea on a serving tray.)

NICHETTE: I always told you, Marguerite, that this was the way to be happy. Many a time Gustave and I have said to each other, "When will Marguerite really love someone and settle down?"

MARGUERITE: Well, your wish is fulfilled. I am really in love. I think it was watching you and Gustave that first made me envious.

NICHETTE: We have two dear little rooms in the rue Blanche.

MARGUERITE: Two little rooms.

NICHETTE: And Gustave says that I am not to work and he will buy me a carriage, one of these days.

MARGUERITE: One of these days!

NICHETTE: And we're going to get married, too.

MARGUERITE: One of these days?

NICHETTE: Soon.

MARGUERITE: You will be very happy. *(She pours tea. The teapot plays "Tea for Two.")* Sugar? *(She places twelve sugar cubes in her cup, one by one, hesitates with the thirteenth, decides against it)*

NICHETTE: But aren't you going to get married and do as we do?

MARGUERITE: Whom should I marry?

NICHETTE: Why, Armand, of course!

MARGUERITE: Armand would marry me tomorrow if I wished it. But I love him too much for that.

NICHETTE: But so long as you are happy, what does it matter?

MARGUERITE: I *am* happy. I can tell you because I know you will understand. *(Takes off wooden shoes)* The Marguerite that used to be and the Marguerite of today are two different beings. I used to spend enough money on camellias to keep a poor family for a year.

(Nanine enters with dish of strawberries.)

But, now, a little flower like this that Armand gave me this morning is enough to fill my whole day with perfume. What do you call this flower, Nanine?

NANINE: Bittersweet. *(Exits)*

MARGUERITE: And yet money-money-money-money. It was the Baron de Varville who paid for everything. Now I'm in debt. Why can't anything ever be perfect?

NICHETTE: If only you could be content with two little rooms like ours.

MARGUERITE: Listen, Nichette, I came up from grinding poverty and it stinks. I never want to go back to work in a shop and live in two little rooms with cucarachas and ratónes. No, no, I'll never go back! There are only two ways a woman may rise from the gutter and become a queen: prostitution or the stage. And, believe me, Nichette, I'd rather peddle my coosie in the streets than become an actress!

NICHETTE: There is another way a woman may rise, Marguerite. A woman may marry.

MARGUERITE: Marriage is nothing but legalized prostitution. *(Salutes with fist. Throws a strawberry up and catches it in her mouth)*

NICHETTE: I think you're wrong, Marguerite, terribly wrong.

MARGUERITE: Perhaps . . . perhaps . . .

NICHETTE: If only you would come to visit our two little rooms, I'm sure you would change your mind.

MARGUERITE: Perhaps I will . . . one of these days.

NANINE *(Entering)*: There is a gentleman here who wishes to speak to you, Madame.

MARGUERITE: That will be my lawyer. I was expecting him. *(To Nichette)* Please excuse me.

NICHETTE: I really must be going. I want to have Gustave's dinner ready for him when he gets home from the office.

MARGUERITE: Cooking? Sister, have you no pride?

NICHETTE: Pride? That's one luxury a woman in love can't afford. Toodle-oo, Marguerite!

MARGUERITE: Ta-ta, Nichette!

(Nichette exits. Prudence enters.)

PRUDENCE: I've sold your diamond earrings. Here's your receipt. Here are the earrings. *(Pulling earrings from Marguerite's ears)* Here's my commission. I'm off! Good-bye, Marguerite. You know where to find me if you need me. L'amour, l'amour. *(Exits)*

DUVAL *(Entering)*: Mademoiselle Marguerite Gautier?

MARGUERITE: Yes, I am she. To whom do I have the honor of speaking?

DUVAL: To Monsieur Duval.

MARGUERITE: Monsieur Duval?

DUVAL: Yes, Madame, I am Armand's father. Is Armand here?

MARGUERITE *(Troubled)*: No, Armand is often here. But just now he is away, at Paris.

DUVAL: Good. I want to speak to you alone. You see, I know what's going on here. My son is ruining himself for you.

MARGUERITE: You are mistaken, sir. I accept nothing from Armand.

DUVAL: Am I to understand, then, as your habits of luxury are well known, that my son is mean enough to help you spend what you receive from others?

MARGUERITE: You must excuse me, sir. Your manner of addressing me is not what I should have expected from a gentleman. I must ask your permission to withdraw. *(Turns to exit)*

DUVAL: Your indignation is cleverly assumed, Madame. They were right when they told me you were dangerous.

MARGUERITE: Dangerous to myself, perhaps, but not to others.

DUVAL: Then will you explain to me the meaning of this letter? *(Hands her the letter)* It is from my lawyer informing me that my son wishes to turn over to you the inheritance he received from his mother.

MARGUERITE: I assure you that, if Armand has done such a thing, it is entirely without my knowledge. He knew that, if he had offered it to me, I should have refused it.

DUVAL: That was not always your method, I think.

MARGUERITE: It is true, but now . . .

DUVAL: Now?

MARGUERITE: Now that I have learned what true love means.

DUVAL: Fine phrases, Madame.

MARGUERITE: You force me to disclose to you that which I should have preferred to keep secret. Ever since I knew and loved your son, I have been selling my horses, my carriage, my gowns and my jewels. A moment ago, when I was told that someone wished to speak with me, I concluded that it was in connection with the sale of furniture, pictures and the rest of the luxury with which you have reproached me. I was not expecting you, sir, so you may be quite sure that this paper was not prepared especially for you, but if you doubt what I say, read this . . . *(Gives him the bill of sale which Prudence has drawn up)*

DUVAL *(Reading)*: A bill of sale on your jewels, the purchaser to pay your creditors, the balance to be given to you? *(Looks at her in astonishment)* Have I been mistaken?

MARGUERITE: You have. It is Armand who changed me.

DUVAL: Forgive me, Madame, for my discourtesy a moment ago. I was not acquainted with you and quite unprepared for what I was to find. I was deeply hurt by my son's silence and ingratitude of which I judged you to be the cause. I beg your pardon.

MARGUERITE: Thank you.

(Pause.)

DUVAL: And what if I ask you to give Armand a greater proof of your love?

MARGUERITE: No! No! You are going to ask something terrible of me. I knew I was too happy.

DUVAL: Let us speak together now like two friends.

MARGUERITE: Yes . . . friends.

DUVAL: I speak to you as a father who asks you for the happiness of his two children.

MARGUERITE *(Thinks he means her)*: Of his two children?

DUVAL: Yes, Marguerite, of his two children. I have a daughter, young, beautiful, pure. *(Realizes he's not talking about her)* She is to be married and she, too, has made her love the dream of her life. Society is exacting in certain respects, especially provincial society. The family of my future son-in-law have learned of the manner in which Armand is living; they have given me to understand that the marriage cannot take place if it continues. Marguerite, in the name of your love, grant me the happiness of my child.

MARGUERITE: How can I refuse what you ask with so much gentleness and consideration? I understand. You are right. I will go back to Paris. I will leave Armand for a while. Besides, the joy of our reunion will help us to forget the pain of parting.

DUVAL: Thank you, Marguerite, thank you, but there is still something that I must ask of you.

MARGUERITE: Can you ask anything more of me?

DUVAL: A temporary parting is not enough.

MARGUERITE: You mean you want me to leave Armand altogether?

DUVAL: You must.

MARGUERITE: Never! You don't know how we love each other.

DUVAL: My son is as dear to me as he can possibly be to you.

MARGUERITE: But you have friends and a family. I have only Armand. I'm ill. I have only a few years to live. To leave Armand would kill me.

DUVAL: Come, come, let's not exaggerate. You're not going to die. What you feel is the melancholy of happiness, knowing that even love can't last forever. No woman is worthy of a man if she lets him ruin himself. Think of Armand's career. He will never go through doors you cannot go through. He can't present you to his family and friends. You're killing his right to a normal life.

MARGUERITE: You're not telling me anything I haven't said to myself a hundred times—but I never let myself go through to the end. *(To herself)* A woman once she has fallen can never rise again. *(To Duval)* But a man can go back, he can always go back!

DUVAL: What career would remain open to him? What will be left to you both when you are old? Who can promise that he will not be less dazzled when time casts the first shadow over your beauty? Has not your own experience taught you that the human heart cannot be trusted?

MARGUERITE: My God!

DUVAL: No unprotected woman can afford to waste the best years of her life. What will your old age be, doubly deserted, doubly desolate?

MARGUERITE: What must I do? Tell me.

DUVAL: You must tell Armand that you no longer love him.

MARGUERITE: He won't believe me.

DUVAL: Leave him.

MARGUERITE: He'll follow me.

DUVAL: In that case . . .

MARGUERITE: Do you believe that I love Armand with a love that is truly unselfish?

DUVAL: Yes, Marguerite.

MARGUERITE: Then, sir, will you kiss me, just once, as you would your own daughter? And believe me when I tell you it is the only really pure kiss that I have ever received. And promise me that one day you will tell this beautiful and pure young girl that somewhere in the world there is a woman, who had only one thought, one hope, one dream in life, and that for her sake she renounced them all *(Throws spray of bittersweet off)*, and that she died of it. Because I shall die of it and then, perhaps, God will forgive me.

DUVAL *(Moved in spite of himself)*: Poor girl! *(Kisses her)*

MARGUERITE: I swear that he shall never know what has passed between us. One last favor.

DUVAL: Ask it.

MARGUERITE: In a little while, Armand will experience one of the greatest sorrows he has ever known, or perhaps ever will know. He will need someone who loves him. Will you be here, sir, at his side?

DUVAL: What are you going to do?

MARGUERITE: If I told you, it would be your duty to prevent it.

DUVAL: You are a noble girl. But I am afraid.

MARGUERITE: Fear nothing, sir. He shall hate me. *(Rings for Nanine)*

DUVAL: I shall never forget what I and my family owe you.

MARGUERITE: Make no mistake, monsieur, whatever I do is not for you. Everything I do is for Armand.

DUVAL *(Offering her money)*: Is there nothing I can do for you in acknowledgment of the debt that I shall owe you?

MARGUERITE *(Rejecting the money)*: When I am dead and Armand curses my memory, tell him that I loved him and that I proved it. We shall never meet again. Good-bye.

(Duval exits. Marguerite is alone.)

Venus Castina give me strength. *(Writes a letter)*

NANINE *(Entering all smiles)*: You rang for me, Madame?

MARGUERITE *(Weeping)*: Yes, there is something I want you to do for me.

NANINE: What is it?

MARGUERITE: Take this letter, Nanine.

NANINE: Why, you're weeping. I don't know what's in it, but I can see that the thought of it makes your blood run cold.

MARGUERITE: Read the address.

NANINE: The Baron de Var . . . Now what do you want to send this for? I thought you were so happy with Monsieur Duval.

MARGUERITE: I was.

NANINE: Then what are you doing, you foolish girl?

MARGUERITE: I'm going to make my love hate me, Nanine. Make him hate me! Make him hate me! *(Sobs)*

NANINE: But . . .

MARGUERITE: Hush. Go at once!

(Nanine exits.)

And now for Armand. *(Begins writing a second letter)*

ARMAND *(Entering)*: Ah, Marguerite, I'm back.

MARGUERITE: Already?

ARMAND: What's the matter? You don't seem glad to see me.

MARGUERITE: I saw you this morning and last night and yesterday and the day before that.

ARMAND: How was your day?

MARGUERITE: Well, this morning Prudence and I walked down the road to see the new cow. And this afternoon, I washed my hair. Those were the two big events of my day.

ARMAND: You seem so strange. What's the matter?

MARGUERITE: I'm bored.

ARMAND: Bored? But this morning you said you liked the country.

MARGUERITE: That was this morning.

ARMAND: Are things so different now?

MARGUERITE: Yes, things are different now. This is no life for me.

ARMAND: What does this mean?

MARGUERITE: I'm going back to Paris.

ARMAND: But you said it would kill you if you went back to Paris.

MARGUERITE: Perhaps it will. But if I'm going to die, I'd rather die gaily than of boredom. Wasn't one summer all you wanted, dahling?

ARMAND: I won't let you go. (*He takes her in his arms and holds her very tight*)

MARGUERITE: You must let me go, Armand. You must. It's better this way, better for both of us.

ARMAND: You've put tears on my hand.

MARGUERITE: I had to cry a little. (*Wipes tear from her eye and flicks it off her finger*) There, I'm better now. Believe me, I've loved you as long as I can. It's not my fault that I can't love you forever. We don't make our own hearts, Armand.

ARMAND (*Releasing her*): No, Marguerite, you can't help it that you can love me only a little while. Just as I can't help it that I will love you for the rest of my life.

MARGUERITE (*Bitterly*): That's the way it is. I'm going.

ARMAND: I can't let you go!

MARGUERITE: You must. The Baron de Varville is expecting me.

ARMAND: The Baron de Varville?!! I could kill you for this.

MARGUERITE: I'm not worth killing. You can't give me the things in life I want. I can't part with my horses, my carriage, my gowns and my jewels. I thought I could, but I can't.

ARMAND: You filthy slut!

(*Marguerite runs out the door.*)

(*Calling after her*) Marguerite, forgive me! I didn't mean it! Marguerite, don't leave me! Please don't leave me!

(Duval, Sr. has entered at the back. Armand turns, sees his father and collapses into his arms in tears.)

Father!

SCENE 2

A soirée at Olympe's house in Paris, six months later.

PRUDENCE: What a wonderful party!

GASTON: Yes, splendid, splendid. I've been losing all my money.

PRUDENCE: That's all right. Gambling is a gentleman's vice.

GASTON: Olympe has outdone herself tonight. This is the most extravagant soirée of the season.

PRUDENCE: I wonder if Saint Gaudens knows what it is costing him.

OLYMPE *(Overhearing)*: His wife does!

(They all laugh.)

PRUDENCE: Very witty!

GASTON: What a charming gown you are wearing tonight, Olympe.

OLYMPE: Thank you. It's from Prudence's shop. A Duvernoy original. I wanted to wear my gown by Gongora, but Saint Gaudens wouldn't hear of it.

SAINT GAUDENS: My dear, it wasn't you. A grande bateau-mouche tricked out in Punch and Judy orchids. Foh!

OLYMPE: Whenever Saint Gaudens doesn't like the dress I'm wearing, I take it off!

SAINT GAUDENS: Gaston, do you think a demimondaine such as this one might want to give up her former life and lead a simple and pure existence?

GASTON: Put a duck on a lake among swans and you will observe that the duck misses its mire and will return to it.

SAINT GAUDENS: Homesick for the mud. Then you don't believe in repentant Magdalenes.

GASTON: I do. In the desert!

OLYMPE: I like poise, don't you? I always insist upon it. For instance, a woman should always leave a man before he leaves her.

PRUDENCE: And here I am, six months later, and still in the same dress.

OLYMPE: Fermez la bouche. Nobody's going to buy you a new one.

BUTLER *(Announcing)*: Monsieur Armand Duval.

GASTON: Look, there's Armand.

SAINT GAUDENS: Hurumph!

GASTON: But where is Marguerite?

OLYMPE *(Mit schadenfreude)*: Haven't you heard? They've broken up!

GASTON: Impossible.

PRUDENCE: It's quite true. It happened last summer at Auteuil.

GASTON: Then they've really parted. Will Marguerite be here tonight?

PRUDENCE: No, not a chance.

OLYMPE: Don't be too sure, Prudence. I invited the Baron de Varville.

GASTON: Then Varville won her after all.

OLYMPE: "Bought" is more the word, I should say.

SAINT GAUDENS: Don't be a camp, Olympe.

OLYMPE: How can you reproach me? I've been a very good friend to Marguerite. Didn't I buy her horses, her carriage, her gowns and her jewels when she needed the money?

PRUDENCE: It is true.

OLYMPE *(Pointing out various items of jewelry she is wearing)*: See, these and this one and this one. I got them for peanuts. Even this gown belonged to her.

PRUDENCE: The Baron has given her back everything that she lost—her horses, her carriage, her gowns and her jewels. Ah, l'amour, l'amour! For what happiness is worth in this world, she is happy. But she never sleeps.

OLYMPE: She goes everywhere: theaters, balls, orgies and operas.

PRUDENCE: She won't listen to her doctor. She won't last long at this rate. Ah, l'amour, l'amour, toujours l'amour!

GASTON *(Greeting Armand)*: Well, Armand, what a surprise to see you. I thought you'd left Paris.

ARMAND: Well, you were wrong.

GASTON: I hear you've broken with Marguerite.

ARMAND: You heard right.

GASTON: Do you ever see her?

ARMAND: No, never.

GASTON: I hear she's coming here tonight.

ARMAND *(Starts)*: Then I *shall* see her.

GASTON: Of course, she'll be with Varville.

ARMAND: So much the better. *(Intensely)* Listen, Gaston, I'm going crazy. Ever since Marguerite left me, I have hardly slept. And when I do sleep, I have nightmares.

GASTON: Dear boy.

ARMAND: I came here tonight because I knew she would be here. I want to punish her for leaving me.

GASTON: Armand, be careful. She is a woman, and any act of revenge on your part will seem like cowardice.

ARMAND: Then let her escort protect her. I would give anything for an excuse to kill him.

BUTLER: Madame Marguerite Gautier. The Baron de Varville.

(Armand goes over and puts his arm around Olympe, who plays up to him. Marguerite enters wearing the same gown as Olympe but much more fabulous. There is a momentary confrontation between the two women.)

MARGUERITE *(To Varville)*: I don't feel well. I want to go home.

OLYMPE *(Turning on Prudence, furiously)*: I thought you said this gown was an original!

PRUDENCE *(Sheepishly)*: Well, it was. The first time I made it.

OLYMPE *(Wringing Prudence's neck)*: You treacherous old harridan! *(Spinning around furiously)* I won't be outdone in my own home! *(During her tantrum, her dress becomes disheveled and one tit is exposed; she hides it with her fan. Regaining her composure, she faces Marguerite)* You made me lose my poise and for this, I shall never forgive you! *(Starts out)*

SAINT GAUDENS: Where are you going?

OLYMPE: I'm going to change into my Gongora with the Punch and Judy orchids! *(Exits)*

MARGUERITE: Please, Varville, I want to go home. I'm ill.

VARVILLE: Your illness bores me, my dear.

(Marguerite drops her fan.)

You've dropped your fan.

MARGUERITE: What?

VARVILLE: You've dropped your fan

MARGUERITE: Oh, have I? *(Bends over and picks it up)*

GASTON: Good evening, Marguerite.

MARGUERITE *(Drying her eyes)*: Good evening, dear Gaston, I'm so glad to see you.

GASTON: You're weeping. What is the matter?

MARGUERITE: It's nothing. I'm just unhappy, that's all.

GASTON: What are you doing here?

MARGUERITE: I am not my own mistress. Besides, I do all I can to forget.

GASTON: Take my advice and leave at once! I fear there may be some trouble between Armand and the Baron, perhaps a duel.

MARGUERITE: A duel between Armand and Varville?

GASTON: Make some excuse. Say you are ill.

MARGUERITE: You are right. *(To Varville, who has been cruising the butler)* Varville, I'm terribly ill. We must leave at once.

VARVILLE: We're staying right where we are. I'm not missing the best soirée of the season because of Armand Duval.

(Olympe enters in an outrageous Gongora gown with Punch and Judy orchids.)

GASTON: Is this a woman or a circus tent? *(Pops one of the balloons that hold up her skirt)*

OLYMPE: You stop that. *(Hanging around Armand's neck and talking baby talk)* Look, Armand's been winning at cards.

ARMAND: Yes, I'm testing the old saying, "Lucky at cards, unlucky in love."

OLYMPE: How do you like me, Armand?

ARMAND: I like you as well as you like my money.

OLYMPE: Come, let's greet the Baron de Varville and Marguerite Gautier together.

ARMAND: I will on one condition.

OLYMPE: I'll do anything as long as it's *not* within reason.

ARMAND *(Imitating her baby talk)*: If you don't stop talking like that, I'm going to knock your little teeth down your throat. *(Drops the baby talk)* I want you to insult Marguerite.

OLYMPE: I'd be delighted.

(Armand and Olympe, petting each other, go to greet Varville and Marguerite.)

Good evening, Marguerite, Baron.

MARGUERITE: Good evening, Olympe.

ARMAND: Marguerite, Baron. *(Bows)*

VARVILLE: Good evening. *(Bows stiffly)*

MARGUERITE: Good evening.

VARVILLE: We've just come from the Opera, where we heard Berenice Blowell.

OLYMPE: What did she sing?

VARVILLE: *Manon Lescaut.*

ARMAND: Ah, yes, *Manon Lescaut*, the story of a vile woman incapable of loyalty, who sold her young lover for an old man's gold.

OLYMPE: How very unoriginal. And most untrue. Women never betray their lovers.

ARMAND: Some do.

OLYMPE: Of course, but then there are lovers and lovers.

ARMAND: Just as there are women and women.

(Marguerite drops her fan again.)

VARVILLE: You dropped your fan again, my dear.

(Armand, intercepting Marguerite, picks up the fan and returns it to her.)

MARGUERITE: Thank you.

ARMAND: Any gentleman would do the same.

(Varville makes a threatening movement toward Armand. Marguerite and Olympe draw the two men apart.)

GASTON: Armand, would you care for a hand of baccarat?

ARMAND: Yes, I intend to make my fortune tonight. Then when I am really rich, I intend to go and live in the country.

OLYMPE: Alone?

ARMAND: No, with someone who went with me once before and left me. It all depends on how much I win. If I am wealthy, perhaps I can buy her back.

GASTON: Be quiet, Armand. Look at that poor girl.

ARMAND: It's an amusing story. You would enjoy it. There is an old buffoon who makes his appearance right at the very end—a sort of deus ex machina . . .

VARVILLE: Sir!

MARGUERITE *(Aside to Varville)*: If you challenge Monsieur Duval to a duel, you will never see me again as long as you live.

ARMAND: You addressed yourself to me, sir?

VARVILLE: I did. *(Spitting out all his "T's")* Your luck tonight tempts me to try my own. *(Turning to Marguerite)* I understand perfectly how you intend *(Marguerite deflects his spit with her fan)* to use your winnings and I should be happy to help you increase them. Therefore, I propose to bet against you.

ARMAND: I accept with all my heart, sir. But remember, the reverse of the old saying may also be true. "Lucky in love, unlucky at cards."

(Armand and Varville begin gambling.)

MARGUERITE: My God, what are they doing?

PRUDENCE *(Aside to Butler)*: Say dinner is served.

BUTLER: I beg your pardon?

PRUDENCE: Say dinner is served. *(Gives him a good swift kick in the hams)*

BUTLER *(Blurts out)*: Dinner is served!

PRUDENCE: Thank heavens! I'm famished. Dinner is ready, everyone. Come into the next room and eat! *(She herds everyone out)* Ah, l'amour, l'amour!

MARGUERITE: Gaston, dahling, please ask Armand to come in here a moment. I must speak to him.

GASTON: I will. *(Exits)*

VARVILLE *(To Marguerite)*: Are you coming, my dear?

MARGUERITE: Go ahead without me. I need a moment to repair my maquillage.

VARVILLE: All right. But if you are longer than five minutes, I'll come back for you. *(Exits)*

ARMAND *(Entering)*: You sent for me?

MARGUERITE: Yes, Armand, I want to speak to you.

ARMAND: What do you want?

MARGUERITE: I want to beg you to please stop this.

ARMAND: Stop what?

MARGUERITE: This torture. I can't bear it.

ARMAND: I'm sure I don't know what you mean.

MARGUERITE: You *do* know what I mean. This continuous punishment. I can't bear it. I can't bear it.

ARMAND: What business is it of yours what I do? We mean nothing to each other anymore.

MARGUERITE: That's not true, Armand. I love you. I have always loved you.

ARMAND: Then come away with me at once!

MARGUERITE: Oh, I would give my life for one hour of such happiness, but it's impossible.

ARMAND: It will be humiliating for me, but I will do anything to have you back. You can take everything I own. You name your price.

MARGUERITE: Armand, stop!

ARMAND *(On his knees)*: Please, Marguerite. Since I have loved you, I can love no other. Help me! Help me!

MARGUERITE: I can't, Armand. I have promised not to.

ARMAND: Who have you promised?

MARGUERITE: Someone to whom I owe all the respect in the world.

ARMAND *(Incensed)*: The Baron de Varville?

MARGUERITE *(Lying)*: Yes.

(Armand throws open the doors to the next room.)

ARMAND: Come in here, all of you. I have an announcement to make!

MARGUERITE: What are you doing?

(All enter, puzzled.)

ARMAND: You see this woman?

ALL *(Pointing simultaneously to Marguerite)*: Marguerite Gautier?

ARMAND: Yes, Marguerite Gautier! She spent a summer in the country with me once. I gave her everything I had. I loved her as I have never loved anyone and as I shall never love again. But that love was not enough for her. It meant less to her than horses, a carriage and the diamonds around her neck. I have not yet paid her for the summer we spent together. You are my witnesses. I owe this woman nothing.

(Armand slaps Marguerite across the face with the bundle of franc notes he won and throws them at her. They fall about her in a flurry.)

VARVILLE *(To Armand)*: Congratulations, young man. You have treated her as she deserved.

(Armand slaps Varville across the face. Marguerite faints. Curtain.)

⟿ Act Three

Marguerite's bedroom. Paris, six months later. New Year's Day.
The light of dawn reveals snow falling outside the window of
Marguerite's apartment. Marguerite is in bed asleep; Nanine has fall-
en asleep in a chair. Gaston enters wearing a skeleton's head on the back
of his head. The occasional sound of a last reveler tooting his party
horn is heard offstage along with a cry of "Happy New Year" and a
snatch of "Auld Lang Syne" sung drunkenly. A bit of confetti might
blow past the window. Gaston wears a party hat with bits of confetti in
his hair and a few serpentines around his neck. He may be a little drunk
on champagne, but not unbecomingly so.

GASTON: She is still asleep. What time is it? Seven o'clock. Not yet
  daylight. *(The sound of loud snoring from Nanine)* Faithful
  old Nanine. *(Lights candle)* It is better to light one candle
  than to curse the darkness. *(He picks up Marguerite's purse
  from the mantel)* Here's her purse. *(Looking inside)* Empty!
  *(He reaches deep inside his pockets and pulls out some franc
  notes, turning his pockets inside out in the process. Stuffs the
  notes into her purse)*
MARGUERITE *(Waking)*: I'm thirsty, Nanine.
GASTON *(Giving her some tea)*: Here you are, old girl.
MARGUERITE: I'm cold. Nanine, throw another faggot on the fire!
NANINE *(Waking)*: There are no more faggots in the house. *(Falls
  asleep)*
MARGUERITE *(Plaintively looking out at the audience)*: No faggots
  in the house? Open the window, Nanine. See if there are any
  in the street. *(Seeing Gaston)* Gaston, what are you doing here?

GASTON: Drink this first, and then I'll tell you. I am a born nurse.

MARGUERITE: But where is Nanine?

GASTON: Asleep. How do you feel this morning?

MARGUERITE: Better, Gaston dear. But why should you tire yourself like this?

GASTON: Tire myself? Nonsense! I've been out all night partying. I just wanted to wish you a Happy New Year.

MARGUERITE: New Year?

GASTON: I wanted to bring you flowers. But I couldn't find a single camellia in Paris. It seems there was a killing frost last night in the flower market.

MARGUERITE: I'm cold.

GASTON: Drink this.

MARGUERITE: It's strange that you should come here to take care of me. I always thought that you were just a scatterbrain who cared for nothing but pleasure.

GASTON: You were quite right.

(Marguerite laughs and then coughs.)

Now, I'll tell you what we'll do.

MARGUERITE: What?

GASTON: You must try to sleep a little longer. There will be plenty of sunshine in the early part of the afternoon. Wrap yourself up well, and I will come back and take you for a drive. And then who'll sleep tonight? . . . Marguerite! Now I must go and call on my mother, and God knows what kind of a reception I'll get. I haven't been to see her in over a fortnight. I shall lunch with her and then call for you at one o'clock. How will that suit you?

MARGUERITE: I shall try to have enough strength.

GASTON: You will. Of course, you will. *(To Nanine)* Marguerite is awake. *(To Marguerite)* Until this afternoon then. *(Exits)*

MARGUERITE: Until this afternoon. Are you tired, my poor old Nanine?

NANINE: A little, Madame.

MARGUERITE: Open the window, Nanine, and let in the morning air. I should like to get up.

NANINE: The doctor said you weren't to get out of bed.

MARGUERITE: Dear doctor. Always giving me good advice.

NANINE: He's going to have you well by spring.

MARGUERITE: When God said it was a sin to tell lies, he must have made an exception for doctors. I suppose they have a special dispensation from the pope every time they visit a patient. What have you got there?

NANINE: Presents, Madame.

MARGUERITE: Oh, yes, it's New Year's Day. How much can happen in a year! . . . A year ago today, we were sitting around the table singing and laughing . . . Where are the days, Nanine, when we still laughed? *(Opens parcels)* A ring with a card from Saint Gaudens. A *bracelet*! From the Baron de Varville. He sent it all the way from Siberia. It's cold. What would he say if he could see me like this? . . . And marrons glacés! Well, men are not so forgetful, after all. Joseph has a little niece, hasn't he, Nanine?

NANINE: Yes, Madame.

MARGUERITE: Give him these marrons glacés, for the little girl. It's been a long time since I've wanted any. Is that all?

NANINE: There is a letter.

MARGUERITE: A letter! *(Takes letter, opens it and reads)* "My dearest Marguerite, I have called again and again, but was not allowed to see you. I cannot bear the thought that you will have no share in the happiest day of my life. I am to be married on the first of January. It is the New Year's gift that Gustave was keeping as a surprise for me. I do hope that you will be able to come to my wedding—such a simple, quiet wedding in the Chapel of Sainte Thérèse, in the Madeleine. I kiss you, dear, with all the fervor of my most happy heart. Toodle-oo. Nichette." And so, there is happiness for everyone in the world except for me. But there, I am ungrateful. Please, shut the window, I'm cold. *(The bell rings)* Ah, there is the bell. See who it is, Nanine.

NANINE *(Coming back)*: Madame Duvernoy would like to see you.

MARGUERITE: Let her come in. Pretty please, let her in. Just this once. *(Etc. Nanine relents)* There's the good Nanine.

PRUDENCE *(Entering)*: Well, my dear Marguerite, how are you this morning?

MARGUERITE: Better, thank you, Prudence. And how are you?

PRUDENCE: Rotten, thank you. I drank too much champagne last night at Olympe's and I've got the worst hangover. My stomach, oh my God, I don't know when I've had such indigestion. Olympe has a new chef who is a genius, an absolute artist of genius. But he's ruined my stomach. And then, there's a headache to top it all off. And my sciatica has been acting up again. I'm feeling terrible. I'm really enjoying very poor health.

MARGUERITE: I'm sorry to hear it.

PRUDENCE: Have you heard? The Baron de Varville has recovered from the duel. Fortunately, it was only a scratch and Armand can return from exile. The Baron has taken up with little boys. He likes to get kicked in the rump by little boys! All that money he used to spend on jewels is now being wasted on toys. Ah l'amour, l'amour! Send Nanine away for a moment. I want to speak to you alone.

MARGUERITE: You can finish the other room first, Nanine. I'll call you if I need you.

(Nanine exits.)

PRUDENCE: I wonder if you would do me a favor, Marguerite?

MARGUERITE: What is it?

PRUDENCE: You have money in hand, don't you?

MARGUERITE: You know that I have been very short of money for some time.

PRUDENCE: It's New Year's Day and I have some presents to buy. I'm badly in need of two hundred francs. Do you think you could lend it to me until the end of the month?

MARGUERITE: Until the end of the month!

PRUDENCE: If it's not inconvenient.

MARGUERITE: Well, I do rather need what little money I have left.

PRUDENCE *(In a snit)*: Very well, then, we'll say no more about it. *(Pause)* I didn't want to mention it, but you do owe me two hundred francs for the bonnet I made for you last Easter.

MARGUERITE: Bonnet?

PRUDENCE: Of course, it was violet voile with Costa Rica roses. Don't tell me you've forgotten it.

MARGUERITE: How could I forget the Costa Rica roses.

PRUDENCE: Why, here's your purse.

MARGUERITE: It's empty.

PRUDENCE *(Looking inside the purse)*: Nonsense! It's full of money!

MARGUERITE: Full of money? . . . Gaston! How much is there?

PRUDENCE: Five hundred francs!

MARGUERITE: Then take the two hundred that you need.

PRUDENCE: Are you sure the rest will be enough for you?

MARGUERITE: I shall have all I need. Don't worry about me.

PRUDENCE: You are looking better this morning.

MARGUERITE: I feel better.

PRUDENCE: It won't be long now before spring will be here. Warm weather and a little country air will soon put you right.

MARGUERITE: Yes, that's what I need.

PRUDENCE *(Going out)*: Well, good-bye, dear. And thank you again.

MARGUERITE: Send Nanine to me.

(Nanine enters.)

NANINE: Has she been asking you for money again?

MARGUERITE: Yes.

NANINE: Did you give it to her?

MARGUERITE: Money is such a little thing to give, and she needed it badly, she said. But we need some too, don't we? We must buy some New Year's presents. Take this bracelet that has just come. Sell it and come back as quickly as you can.

NANINE: But what about you?

MARGUERITE: I shall not need anything. Oh, Nanine. Sweet Nanine. Perfect Nanine. You will not be gone very long. You know the way to the pawnbroker's. He's bought enough from me these last three months.

(Nanine exits. Butler has been standing in the background listening.)

BUTLER *(Coming forward)*: Excuse me, Madame, I am a man of few words. Nanine and I have put away a little money for our old age. It isn't much. But it might be enough for a pilgrimage to Lourdes. Please accept our life's savings.

MARGUERITE: Yes, it is a miracle that I need. Thank you, Joseph. But there is only one miracle that can save me . . . Armand's return.

NANINE *(Entering)*: Here is the money, Madame. I had to smuggle it past the bailiff waiting downstairs.

MARGUERITE *(Putting the money into an envelope with a note)*: Take this to Nichette at the Chapel of Sainte Thérèse in the Madeleine. Tell her not to open it until after the wedding.

BUTLER: Yes, Madame. *(Exits with Nanine)*

MARGUERITE: If only I had some word from Armand. That hope alone keeps me alive. How changed I am. The doctor said that I am very ill. But one may still be very ill and have a few more months to live. If only Armand would come and save me. It is the first day of the new year; a day to hope and look forward in.

(Laughter is heard outside the window.)

I hear people laughing far away.

NANINE *(Entering)*: Madame . . .

MARGUERITE: Yes, Nanine?

NANINE: You feel better today, don't you?

MARGUERITE: Why?

NANINE: If I tell you something, will you promise to keep quite calm and quiet?

MARGUERITE: What is it?

NANINE: I want to prepare you. I'm afraid a sudden joy might kill you.

MARGUERITE: Did you say a joy, Nanine?

NANINE: Yes.

MARGUERITE: Armand! You've seen Armand? He's coming to see me? *(Nanine nods and gives Marguerite a bunch of camellias)* He mustn't see me like this. My hair, bring me a brush. Help me up.

NANINE: No, Madame, you must not get up. You're too weak.

MARGUERITE *(Adamant)*: Don't just stand there, help me, Nanine. *(Nanine supports Marguerite as she struggles over to her vanity table and paints her lips and cheeks)* Please, Nanine. Ma solitaire. Ne pas le gros, l'énorme. My camellias. There isn't much time. Send him in, hurry!

(Duval, Sr. appears in the doorway.)

DUVAL: Madame, you have kept your word to the utmost limit of your strength, and I fear recent events have injured your health. I have written to Armand, telling him the whole story. He was far away but he has returned to ask your forgiveness, not only for himself but for me, too. Go to her, Armand!

(Armand enters remorsefully and crosses to Marguerite.)

MARGUERITE: At last, Armand! It's not possible that you've come back, that God has been so good to me.

ARMAND: If we had not seen Nanine, I should have remained outside and never dared to come near you. Have pity, Marguerite! Don't curse me! If I had not found you again, I should have died because it would have been I who killed you. My father has told me everything. Tell me that you forgive us both. Oh, how good it is to see you again!

MARGUERITE: Forgive you, darling! It was all my fault! But what could I do? I wanted your happiness so much more than my own. Your father won't part us again, will he? You do not see the Marguerite that you used to know, dear, but I am still young. I will grow beautiful again now that I am happy.

ARMAND: I will never leave you again, Marguerite. We will go to the country at once and never come back to Paris anymore. My father knows what you are now, and will love you as the good angel of his son. My sister is married. The future is ours.

MARGUERITE: We must lose no time, beloved. Life was slipping away from me, but you came and it stayed. You haven't heard, have you? Nichette is to be married, this morning, to Gustave. Let's go to see her married.

ARMAND: And repeat those vows along with them, silently, in our hearts.

MARGUERITE: It would be so good to go to church, to pray to God, and look on a little at the happiness of others. Tell me again that you love me.

ARMAND: I love you, Marguerite. All my life is yours.

MARGUERITE: Bring my outdoor things, Nanine. I want to go out.

ARMAND: You are a good girl, Nanine. You have taken faithful care of her. Thank you.

(Nanine exits.)

MARGUERITE: We used to speak of you every day. No one else dared mention your name. But Nanine would comfort me and tell me that I would see you again. And she was right. You have traveled a long way and seen many strange lands with strange customs. You must tell me about them and perhaps take me there one day. *(She sways)*

ARMAND: What is it, Marguerite? You are ill!

MARGUERITE *(With difficulty)*: No, it's nothing. Happiness hurts a little at first and my heart has been desolate for so long. *(She throws back her head)*

ARMAND: Marguerite, speak to me. Marguerite!

MARGUERITE *(Coming to herself)*: Don't be afraid, dear. I always used to have these moments of faintness, don't you remember?

ARMAND *(Taking her hand)*: You are trembling!

MARGUERITE: It's nothing. Come, Nanine, give me my shawl and bonnet. We're going to the country! *(Nanine enters, she begins to weep)* Don't just stand there, Nanine. Hurry, we're going to the country! *(Tries to walk)* I can't. I can't. I can't.

(Marguerite drops. Armand catches her and carries her to the chaise.)

ARMAND *(In terror)*: Oh God! Oh, my God! Run for the doctor, Nanine! At once!

MARGUERITE: Yes, yes! Tell him that Armand has come back! That I want to live! That I must live . . . *(Nanine exits)* But if your coming hasn't saved me, nothing will. I have lived for love. Now I'm dying of it.

ARMAND: Hush, Marguerite. You will live. You must.

MARGUERITE: Sit down here beside me, as close as you can. Just for a moment. I was angry at death. But now I see that it had to come. I'm not angry anymore because it has waited long enough for me to see you again. If I had not been going to die, your father would never have written to you to come back.

ARMAND: Marguerite, don't talk like that! I can't bear it! Tell me that you are not going to die! That you don't believe it, that you will not die!

MARGUERITE: Even if I did not wish it, dear, it would have to be because it is God's will. If I had really been the girl you should have loved, I might have grieved more at leaving a world where you are and a future so full of promise. Then we might have lived happily ever after. But perhaps it's better that I die. Then there'll be no stain on our love. Believe me, God sees more clearly than we do.

ARMAND: Don't, Marguerite, don't.

MARGUERITE: Must I be the one to give you courage? Come, do as I tell you. On my vanity table you will find a miniature of me, painted in the days when I was still pretty. *(Armand picks up the painting)* Keep it, it will help your memory later. If ever you should love and marry some young and beautiful girl, as I hope you may, and if she should find the portrait and ask who it is, tell her it is a friend, who, if God in her starry heaven permits, will never cease to pray for you and her. And if she should be jealous of the past, because we women sometimes are, and ask you to give up the picture, do so, dearest. I forgive you now, already. A woman suffers too deeply when she feels she is not loved . . . Are you listening, Armand, my darling, do you hear me?

(Enter Nichette, timidly at first and then more boldly as she sees Marguerite smiling and Armand at her feet.)

NICHETTE: Marguerite, you wrote to me that you were dying, but I find you up and smiling.

ARMAND *(Aside)*: Ah, Nichette, I am so miserable!

MARGUERITE: I am dying, but I am happy too, and it is only my happiness that you can see . . . And so you are married! . . . Look at that . . . What a strange life this first one is. What will the second be? . . . You will be even happier than you were before. Speak of me sometimes, won't you? Armand, give me your hand. Believe me, it's not hard to die. That's strange.

(Enter Gaston.)

Here is Gaston come back for me! I am so glad to see you
again, dear Gaston. Happiness is ungrateful. I had forgotten
you . . . Thank you for filling my purse with money . . . He
has been so good to me, so kind . . . Ah! . . . It's strange.

ARMAND: What?

MARGUERITE: I'm not suffering anymore. I feel better, so much
better than I have ever felt before . . . I am going to live.

(Appears to sleep)

GASTON: She is asleep.

ARMAND *(With anxiety at first, then with terror)*: Marguerite!
Marguerite! Marguerite! Don't leave me! Please don't leave me!

GASTON: She loved you dearly, poor girl.

NICHETTE *(On her knees beside Marguerite)*: Much will be forgiven
you, for you loved much. Toodle-oo, Marguerite.

*(Tableau vivant. All lights dim out leaving the little statue of
the Madonna on Marguerite's vanity in the flickering light of a
votive candle.)*

CURTAIN

BLUEBEARD

*A Melodrama
in Three Acts*

1970

Bluebeard: A Melodrama in Three Acts was first presented by The Ridiculous Theatrical Company at La MaMa E.T.C. in New York City on March 26, 1970. Scenic design was by Christopher Scott and Sam Yahn, costume design was by Mary Brecht, lighting design was by Leandro Katz and original music and sound design were by David Scott. It was directed by Charles Ludlam. The cast was as follows:

KHANAZAR VON BLUEBEARD	Charles Ludlam
SHEEMISH	John Brockmeyer
MRS. MAGGOT	Eleven
SYBIL	Black-Eyed Susan
MISS FLORA CUBBIDGE	Lola Pashalinski
RODNEY	Bill Vehr
LAMIA THE LEOPARD WOMAN	Mario Montez
GOOD ANGEL	James Morfogen
BAD ANGEL	Fredrick "Dude" Teper
HECATE	Lohr Wilson
HER TRAIN	James Morfogen
	Fredrick "Dude" Teper

Characters

KHANAZAR VON BLUEBEARD

SHEEMISH

MRS. MAGGOT

SYBIL

MISS FLORA CUBBIDGE

RODNEY

LAMIA THE LEOPARD WOMAN

GOOD ANGEL

BAD ANGEL

HECATE

HER TRAIN

Note

Often Bluebeard's first name, Khanazar, is pronounced with a hard, rolled "Kh" sound, as if one is clearing his throat or about to spit.

Act One

SCENE I

SHEEMISH, MRS. MAGGOT

The alchemical laboratory of Dr. Bluebeard, located on an island off the coast of Maine.

The house is a lighthouse still in use. Revolving light, test tubes and other laboratory equipment including an operating table. Sheemish, the butler, and Mrs. Maggot, the housekeeper, are dusting and sweeping. Mrs. Maggot bumps the table, causing a test tube to fall and break.

SHEEMISH: Now see what you've done! Clean it up at once. For if Khanazar, the Bluebeard, finds anything broken, he will surely send you to the House of Pain.

MRS. MAGGOT *(Terribly frightened)*: No, no, not the House of Pain!

SHEEMISH *(Sadistically)*: Yes, yes, the House of Pain. If I should mention the fact that you broke this little glass tube, I'm sure the master would send you to the House of Pain.

MRS. MAGGOT *(More frightened)*: No, no, not the House of Pain! Please, Sheemish, don't tell, I beg of you.

SHEEMISH *(Calculatingly)*: Very well. I will not tell . . . as long as you realize that I am doing you a favor . . . and that I will expect a favor in return.

MRS. MAGGOT: Anything, I'll do anything you ask, but please, please do not tell.

SHEEMISH: Replace the little glass tube. Substitute something for the sticky liquid inside. Do this quickly, for the good ship

Lady Vain will dock here at three o'clock this afternoon, drop off a female passenger, and return to the mainland.

(Mrs. Maggot puts test tube under her skirt and urinates in it.)

We must prepare the guest room for tonight . . . and the bridal chamber for tomorrow.

MRS. MAGGOT: You mean he's found another . . . another . . . ?
(She begins to weep)

SHEEMISH: Say it, Mrs. Maggot! Wife. Say it: wife! Wife! Wife!

MRS. MAGGOT: I can't. I can't bear to say it. *(Falling to her knees)* Lord of my prayers! God of my sacrifice! Because you have done this thing, you shall lack both my fear and my praise. I shall not wince at your lightnings nor be awed when you go by.

SHEEMISH: Curse not our god, Khanazar, the Bluebeard.

MRS. MAGGOT: Why should I not curse him who has stolen from me the gardens of my childhood?

SHEEMISH: Remember the House of Pain and hold your tongue. *(Mrs. Maggot holds her tongue with her fingers)* You have replaced the little glass tube. It looks exactly as it did before the little accident. Even the sticky liquid is the same color and viscosity. You and I are the only ones who know. Come, the guest room. And, Mrs. Maggot, forget about the past.

MRS. MAGGOT: Since the operation I can't remember it anyway.

SHEEMISH: And think as I do, of the future.

MRS. MAGGOT:
The future is so very far.
The present is what must be feared.
For we are slaves of Khanazar,
And dread the wrath of the Bluebeard.

(Exeunt.)

SCENE 2

LAMIA THE LEOPARD WOMAN

Enter Lamia the Leopard Woman, wearing more leopard than the costume designer thought advisable. She riffles through Bluebeard's papers.

SCENE 3

KHANAZAR, THE BLUEBEARD

BLUEBEARD *(Entering and seeing Lamia)*: I thought I told you
never to come to this side of the island again! *(Draws gun and
fires. Lamia runs out)* Give up your passions, Bluebeard, and
become the thing you claim to be. Is to end desire desire's
chiefest end? Does sex afford no greater miracles? Have all my
perversions and monstrosities, my fuckings and suckings,
led me to this? This little death at the climax followed by
slumber? Yet chastity ravishes me. And yet the cunt gapes
like the jaws of hell, an unfathomable abyss; or the boy-ass
used to buggery spread wide to swallow me up its bung; or
the mouth sucking out my life! Aaagh! If only there were
some new and gentle genital that would combine with me
and, mutually interpenetrated, steer me through this storm in
paradise! *(The sound of a foghorn)* They said I was mad at
medical school. They said no third genital was possible. Yang
and yin, male and female, and that's that. *(Laughs maniacally)*
Science suits a mercenary drudge who aims at nothing but
external trash. Give me a dark art that stretches as far as does
the mind of man; a sound magician is a demigod.

(Foghorn again.)

SCENE 4

BLUEBEARD, GOOD ANGEL, BAD ANGEL

GOOD ANGEL:
On, Bluebeard, lay these thoughts aside,
And think not on them lest it tempt thy soul
And heap God's heavy wrath upon thee.
Take half—one sex, that's all—for that is nature's way.

(Foghorn.)

BAD ANGEL:

> Go forward, Bluebeard, in that famous art
> Wherein all nature's treasure is contained:
> Be thou on earth as God is in the sky,
> Master and possessor of both sexes.

(Angels exit.)

SCENE 5

BLUEBEARD

BLUEBEARD:

> Love must be reinvented, that's obvious.
> Sex to me no longer is mysterious
> And so I swear that while my beard is blue,
> I'll twist some human flesh into a genital new.

SCENE 6

BLUEBEARD, SHEEMISH, MRS. MAGGOT

SHEEMISH: Master, Master.

BLUEBEARD *(Enraged)*: Swine! How dare you enter my room without knocking? *(Lashes whip)* Have you forgotten the House of Pain?

SHEEMISH *(Clutching his genitals)*: No, no, not the House of Pain! Mercy, Master.

BLUEBEARD: How can I show you mercy when I am merciless with myself? I see in you nothing but my own failure; another experiment down the drain.

SHEEMISH *(On his knees, pathetically)*: Forgive me. *(Whimpers)*

BLUEBEARD: Aaagh, get up. Tell me what you want.

SHEEMISH: The good ship *Lady Vain* has docked here on the rocky side of the island.

BLUEBEARD *(Anticipating)*: Yes . . .

SHEEMISH: There are two women . . .

BLUEBEARD *(In ecstasy)*: Ah, resolve me of all ambiguities. Perform what desperate enterprises I will!

MRS. MAGGOT: And a man.

BLUEBEARD: Huh? A man? There is no man! *(Lashes her with whip)* You are mistaken, there is no man.

(Loud knocking at the door.)

MRS. MAGGOT: It's them.

SHEEMISH *(Correcting her)*: It is they.

BLUEBEARD *(Looking through spy hole)*: Sybil said nothing about a man. *(Loud knocking, howling wind and the sound of rain)* Go away! Go away! Leave me in peace!

SCENE 7

BLUEBEARD, SHEEMISH, MRS. MAGGOT, RODNEY PARKER, SYBIL, MISS FLORA CUBBIDGE

RODNEY'S VOICE: Baron Bluebeard, please open the door!

BLUEBEARD: Leave me alone! Go away!

SYBIL'S VOICE: Dear Uncle, please let us in for the love of God. It's bitter without.

BLUEBEARD *(Aside)*: And I am bitter within!

MISS CUBBIDGE'S VOICE: We'll catch our death of cold!

MRS. MAGGOT *(In confusion)*: What should we do, Master?

SHEEMISH *(Calling down from a lookout point)*: We must let them in for their ship, the *Lady Vain*, its sails big-bellied, makes way from our port. I think it will go down in the storm.

BLUEBEARD: Aagh, very well, come in then. But you can't stay. *(Opens the door)*

(Enter Sybil, Rodney and Miss Cubbidge, wet.)

SYBIL *(Rushing to Bluebeard)*: Oh Uncle Khanazar, my dear Uncle Khanazar, why wouldn't you let us in? How glad I am to see you. Who would have thought of you?

BLUEBEARD: Why, Sybil, I hope you always thought of me.

SYBIL: Dear Uncle, so I do; but I meant to say of seeing you— I never dreamed I would while you were quartered here at ... at ... what is the name of this island anyway?

BLUEBEARD *(Lying)*: I don't believe it has a name. I've never thought to give it one.

RODNEY: The sailors called it "The Island of Lost Love."

SYBIL: It's true our ship was almost lost in the fog.

RODNEY: And we are in love.

BLUEBEARD *(Aside)*: Grrrr!

SYBIL: Oh, excuse me, Uncle, this is my fiancé, Rodney Parker.

BLUEBEARD *(Icily)*: Howdyedo?

RODNEY *(Running off at the mouth)*: Sybil has told me so much about you. She says you were the great misunderstood genius at medical school. But that you suddenly gave it all up, threw it all away to live here in almost total seclusion—

SYBIL *(Interrupting)*: And this is Miss Cubbidge, my beloved traveling companion and tutor.

MISS CUBBIDGE *(Shaking his hand violently)*: I am incensed to meet you, Baron Bluebeard. Sybil told me that you were with her father at medical school when the terrible fire . . .

BLUEBEARD *(Flaring up)*: Don't squeeze my hand! I work with my hands. *(Then politely)* If you will excuse me. I expected only one guest. *(Turning to Mrs. Maggot and Sheemish, who bow with sinister smiles)* Now, there are extra preparations to be made. Mrs. Maggot and Sheemish will show you to your rooms. *(Kisses Sybil's hand, shakes Miss Cubbidge's hand, and ignores Rodney's hand)* We will sup when the moon rises over Mount Agdora. *(Exits)*

RODNEY: Did you see that? I offered him my hand, but he refused it.

SYBIL: I'm sure Uncle Khanazar meant nothing by it. He's so involved in his work and he's unused to human companionship.

SCENE 8

SYBIL, RODNEY, MISS CUBBIDGE, MRS. MAGGOT, SHEEMISH

RODNEY *(Aside to Sybil)*: What about these serving people he keeps around here?

SYBIL *(Aside to Rodney and Miss Cubbidge)*: Yes, of course. *(Then strangely)* But then they hardly seem human, do they?

MISS MAGGOT *(Dykey)*: This way to the washroom, ladies. Follow me to the washroom, ladies.

MISS CUBBIDGE: Shall we wash away that which we acquiesced during our long adjunct? I refer, of course, to the dust of travel.

SYBIL: Until dinner, Rodney dear.

RODNEY: Sybil, there is something that I must discuss with you.

SYBIL: Excuse me until then, dear Rodney, I must freshen up. *(Throws him a kiss and exits)*

SCENE 9

RODNEY, SHEEMISH

RODNEY: Ah, I'm convinced of it! Sybil is in love with him.

SHEEMISH: With whom?

RODNEY: Excuse me, I was thinking aloud. Thinking, thinking, thinking, that's all I ever do. My head thunders with thinking. I must stop thinking. I needs must shout it. *(Very loud)* Why did she come here? To look for him. Nothing I could do but she must come to look for him. I think this jealousy will drive me mad!

SHEEMISH: Shall I tell you between our two selves what I think of it? *(Joins Rodney on the sofa and passes him a bottle of whiskey, which they share during scene)* I'm afraid she'll get little return for her love; her journey to this foggy island will be useless.

RODNEY *(Overjoyed)*: But what is the reason? Do tell me, Sheemish, what makes you take such a gloomy view of the situation?

SHEEMISH: His feelings are cold.

RODNEY *(Enraged again)*: You think he will betray her innocent love?

SHEEMISH: He has no heart, that man.

RODNEY: But how could a gentleman do such a vile thing?

SHEEMISH: I have been his servant on this island nineteen years and I will say this—just between us—that in my master, Baron Khanazar, the Bluebeard, you see the vilest scoundrel that ever cumbered the earth, a madman, a cur, a devil, a Turk, a heretic, who believes in neither Heaven, Hell, nor werewolf; he lives like an animal, like a swinish gourmet, a veritable vermin infesting his environs and shuttering his ears to every Christian remonstrance and turning to ridicule everything we believe in.

RODNEY *(Quite drunk and slurring his speach)*: But surely there's nothing between them. He wouldn't marry his own niece, Sybil. What a ridiculoush idea! *(Laughs)*

SHEEMISH *(Ominously and with candor)*: Believe me, to satisfy his passion he would have gone further than that, he would have married you as well and her dog and cat into the bargain. Marriage means nothing to him. It is his usual method of ensnaring women! *(Sound of footsteps)* But here he comes taking a turn in the palace. *(Bluebeard enters and does a 360-degree turn and exits the way he enters)* Let us separate—what I have spoken I have spoken in confidence. I am his slave, but a master who has given himself over to wickedness is a thing to be dreaded. If you repeat a word of this to him, I will swear you made it up.

(Rodney exits.)

SCENE 10

SHEEMISH, BLUEBEARD

BLUEBEARD: I have been in my laboratory putting things in readiness, for I have found the ideal subject for my next experiment . . . or should I say my next work of art?

SHEEMISH *(With dread)*: Oh, Master.

BLUEBEARD: What is it?

SHEEMISH: I'm afraid. I'm afraid. I'm afraid. *(Leaps into Bluebeard's arms)*

BLUEBEARD *(Throwing him off)*: Down, down, you fool. Never mind the disagreeable things that may happen. Let us think of the pleasant ones. This girl is almost the most charming creature imaginable. Add to that a few of my innovations! I never saw two people so devoted, so completely in love. The manifest tenderness of their mutual affection inspired a like feeling in me. It affected me deeply. My love began as jealousy. I couldn't bear to see them so happy together; vexation stimulated my desire and I realized what a pleasure it would give me to disturb their mutual understanding and break up an attachment so repugnant to my own susceptibilities.

SHEEMISH: Have you no desire for Miss Cubbidge?

BLUEBEARD: She is not without a certain cadaverous charm. *(Footsteps)* Shhh! Quickly, the spy hole, see who it is.

SHEEMISH: The sun is in my eyes, but I know the sound of her footsteps. It is only Mrs. Maggot.

SCENE II

MRS. MAGGOT, SHEEMISH

Mrs. Maggot and Sheemish bring on a table and chairs. Then they set the table for dinner.

MRS. MAGGOT *(Carrying in a platter)*: Yum, yum, yum . . . I'm nibbling . . . yum . . . mutton good! Lovely . . . yum . . . yum . . . yum.

SHEEMISH: It is the first time meat has been seen in the palace in nineteen years.

MRS. MAGGOT: Twenty for me! Twenty years and never any meat. I've withered. You fed yourself on the fat in your hump, didn't you? Ach. Ouf. *(She is seized by a violent coughing fit)* Swallowed the wrong way.

SHEEMISH: Heaven has punished you, glutton. Stop, before you eat the knives and the tablecloth.

MRS. MAGGOT: My illness, not my sin! Look, Sheemish, a chicken! Ah, the drumstick! *(With her mouth full)* Those who have a stomach, eat; those who have a hump, glue themselves to keyholes.

SHEEMISH: Watch what you say to me. My hump contains a second brain to think my evil thoughts for me. It hasn't forgotten the broken test tube and our little secret.

MRS. MAGGOT: You must teach me to spy through keyholes. Which eye does one use, the right or the left? They say in time one's eye becomes shaped like a keyhole. I prefer eavesdropping. There, see my ear, a delicate shell. *(She shows her ear trumpet, which has an actual ear on the end of it)*

SHEEMISH: When others are present you are as deaf as a bat—but when we are alone you are cured and hear perfectly.

MRS. MAGGOT: It's a miracle! Look at that pork chop!

(Sheemish grabs her and throws her onto the table. Climbing on top of her, he forces a huge piece of meat into her mouth.)

SHEEMISH: Here, glutton, eat this! Someday your mouth will be full of maggots and greenish pus.

(Laughter of the dinner guests is heard off.)

But here come the guests to dinner. Let us have a truce until the next time that we are alone.

MRS. MAGGOT: Peace!

SCENE 12

MRS. MAGGOT, SHEEMISH, BLUEBEARD, RODNEY, SYBIL, MISS CUBBIDGE

The dinner guests and Bluebeard enter. Mrs. Maggot and Sheemish just manage to get off the table in the nick of time. Miss Cubbidge enters on Bluebeard's arm, Sybil on Rodney's arm.

BLUEBEARD: Work, work, work. I have thought of nothing else these nineteen years. My work, my work, and nothing else.

SYBIL: Beware, Uncle, all work and no play makes Jack a dull boy.

MISS CUBBIDGE: True, Sybil, but all play and no work makes Jack a mere toy.

BLUEBEARD: No danger there. I never cease in my experimenting. My dream is to remake Man. A new man with new possibilities for love.

SYBIL: "Love for a man is a thing apart. 'Tis woman's whole existence."

MISS CUBBIDGE *(Applauding)*: Lord Byron!

BLUEBEARD: Won't you all be seated?

(Bluebeard seats Miss Cubbidge at the table. Rodney seats Sybil.)

MRS. MAGGOT *(To Sybil)*: Why, dearie, what an unusual locket.

SYBIL: Yes. It's lapis lazuli. My mother gave it to me the night she died when the terrible fire—

MISS CUBBIDGE *(Interrupting)*: Don't, Sybil . . .

SYBIL: I never knew my mother.

RODNEY: Strange, all the places are set to one side of the table.

BLUEBEARD: That is because of a little surprise I have for you. There will be an entertainment tonight while we are taking our evening meal, a little play I wrote myself.

SYBIL: What, a play?

RODNEY: Jolly!

MISS CUBBIDGE: Wrote it yourself? You've a touch of erosion, I see, Baron. And yet you studied medicine?

BLUEBEARD: I write for amusement only.

MISS CUBBIDGE: Were you indoctrinated? I mean, did you receive the doctorate? On what theme did you write your dissipation? Which degree did you receive?

BLUEBEARD: I received the third degree.

(Mrs. Maggot places a platter of meat on the table.)

RODNEY: This meat looks delicious.

BLUEBEARD *(Having a seizure)*: Meat? Meat? *(Turning on Mrs. Maggot)* You dare to serve them meat?

MRS. MAGGOT: Eh?

BLUEBEARD *(In a blind rage)*: Take it away at once, blockhead! Do you want to ruin my experiment? *(He throws the meat at Mrs. Maggot and then leaps up on the dinner table like a wild man, roaring)* What is the Law?

(Mrs. Maggot and Sheemish bow before Bluebeard as though he were an idol on an altar; they link their arms together and chant, swaying back and forth rhythmically:)

MRS. MAGGOT AND SHEEMISH: We are not men. We are not women. We are not men. We are not women. His is the hand that makes. We are not men. We are not women. His is the

House of Pain. We are not men. We are not women. That is
the Law!

BLUEBEARD *(Rolling his eyes savagely)*: Now get out! *(Turning on
the guests)* All of you!

MISS CUBBIDGE *(Horrified)*: What about dinner?

BLUEBEARD: I've lost my appetite!

RODNEY: What about the play?

BLUEBEARD: I detest avant-garde theater.

SCENE 13

BLUEBEARD, MISS CUBBIDGE, SYBIL, RODNEY, SHEEMISH,
MRS. MAGGOT, LAMIA

The face of Lamia the Leopard Woman appears at the window.

RODNEY: Look, there's a face at the window!

*(Miss Cubbidge screams, Sybil faints in Rodney's arms,
Bluebeard fires his revolver at Lamia. Tableau vivant.
The curtain falls.)*

⟶ *Act Two*

SCENE I

SYBIL, RODNEY

SYBIL: Rodney, you have come to speak to me about my letter to you.

RODNEY: Yes, you could have told me face-to-face. People living in the same house, even when they are the only people living on a deserted island, as we are, can be further apart than if they lived fifty miles asunder in the country.

SYBIL: I have thought much of what I then wrote and I feel sure that we had better—

RODNEY: Stop, Sybil . . . do not speak hurriedly, love. Shall I tell you what I learned from your letter?

SYBIL: Yes, tell me if you think it is better that you should do so.

RODNEY: I learned that something had made you melancholy since we came to this island. There are few of us who do not encounter, every now and again, some of that irrational spirit of sadness which, when overindulged, leads men to madness and self-destruction. Since I have loved you I have banished it utterly. Do not speak under the influence of that spirit until you have thought whether you too can banish it.

SYBIL: I have tried, but it will not be banished.

RODNEY: Try again, Sybil, if you love me. If you do not . . .

SYBIL: If I do not love you, I love no one upon earth. *(Sits quietly, looking into his face)*

RODNEY: I believe it. I believe it as I believe in my own love for you. I trust your love implicitly, Sybil. So come, return with me to the mainland and let us make an early marriage.

SYBIL *(Strangely, as if in a trance)*: No, I cannot do so.

RODNEY *(Smiling)*: Is that melancholy fiend too much for you? Sybil, Sybil, Sybil.

SYBIL *(Snapping out of it)*: You are noble, good and great. I find myself unfit to be your wife.

RODNEY: Don't quibble, Sybil.

SYBIL *(Falling to her knees)*: I beg your pardon on my knees.

RODNEY: I grant no such pardon. Do you think I will let you go from me in that way? No, love, if you are ill, I will wait till your illness is gone by; and if you will let me, I will be your nurse.

SYBIL: I am not ill. *(Her hands stray unconsciously to her breasts and yoni)*

RODNEY: Not ill with any defined sickness. You do not shake with ague, nor does your head rack you with aching; but yet you must be ill to try to put an end to all that has passed between us for no reason at all.

SYBIL *(Standing suddenly)*: Mr. Parker . . .

RODNEY *(Deeply hurt)*: If you will call me so, I will think it only part of your malady.

SYBIL: Mr. Parker, I can only hope that you will take me at my word. I beg your forgiveness and that our engagement may be over.

RODNEY: No, no, no, Sybil. Never with my consent. I would marry you tomorrow, tomorrow or next month, or the month after. But if it cannot be so, then I will wait . . . unless . . . there is some other man. Yes, that! and that alone would convince me. Only your marriage to another man could convince me that I had lost you. *(He kisses her on the lips)*

SYBIL *(Turning away and surreptitiously wiping away the kiss)*: I cannot convince you in that way.

RODNEY *(Prissily wipes his lips on a lace hankie and carefully folds it and replaces it in his breast pocket, relieved)*: You will convince me in no other. Have you spoken to your uncle of this yet?

SYBIL: Not as yet.

RODNEY *(Anxiously)*: Do not tell him. It is possible you may have to unsay what you have said.

SYBIL: No, it is not possible.

RODNEY: I think you must leave this island. The foggy air is no good for you. Living on an island can make one grow so insular.

SYBIL: Or insolent.

RODNEY: You need the sun, I think. You have grown so pale. You need a change.

SYBIL: Yes, you treat me as though I were partly silly and partly insane, but it is not so. The change you speak of should be in my nature and in yours. *(Rodney shakes his head and smiles)* *(Aside)* He is perfect! Oh, that he were less perfect!

RODNEY: I'll leave you alone for twenty-four hours to think this over. I advise you not to tell your uncle. But if you do tell him, let me know that you have done so.

SYBIL: Why that?

RODNEY *(Pressing her hand)*: Good night, dearest, dearest Sybil. *(Exits)*

SCENE 2

SYBIL, BLUEBEARD

BLUEBEARD: What, Sybil, are you not in bed yet?

SYBIL: Not yet, Uncle Khanazar.

BLUEBEARD: So Rodney Parker has been here. I smell his cologne in the air.

SYBIL: Yes, he has been here.

BLUEBEARD: Is anything the matter, Sybil?

SYBIL: No, Uncle Khanazar, nothing is the matter.

BLUEBEARD: He has not made himself disagreeable, has he?

SYBIL: Not in the least. He never does anything wrong. He may defy man or woman to find fault with him.

BLUEBEARD: So that's it, is it? He is just a shade too good. I have noticed that myself. But it's a fault on the right side.

SYBIL *(Deeply troubled)*: It's no fault, Uncle. If there be any fault, it is not with him.

BLUEBEARD: Being too good is not one of my faults . . . I am very bad.

SYBIL *(Starry-eyed)*: Are you bad? Are you really bad?

BLUEBEARD: When I am good, I am very, very good; but when I'm bad, I'm not bad. I'm good at being bad . . . I do it well.

SYBIL *(Again as if in a trance)*: Tonight, at dinner, your words carried me away . . . *(Their lips almost meet, but she yawns, breaking the spell and he yawns sympathetically)* . . . But I am yawning and tired and I will go to bed. Good night, Uncle Khanazar.

BLUEBEARD: Good night, Sybil. *(Aside)* And rest, for a new life awaits you!

(Sybil exits.)

SCENE 3

BLUEBEARD, MISS CUBBIDGE

MISS CUBBIDGE: Oh, excuse me. I didn't realize that the parlor was preoccupied. *(Starts out)*

BLUEBEARD: Come in, Miss Cubbidge. I do not desire to be alone.

MISS CUBBIDGE: No, I think I'd better go and leave you to your own devices.

BLUEBEARD: Please stay. I think I know what you are thinking.

MISS CUBBIDGE: I'll do my own thinking, thank you; and my own existing.

BLUEBEARD: Miss Cubbidge, I don't think you like me.

MISS CUBBIDGE: I can sympathize with neither your virtues nor your vices.

BLUEBEARD: What would you say if I told you that I need a wife?

MISS CUBBIDGE: I do not believe in sudden marriages.

BLUEBEARD: People often say that marriage is an important thing and should be much thought of in advance, and marrying people are cautioned that there are many who marry in haste and repent at leisure. I am not sure, however, that marriage may not be pondered over too much; nor do I feel certain that the leisurely repentance does not as often follow the leisurely marriages as it does the rapid ones. Why, you yourself might marry suddenly *(Kneeling before her on one knee)* and never regret it at all.

MISS CUBBIDGE: My health might fail me under the effects of so great a change made so late in life.

BLUEBEARD: Miss Cubbidge, how can you live without love?

MISS CUBBIDGE: It is my nature to love many persons a little if I've loved few or none passionately, Baron Bluebeard.

BLUEBEARD: Please, call me Khanazar; and may I call you . . .

MISS CUBBIDGE *(Shyly)*: Flora.

BLUEBEARD: Ah, Flora! It is only possible to be alone with you in nature. All other women destroy the landscape; you alone become part of it.

MISS CUBBIDGE *(Aside)*: Could any woman resist such desuetude? *(Giggling)* Why, Baron Blue—

BLUEBEARD *(Interrupting)*: Khanazar.

MISS CUBBIDGE *(Giggling)*: Khanazar.

BLUEBEARD: Flora, you are part of the trees, the sky; you are the dominating goddess of nature. Come to me, Flora, you lovely little fauna, you.

MISS CUBBIDGE *(Recovering herself)*: Mr. Bluebeard, I shall certainly not come to you.

BLUEBEARD *(Suddenly)*: Look, do you see what it is I am holding in my hand?

MISS CUBBIDGE *(Alarmed)*: A revolver!

BLUEBEARD: Take it, press it to my temple and shoot, or say you will be mine.

MISS CUBBIDGE *(Frightened, with the revolver in her hand)*: I can't shoot you, but I cannot be yours, either.

BLUEBEARD: It is one or the other. Blow my brains out. I will not live another day without you.

MISS CUBBIDGE: Recuperate your gun at once. It isn't loaded, is it?

BLUEBEARD: Pull the trigger! There are worse things awaiting Man than death.

MISS CUBBIDGE: To what do you collude?

BLUEBEARD: All tortures do not matter . . . only not to be dead before one dies. I will not live without your love. *(He pretends to weep)*

MISS CUBBIDGE: Don't weep, Baron Bluebeard . . . er . . . Khanazar. 'Tisn't manly. Try to be more malevolent.

BLUEBEARD: Marry me, marry me, Flora, and make me the happiest man on earth.

MISS CUBBIDGE: How can I marry you?

BLUEBEARD *(Hypnotically)*: Easily. Just repeat after me. I, Flora Cubbidge . . .

MISS CUBBIDGE: I, Flora Cubbidge . . .

BLUEBEARD: Do solemnly swear . . .

MISS CUBBIDGE: Do solemnly swear . . .

BLUEBEARD: To take this man, Baron Khanazar von Bluebeard, as my lawful wedded husband . . .

MISS CUBBIDGE: To take this man, Baron Khanazar von Bluebeard, as my lawful wedded husband . . .

BLUEBEARD: To love, honor, and obey; for better or for worse; for richer or poorer; in sickness and in health; from this day forward . . . *(He begins to undress her)*

MISS CUBBIDGE: To love, honor, and obey; for better or for worse; for richer or for poorer; in sickness and in health; from this day forward . . .

BLUEBEARD: Until death us do part.

MISS CUBBIDGE: Till death us do part.

BLUEBEARD *(Licentiously)*: I may now kiss the bride.

MISS CUBBIDGE: What about your vows?

BLUEBEARD: Don't you trust me?

MISS CUBBIDGE: I do. I do. I do.

(They begin to breathe heavily as they undress slowly. They move toward each other, wearing only their shoes, socks, stockings and her merry widow. They clinch and roll about on the floor making animal noises.)

BLUEBEARD: Was ever woman in this manner wooed? Was ever woman in this manner won?

MISS CUBBIDGE *(Aside)*: There are things that happen in a day that would take a lifetime to explain.

(There follows a scene of unprecedented eroticism in which Miss Cubbidge gives herself voluptuously to Baron von Bluebeard.)

BLUEBEARD: In my right pants pocket you will find a key. It is the key to my laboratory. Take it. And swear to me that you will never use it.

MISS CUBBIDGE: I swear! I must return to Sybil at once. She sometimes wakes up in a phalanx.

BLUEBEARD: Won't you sleep here tonight, with me?

MISS CUBBIDGE: No, I can't sleep in this bed. It has cold, wet spots in it. Good night, Baron . . . husband.

BLUEBEARD: Good night, Miss Cubbidge.

MISS CUBBIDGE: Please don't mention our hymeneals to Sybil. I must find the right words to immure the news to her.

BLUEBEARD: Believe me, I'll confess to none of it.

MISS CUBBIDGE: Thank you. I believe that you have transformed me to a part of the dirigible essence. You have carried me aloft and I believe I am with Beatrice, of whom Dante has sung in his immortal onus. Good night. *(Exits)*

SCENE 4

BLUEBEARD

BLUEBEARD: It is a lucky thing for me that I did not take the vows or this marriage might be binding on me as it is on her. I cannot sleep tonight. There is work to be done in my laboratory. Good night, Miss Cubbidge, wherever you are. And good night to all the ladies who do be living in this world. Good night, ladies. Good night, sweet ladies. *(Exits into laboratory)*

SCENE 5

RODNEY, LAMIA, MRS. MAGGOT

Entering surreptitiously, Mrs. Maggot crosses, lighting a candelabra.

LAMIA: SHHH! Take care of the deaf one . . . She hears nothing of what you shout and overhears everything that you whisper.

RODNEY: What is it that you wish to tell me?

LAMIA: He is mad, I tell you, mad! And he will stop at nothing.

RODNEY: Who?

LAMIA: The Bluebeard, Khanazar. If you love that girl, convince her to leave this island at once.

RODNEY: But why?

LAMIA: Look at me. I was a woman once!

RODNEY: But you are a woman. So very much a woman. You are all woman.

LAMIA: No, no, never again will I bear the name of woman. I was changed in the House of Pain. I was a victim of his sex-switch tricks and his queer quackery.

RODNEY: Quackery—Sybil told me that he was a brilliant physiologist.

LAMIA: Even in Denmark they called him a quack. He wasn't satisfied with sex switches. He wants to create a third genital organ attached between the legs of a third sex. I am an experiment that failed.

RODNEY *(Seductively)*: You look like a woman to me.

LAMIA: I wish I could be a woman to you. *(Aside)* Perhaps when Bluebeard is defeated I will. *(Aloud)* He uses the same technique on all his victims. First he married me. Then he gave me the key to his laboratory, forbidding me ever to use it. Then he waited for curiosity to get the better of me. All women are curious.

RODNEY: Men marry because they are tired, women because they are curious.

LAMIA: Both are disappointed.

RODNEY: Does he ever use men for his experiments?

LAMIA: At first he did. Sheemish was the first. But when that experiment failed he turned to women. We are all experiments that have failed. He has made us the slaves of this island.

RODNEY *(Realizing)*: The Island of Lost Love!

LAMIA: Save yourself and save the woman you love. Take the advice of the Leopard Woman and go.

RODNEY: How did a nice girl like you get mixed up in a mess like this?

LAMIA: I was entertaining in a small bistro nightclub called The Wild Cat's Pussy. I was billed as Lamia the Leopard

Woman. It was only fourteen beans a day but I needed the
scratch. I sang this song. *(Sings:)*

Where is my Leopard Lover?
When will I spot the cat for me?
I'm wild when I'm under cover.
Where is the cat who will tame me?
Where is my wild cat lover?
Leopard hunting is all the rage.
Where is my wild cat lover?
I'm free but I want to be caged.
If you dig this feline.
Better make a beeline.
I've got the spots to give men the red-hots
Where is my wild leopard hunter?
I'm game if you'll play my game.
Where is that runt cunt hunter?
I'm wild but I want to be tame.

After I sang my set, he signaled and I sat at his table. He
ordered a Tiger's Milk Flip. He was into health food. No
woman can resist him, I tell you.

RODNEY: He seduced you?

LAMIA: Worst, worst, a thousand times worst. I didn't know if I
was coming or going. He has a way with women.

RODNEY: Sybil, great Scott no. Either you're jesting or I'm
dreaming! Sybil with another man? I'll go mad.

LAMIA: His idealism . . . his intensity . . . the Clairol blue of his
beard! His words carried me away. He had a strange look in
his eyes. I felt strange inside. He and I were total strangers!
If you love her, get her off this island before it is too late.

RODNEY: No, not Sybil. I am ashamed to listen to you. Yet she
admires him so . . . I have gone mad!

LAMIA: He came closer . . . closer. "Submit," he said, "in the name
of science and the dark arts. Submit. Submit."

RODNEY *(In a panic)*: Sybil is with him now. You are lying.

LAMIA: If you think I am lying, look. *(She lifts up her sarong,
revealing her altered genitalia: a red squeak box contraption that*

> *Rodney squeaks by pushing)* Look what he did to the Leopard Woman's pussy.

RODNEY: Eeeccht! Is that a mound of Venus or a penis?

LAMIA *(Perplexed)*: I wish I knew.

RODNEY: No, no, he can't do that to Sybil. I must kill him. What am I saying? This is madness. But what consolation is sanity to me? The most faithful of women is after all only a woman. I'll kill you. No, I am mad.

LAMIA: Go and stop him. Save her from the fate that has befallen me.

RODNEY: I will kill myself! *(He tries to strangle himself)* No, I will kill her! Oh, God, it is impossible. I have gone mad! *(He runs out)*

SCENE 6

LAMIA

LAMIA *(Sings)*:

I've lost my leopard lover.
A world of made is not a world of born.
Bluebeard will soon discover
Hell hath no fury like a woman scorned.

SCENE 7

LAMIA, SHEEMISH

LAMIA *(Calling after him)*: Rodney! Rodney! Rodney! He is gone.

SHEEMISH *(Appearing out of the shadows)*: Are you afraid of being alone?

LAMIA *(Fanning herself with a leopard fan)*: How stifling it is! There must be a storm coming.

SHEEMISH: I heard you telling the secrets of the island to Rodney *(Spits)* Parker.

LAMIA *(Furiously hits him over the head with her fan)*: Sneaking little eavesdropper! How dare you?

SHEEMISH: I love you.

LAMIA *(Fanning herself)*: What awful weather! This is the second day of it.

SHEEMISH: Every day I walk four miles to see you and four miles back and meet with nothing but indifference from you.

LAMIA: Your love touches me but I can't return it, that's all.

SHEEMISH *(Accusing)*: But you came four miles here to tell the secrets of the island to Rodney *(Spits)* Parker.

LAMIA: You are a bore.

SHEEMISH *(Twisting her arm)*: You are in love with him!

LAMIA *(In pain)*: Yes, it's true. If you must know. I do love him. I do! *(Aside)* For all the good it will do me. He loves Sybil.

SHEEMISH *(Taking her in his arms roughly and humping her like a dog)*: I want you.

LAMIA *(Fighting him)*: You stupid, vulgar, deformed nincompoop! Do you think I could ever fall for such a one as you? You are as ugly as sin itself. Besides, our genitals would never fit together.

SHEEMISH *(Groping her)*: We can work it out.

LAMIA: Evil cretin! God will punish you. *(She breaks away)*

SHEEMISH: God will not punish the lunatic soul. He knows the powers of evil are too great for us with weak minds. Marry me!

LAMIA: I'd rather blow a bald baboon with B.O. and bunions than marry a monster! *(Lamia exits in a huff)*

SHEEMISH *(Following her)*: Lamia, be reasonable!

SCENE 8

BLUEBEARD, SYBIL

Sybil is seated at a spinet. She plays dramatic music. Bluebeard moves slowly, approaching her from behind. His eyes are ablaze. She senses his approach. She plays with greater emphasis. Her shoulders are bare. He begins kissing them. The music she is playing rises to a crescendo. She stops playing suddenly.

SYBIL: This is ridiculous!

BLUEBEARD *(Swinging a key on a chain back and forth before her eyes as though hypnotizing her)*: Here is the key to my laboratory. Take it and swear to me that you will never use it.

SYBIL *(In a trance)*: Yes, Master!

BLUEBEARD: Ah, my darling, my own one. You will be my wife.

SYBIL: Yes, Master!

BLUEBEARD: You will be the loveliest of all wives. *(Aside)* When I am through with you.

SYBIL: Yes, Master.

BLUEBEARD: I am about to perform the *magnum opus*. The creation of a third genital organ will perhaps lead to the creation of a third sex. You will be my ultimate masterpiece of vivisection! *(He kisses her)*

SCENE 9

BLUEBEARD, SYBIL, MISS CUBBIDGE

MISS CUBBIDGE *(Entering)*: Sir, what are you doing with Sybil there? Are you making love to her too?

BLUEBEARD *(Aside to Miss Cubbidge)*: No, no, on the contrary, she throws herself at me shamelessly, although I tell her that I am married to you.

SYBIL: What is it you want, Miss Cubbidge?

BLUEBEARD *(Aside to Sybil)*: She is jealous of my speaking to you. She wants me to marry her, but I tell her it is you I must have.

MISS CUBBIDGE *(Incredulous)*: What, Sybil?

BLUEBEARD *(Aside to Miss Cubbidge)*: The impressionable little creature is infatuated with me.

SYBIL *(Incredulous)*: What, Miss Cubbidge?

BLUEBEARD *(Aside to Sybil)*: The desperate old maid has got her claws out for me.

MISS CUBBIDGE: Do you . . .

BLUEBEARD *(To Miss Cubbidge)*: Your words would be in vain.

SYBIL: I'd . . .

BLUEBEARD *(To Sybil)*: All you can say to her will be in vain.

MISS CUBBIDGE: Truly . . .

BLUEBEARD *(Aside to Miss Cubbidge)*: She's obstinate as the devil.

SYBIL: I think . . .

BLUEBEARD *(Aside to Sybil)*: Say nothing to her. She's a mad-woman.

SYBIL: No, no, I must speak to her.

MISS CUBBIDGE: I'll hear her reasons.

SYBIL: What . . .

BLUEBEARD *(Aside to Sybil)*: I'll lay you a wager she tells you she's my wife.

MISS CUBBIDGE: I . . .

BLUEBEARD *(Aside to Miss Cubbidge)*: I'll bet you she says I'm going to marry her.

MISS CUBBIDGE: Sybil, as your chaperone I must intercept. It is past your bedtime.

SYBIL: Dear Miss Cubbidge, I have been to bed but I got up because I have insomnia.

MISS CUBBIDGE: So I see. Sybil, I must ask you to leave me alone with *my* husband. The Baron and I married ourselves in an improvident ceremony earlier this evening.

BLUEBEARD *(Aside to Sybil)*: What did I tell you? She's out of her mind.

SYBIL: Dear *Miss* Cubbidge, are you sure you are feeling all right? Are you ill?

MISS CUBBIDGE *(Indignantly)*: I've never felt more supine in my life. Sybil, it does not become a young *unmarried* woman to meddle in the affairs of others.

BLUEBEARD *(Aside to Miss Cubbidge)*: She thinks she is going to marry me.

SYBIL: It is not fit, *Miss* Cubbidge, to be jealous because the Baron speaks to me. I am going to be his wife.

BLUEBEARD *(Aside to Miss Cubbidge)*: What did I tell you?

SYBIL: Baron, did you not promise to marry me?

BLUEBEARD *(Aside to Sybil)*: Of course, my darling.

MISS CUBBIDGE: Baron, am I not your wife, the Baroness von Bluebeard?

BLUEBEARD *(Aside to Miss Cubbidge)*: How could you ask such a question?

SYBIL *(Aside to the audience)*: How sure the old goat is of herself!

MISS CUBBIDGE *(Aside to the audience)*: The Baron is right, how pigheaded the little bitch is!

SYBIL: We must know the truth.

MISS CUBBIDGE: We must have the matter abnegated.

SYBIL AND MISS CUBBIDGE: Which of us will it be, Baron?

BLUEBEARD *(Addressing himself to both of them)*: What would you have me say? Each of you knows in your heart of hearts whether or not I have made love to you. Let her that I truly love laugh at what the other says. Actions speak louder than words. *(Aside to Miss Cubbidge)* Let her believe what she will. *(Aside to Sybil)* Let her flatter herself in her senile imagination. *(Aside to Miss Cubbidge)* I adore you. *(Aside to Sybil)* I am yours alone. *(Aside to Miss Cubbidge)* One night with you is worth a thousand with other women. *(Aside to Sybil)* All faces are ugly in your presence. *(Aloud)* If you will excuse me, there's work to be done in my laboratory. I do not wish to be disturbed. Good night, ladies. *(Exits)*

SCENE 10

SYBIL, MISS CUBBIDGE, SHEEMISH

SHEEMISH *(Appearing out of the shadows)*: Poor ladies! I can't bear to see you led to your destruction. Take my advice, return to the mainland.

SYBIL: I am she he loves, however.

MISS CUBBIDGE: It is to me he's married.

SHEEMISH: My master is an evil sadist. He will do you irreparable harm as he has done to others. He wants to marry the whole female sex so that he can take them to his laboratory and . . .

SCENE 11

SYBIL, MISS CUBBIDGE, SHEEMISH, BLUEBEARD

BLUEBEARD *(Popping back in)*: One more word . . .

SHEEMISH: My master is no evil sadist. He means you no harm. If you ladies think he can marry the whole female sex,

you've got another thing coming. He is a man of his word.
There he is—ask him yourself.

BLUEBEARD: What were you saying, Sheemish?

SHEEMISH *(Aside to Bluebeard)*: You know how catty women are.
I was defending you . . . as best I could.

BLUEBEARD *(To Sybil and Miss Cubbidge)*: She who holds the key
to my heart holds the key to my laboratory. *(Exits)*

SCENE 12

MISS CUBBIDGE, SYBIL, SHEEMISH

MISS CUBBIDGE *(Aside)*: Then he is my husband, for he gave me
the key.

SYBIL *(Aside)*: The key, I have the key! It is me he loves after all.
(Loud) Good night, Madame. If you have the key, you are
his wife.

MISS CUBBIDGE: Good night, Sybil. If it is to you he gave the key,
you are his bethrothed.

(They both exit laughing.)

SCENE 13

SHEEMISH, MRS. MAGGOT

MRS. MAGGOT *(Entering excitedly)*: I overheard laughter. It is the
first time laughter has been heard on this island in nineteen
years. Who was laughing? Who is it that knows a single
moment of happiness on the Island of Lost Love?

SHEEMISH: It was not with joy you heard them laughing, but with
scorn. Bluebeard has got the young woman and her gov-
erness fighting like cats in the alley.

MRS. MAGGOT: I thought they always swore by each other.

SHEEMISH: It's at each other that they swear now. He's married
both of them!

MRS. MAGGOT: Wedding bells must sound like an alarm clock to
him.

SCENE 14

SHEEMISH, MRS. MAGGOT, SYBIL

MRS. MAGGOT: Look, here comes the young one carrying a candle, her long black hair unloosed, her lips slightly parted. A lovely flower that blooms for just one hour.

SHEEMISH: A sleepwalker, a somnambulist.

MRS. MAGGOT: Her eyes are open.

SHEEMISH: But their sense is shut. I believe he has mesmerized her. Let us conceal ourselves, I will keep my eyes peeled.

MRS. MAGGOT: And I my ears. I can't wait to find out what happens next!

(Mrs. Maggot and Sheemish hide.)

SYBIL: I can control my curiosity no longer. I must see what lies behind the door to my lover's laboratory. I know he has forbade me ever to use this key. But how can I stand the suspense? Should not a woman take an interest in her husband's work?

(She unlocks the door with her key and opens it. Bluebeard awaits her.)

MRS. MAGGOT: Shouldn't we try to save her?

SHEEMISH: Would you prefer to take her place in the House of Pain?

MRS. MAGGOT: No, no, not the House of Pain.

SCENE 15

SYBIL, BLUEBEARD, SHEEMISH, MRS. MAGGOT

BLUEBEARD: I trust you have kept your coming here a secret.

SYBIL: Baron!

BLUEBEARD: Curiosity killed the cat. *(Aside)* But it may have a salutary effect on the pussy. *(To Sybil)* Look into my eyes, my little kitten, and repeat after me. *(Hypnotizing her)* I,

Sybil, do solemnly swear to take this man, Baron Khanazar von Bluebeard, as my lawful wedded husband.

SYBIL: I, Sybil, do solemnly swear to take this man, Baron Khanazar von Bluebeard, as my lawful wedded husband.

MRS. MAGGOT *(Moving her ear trumpet like an antenna)*: I hear someone coming. Just in time! Rodney Parker will save her from the fate worse than death!

SHEEMISH *(Aside)*: My rival, Rodney Parker! Now I will have my revenge. *(To Mrs. Maggot)* Detain him!

BLUEBEARD: To love, honor, and obey . . .

MRS. MAGGOT: Oh, cruel! Don't ask me that. I won't do it. Anything but that.

SYBIL: To love, honor, and obey.

SHEEMISH: Even the House of Pain? The test tube! Master, Master . . .

BLUEBEARD: For better or for worse; for richer or for poorer . . .

MRS. MAGGOT: I'll do it.

BLUEBEARD: In sickness and in health . . . from this day forward . . .

SYBIL: For better or for worse; for richer or for poorer . . . in sickness and in health, from this day forward . . .

SCENE 16

SHEEMISH, MRS. MAGGOT, SYBIL, BLUEBEARD, RODNEY

Rodney rushes onto the stage, mad.

RODNEY: Where is he? Where is he?

(Sheemish roughly throws Mrs. Maggot into Rodney.)

MRS. MAGGOT: Eh?

BLUEBEARD: Until death us do part.

SYBIL: Until death us do part.

(Bluebeard blows out the candle and kisses Sybil.)

RODNEY *(Shaking Mrs. Maggot violently)*: Where is Bluebeard?

MRS. MAGGOT: Eh?

RODNEY: Aagh! *(He throws Mrs. Maggot aside)*

BLUEBEARD *(Pressing Sybil to him, demented)*: And now, ye demons, ere this night goes by, I swear I'll conjure or I'll die!

RODNEY *(Sees Bluebeard)*: Damn you, Bluebeard! Damn your soul!

SYBIL: Rodney! Ah! *(She faints)*

(Bluebeard catches her and quickly carries her into the laboratory. Mrs. Maggot trips Rodney, then Sheemish and Mrs. Maggot follow Bluebeard, slamming the door in Rodney's face and locking it. Rodney beats on the door and shouts.)

SCENE 17

RODNEY

RODNEY: Open the door, you pervert! You invert, you necrophiliac! Open up! Bluebeard! Bluebeard! BLUEBEARD!

(Curtain.)

⸺ *Act Three*

SCENE I

BLUEBEARD, SYBIL, SHEEMISH, MRS. MAGGOT

There is no lapse of time between Act Two and Act Three. The scene changes to the interior of Bluebeard's laboratory. Enter Bluebeard, carrying Sybil in his arms. He walks with a hesitant step, looking from side to side, his cheeks quivering, contracting and expanding, his eyes intently focused. Sheemish and Mrs. Maggot scurry about taking care of last-minute details. There is an air of great anticipation.

RODNEY'S VOICE *(From offstage)*: Bluebeard! Bluebeard! Bluebeard! Open this door or I'll break it down! *(Loud knocking)* Bluebeard!

BLUEBEARD *(Laughing)*: That door is lined with double-duty quilted zinc. No mortal arm can break it down. Even a man whose heart is pure and has the strength of ten could not break it down. But a delicate girl with just enough strength to lift a powder puff to her white bosom can open it . . . if she has the key. *(More loud knocking)* Sheemish, take the girl to the operating room, bathe her, and prepare her for surgery.

SHEEMISH: No, Master, please don't ask me to do that. Anything but that.

BLUEBEARD: And be gentle with her. I want no marks left on her lily-white body. If you so much as bruise her, you and I will make an appointment for a meeting here in the House of Pain, hmm?

SHEEMISH: No, no, not the House of Pain! *(He carries Sybil off)*

SCENE 2

BLUEBEARD, MRS. MAGGOT

BLUEBEARD: Mrs. Maggot, bring in the frog, the serpent and the hearts, hands, eyes, feet, but most of all the blood and genitals of the little children. Bring in the serpent first. I need it to trace a magic circle.

MRS. MAGGOT *(Extending her ear trumpet toward Bluebeard)*: Eh?

BLUEBEARD: Perhaps your hearing would be improved by a vacation. *(He covers her ears and mouths the words)* In the House of Pain.

MRS. MAGGOT: No, no, not the House of Pain! *(She quickly hands him a bottle of blood and a paintbrush)*

BLUEBEARD *(Laughs)*: Thank you. Now, leave me. Go and assist Sheemish. *(Mrs. Maggot lingers)* Is there something that you want, Maggot?

MRS. MAGGOT: Yes, Master.

BLUEBEARD: Well, what is it?

MRS. MAGGOT: The lapis lazuli locket the girl is wearing. May I have it?

BLUEBEARD: Yes, take it, scavenger!

MRS. MAGGOT: Do you think she will mind?

BLUEBEARD: No, she will not mind. She will remember nothing of her former life after the operation. Now get out. *(Kicks her in the ass)*

MRS. MAGGOT: Thank you, thank you, Master. *(Exits)*

SCENE 3

BLUEBEARD

BLUEBEARD *(Inscribing a circle of blood)*:
    Now by the powers that only seem to be,
    With crystal sword and flame I conjure thee.
    I kiss the book; oh, come to me!
    Goddess of night: Hecate!

(The sound of a gong is heard and a high-pitched cockcrow that sometimes breaks from the most refined throat. Hecate appears in a flash of light and a puff of smoke.)

SCENE 4

BLUEBEARD, HECATE

HECATE *(Wearing a blue beard)*: Who summons the Slave of Sin?
BLUEBEARD *(Laughing quietly, aside)*: Not for nothing I have worshiped the Dark One. *(To Hecate)* I called, Hecate; I, Khanazar von Bluebeard.
HECATE: How dare you? Don't you know that torture is the price you pay for summoning the Slave of Sin?
BLUEBEARD: All tortures do not matter: only not to be dead before one dies.
HECATE: What is it you want of me, my fool?
BLUEBEARD: Look, here are my books written in blood, there my apparatus. For nineteen long years I've waited and worked for this moment. In there, on the operating table, swathed in bandages, a new sex, waiting to live again in a genital I made with my own hands! *(Maniacally)* With my own hands!
HECATE: What about your own genitalia?
BLUEBEARD: The male genital organ is but a faint relic and shadow, a sign that has become detached from its substance and lives on as an exquisite ornament.
HECATE: And what do you want of me, my fool?
BLUEBEARD: Good fortune.
HECATE: Do not seek for good fortune. You carry on your forehead the sign of the elect.

Seek, probe,
Details unfold.
Let nature's secret
Be retold.

If ever you mean to try, you should try now. *(She vanishes)*

(There is a roll of thunder. Dramatic music from Bartók's Bluebeard's Castle *begins to swell. Bluebeard dons surgeon's coat, gloves and mask and enters the House of Pain. Mrs. Maggot and Sheemish close the doors after him. There is the sound of loud knocking at the door.)*

SCENE 5

MRS. MAGGOT, SHEEMISH

MRS. MAGGOT: Look, Sheemish, the lapis lazuli locket. The Master said I could have it. Pretty, ain't it?

SHEEMISH: What's with you and that locket?

(A bloodcurdling scream issues from the laboratory. We may be sure that it is Sybil writhing under the vivisector's knife. Both Sheemish and Mrs. Maggot freeze for a moment in terror and clutch their own genitals in sympathy.)

Listen, he has begun the operation.

(There is another bloodcurdling scream. Again Mrs. Maggot and Sheemish freeze and clutch their genitals.)

RODNEY'S VOICE *(From offstage)*: What are you doing in there, you monster? *(He beats loudly on the door. Sybil screams again)* Open the door or I'll tear your heart out! *(Knocks loudly)*

SCENE 6

BLUEBEARD, MRS. MAGGOT, SHEEMISH

BLUEBEARD *(Rushes on)*: The test tube! The test tube. Everything depends upon the sticky liquid now. *(He snatches the test tube and hurries back to his work)*

(Mrs. Maggot and Sheemish exchange a guilty look. Another scream is heard. Suddenly Miss Cubbidge and Rodney burst into the room. Miss Cubbidge brandishes the key.)

SCENE 7

MRS. MAGGOT, SHEEMISH, RODNEY, MISS CUBBIDGE

MISS CUBBIDGE: I could control my curiosity no longer.

RODNEY: I'll see to it that he goes to the guillotine. That will shorten him by a head.

MISS CUBBIDGE: He robbed me of my maidenhead. So it's not his head I'll see cut off him! I want him decalced.

(Another scream is heard.)

RODNEY: Let me at him. I'll maim the bloody bugger.

SHEEMISH: Don't be a fool. The girl is on the operating table. If you interfere now, she'll lose her life.

MISS CUBBIDGE *(Aside)*: With Sybil out of the way, the Baron will be mine alone. *(Aloud)* We must save her no matter what the danger.

(Sybil screams again.)

RODNEY: I can't stand it. I'm going in there.

SHEEMISH: Are you crazy?

RODNEY: Yes, I'm crazy.

SHEEMISH: Can't you understand that we are powerless against a supernatural enemy?

SCENE 8

BLUEBEARD, MISS CUBBIDGE, RODNEY, MRS. MAGGOT, SHEEMISH

BLUEBEARD: The time has come. The final stage of transmutation must be completed. Mars, God of War, and Venus, Goddess of Love, are conjunct in the twelfth house. The house of change and transformation. Scorpio, which rules surgery and the genitalia, is at the zenith. This is the horoscope I have been waiting for. The signs are in perfect aspect. The third genital will be born under the most beneficent stars that twinkle in the heavens. Sheemish, bring in the girl, or should I say "subject"?

(Sheemish exits.)

MISS CUBBIDGE: Khanazar, you have deceived me. I—
BLUEBEARD: Quiet! I have no time to talk to an idiot.
RODNEY: If anything goes wrong with this experiment, I swear I'll kill you.
BLUEBEARD: I have already sworn upon the cross to enter into this experiment for life and for death.

(Sheemish carries on Sybil, who is wrapped in bandages like a mummy.)

SCENE 9

RODNEY, SYBIL, SHEEMISH, MISS CUBBIDGE, MRS. MAGGOT,
BLUEBEARD

BLUEBEARD: Gently, gently! Be careful, you fool.
MISS CUBBIDGE *(Gasps)*: Is she . . . is she . . . dead?
BLUEBEARD *(Listens to Sybil's heart and genital through stethoscope)*: No, she is not dead. She's just resting, waiting for new life to come.

(There is the sound of thunder and flashes of lightning. Mrs. Maggot and Sheemish light candles and incense. There are science-fiction lighting effects.)

RODNEY: Is it a new life or a monster you are creating, Baron Prevert?
BLUEBEARD: The word is "pervert." I believe in this monster as you call it.
RODNEY: So, this is the House of Pain.
BLUEBEARD: How do you know when you unlock any door in life that you are not entering a House of Pain? I have thought nothing of pain. Years of studying nature have made me as remorseless as nature itself. All we feel is pain. But we must take risks if we are to progress.
RODNEY: How could you? How could you?
BLUEBEARD: Do you know what it feels like to be God, Parker?
RODNEY *(Spits in Bluebeard's face)*: I spit in your face.

BLUEBEARD: Do you think that the envenomed spittle of five hundred little gentlemen of your mark, piled one on top of the other, could succeed in so much as slobbering the tips of my august toes?

(He turns his back on Rodney and, with the assistance of Sheemish, begins unwinding the bandages that envelop Sybil. When she is completely nude except for her fuck-me pumps, the genital, which is a loofah sponge with a movable bird's claw, begins to move.)

BLUEBEARD: Look, it's moving. It's alive. It's moving. It's alive! It's alive!

(Sybil moves like the bride of Frankenstein, with stiff, jerking movements of the head and neck. First she looks at Sheemish and screams with horror, then she looks at Bluebeard and screams with horror, then she looks at her new genital and growls with displeasure.)

SCENE 10

LAMIA, RODNEY, SYBIL, MRS. MAGGOT, SHEEMISH,
MISS CUBBIDGE, BLUEBEARD

Lamia enters and crawls with catlike stealth over toward Sybil and examines the third genital.

LAMIA: Now no man will ever want her! Rodney is mine. *(She leaps toward Rodney. Bluebeard fires on her and she falls)*
BLUEBEARD: I told you never to come to this side of the island again.
SHEEMISH *(Kneeling over Lamia's body)*: You killed the woman I love.
BLUEBEARD *(Going to her also, feeling her pulse)*: Woman—I wouldn't say she was a woman. She was a leopard, a wild cat. I couldn't make my leopard love me.
SHEEMISH: You killed the woman I love. Now you must die. *(He moves toward Bluebeard threateningly)*
BLUEBEARD *(Backing away)*: No, Sheemish, no! Remember the House of Pain!
SHEEMISH: I no longer fear pain. My heart is broken. *(He seizes Bluebeard by the throat)*

RODNEY *(Looking at Sybil's genital)*: No man will ever want her?

MISS CUBBIDGE *(To Mrs. Maggot)*: What are you doing with the lapis lazuli locket? Sybil's mother gave it to her the night she died when the terrible fire . . . Sybil's real mother had a strawberry birthmark on her left kneecap.

RODNEY: I need never be jealous again!

(Mrs. Maggot pulls up her dress revealing a strawberry birthmark on her left kneecap.)

MISS CUBBIDGE: Margaret, Margaret Maggot? Maggie!

(Sheemish releases Bluebeard in amazement.)

MRS. MAGGOT: The fire? Margaret Maggot? It's all coming back to me. I am Maggie Maggot. *(Turning on Bluebeard)* What have you suffered for that child that you dare to tear her from me without pity? Sybil is my daughter. I am her real mother. If you give me back my child, I shall live for her alone. I shall know how to tame my nature to be worthy of her always. My heart will not open itself to anyone but her. *(On her knees)* My whole life will be too brief to prove to her my tenderness, my love, my devotion.

BLUEBEARD *(Kicking her over)*: I detest cheap sentiment.

MISS CUBBIDGE: This exploits women!

MRS. MAGGOT: Women want an answer!

(They seize Bluebeard, tie ropes to his wrists and stretch him across the stage. Lamia rises and begins strangling him slowly.)

BLUEBEARD: Lamia! I thought you were dead.

LAMIA: My dear, didn't you know? A cat has nine lives.

SYBIL *(The monster speaks haltingly)*: Stop . . . in . . . the . . . name . . . of love. The human heart . . . who knows to what perversions it may not turn, when its taste is guided by aesthetics?

(The women drop the rope. Lamia releases Bluebeard. The sound of the ship's foghorn is heard offstage.)

SHEEMISH *(Looking out the spy hole)*: The *Lady Vain*! The *Lady Vain*! The *Lady Vain* has weathered the storm!

MISS CUBBIDGE *(To Bluebeard)*: I am leaving this moment. Tomorrow I shall be far away. I shall have forgotten everything that happened yesterday. It's enough to say that I will tell nobody, nobody. If, as I hope, you regret the words that escaped you, write to me and I shall despond at once. I leave without rancor, wishing you the best, in spite of all. I am carrying your child. Would that your son will be your good angel. *(Hands him the key to the laboratory)* Adieu! Come, Margaret, Sybil. *(Rodney is diddling Sybil's new genitalia)* Rodney!! We must return to normalcy.

(They exit. There is the sound of a foghorn.)

SCENE II

BLUEBEARD, LAMIA, SHEEMISH

BLUEBEARD *(In a rage, shaking his fists at the heavens)*: I curse everything that you have given. I curse the day on which I was born. I curse the day on which I shall die. I curse the whole of my life. I fling it all back at your cruel face, senseless fate! *(Laughing)* With my curses I conquer you. What else can you do to me? With my last breath I will shout in your asinine ears: be accursed, be accursed! Be forever accursed! I'm a failure, Sheemish, I'm a failure.

SHEEMISH: But, Master, you have heart, you have talent.

BLUEBEARD: Heart! Talent! These are nothing, my boy. Mediocrity is the true gift of the gods. *(Exits)*

SCENE 12

SHEEMISH, LAMIA

SHEEMISH: Come, let us do the best we can, to change the opinion of this unhappy man. *(He exits with Lamia into a magnificent golden shaft of light)*

THE END